Kazumi Okamoto

Academic Culture: An Analytical Framework for Understanding Academic Work

A Case Study about the
Social Science Academe in Japan

BEYOND THE SOCIAL SCIENCES

Edited by Michael Kuhn, Hebe Vessuri, Shujiro Yazawa

ISSN 2364-8775

1   *Michael Kuhn, Shujiro Yazawa (eds.)*
    Theories about and Strategies against Hegemonic Social Sciences
    ISBN 978-3-8382-0586-1

2   *Michael Kuhn*
    How the Social Sciences Think about the World's Social
    Outline of a Critique
    ISBN 978-3-8382-0892-3

3   *Michael Kuhn, Hebe Vessuri (eds.)*
    The Global Social Sciences
    —Under and Beyond European Universalism
    ISBN 978-3-8382-0893-0

4   *Michael Kuhn, Hebe Vessuri (eds.)*
    Contributions to Alternative Concepts of Knowledge
    ISBN 978-3-8382-0894-7

5   *Kazumi Okamoto*
    Academic Culture: An Analytical Framework
    for Understanding Academic Work
    A Case Study about the Social Science Academe in Japan
    ISBN 978-3-8382-0937-1

Kazumi Okamoto

ACADEMIC CULTURE: AN ANALYTICAL FRAMEWORK FOR UNDERSTANDING ACADEMIC WORK

A Case Study about the
Social Science Academe in Japan

ibidem-Verlag
Stuttgart

Bibliografische Information der Deutschen Nationalbibliothek
Die Deutsche Nationalbibliothek verzeichnet diese Publikation in der Deutschen Nationalbibliografie; detaillierte bibliografische Daten sind im Internet über http://dnb.d-nb.de abrufbar.

Bibliographic information published by the Deutsche Nationalbibliothek
Die Deutsche Nationalbibliothek lists this publication in the Deutsche Nationalbibliografie; detailed bibliographic data are available in the Internet at http://dnb.d-nb.de.

The Dissertation is submitted to the Faculty of Humanities and Social Sciences of the Karlsruhe Institute of Technology (KIT).

∞

Gedruckt auf alterungsbeständigem, säurefreien Papier
Printed on acid-free paper

ISSN 2364-8775

ISBN-13: 978-3-8382-0937-1

© *ibidem*-Verlag
Stuttgart 2016

Alle Rechte vorbehalten

Das Werk einschließlich aller seiner Teile ist urheberrechtlich geschützt. Jede Verwertung außerhalb der engen Grenzen des Urheberrechtsgesetzes ist ohne Zustimmung des Verlages unzulässig und strafbar. Dies gilt insbesondere für Vervielfältigungen, Übersetzungen, Mikroverfilmungen und elektronische Speicherformen sowie die Einspeicherung und Verarbeitung in elektronischen Systemen.

All rights reserved. No part of this publication may be reproduced, stored in or introduced into a retrieval system, or transmitted, in any form, or by any means (electronic, mechanical, photocopying, recording or otherwise) without the prior written permission of the publisher. Any person who does any unauthorized act in relation to this publication may be liable to criminal prosecution and civil claims for damages.

Printed in the EU

Acknowledgements

On the completion of this long and exciting intellectual journey, I must mention names of some people without whom I could not have done this all.

First of all, my greatest gratitude goes to Prof. Dr. Martin Fischer, who kindly accepted me as a doctral researcher under his supervision. The fact that this dissertation written in English by a person who has had no German academic background is finally completed certainly proves the main point of this dissertation: Knowledge generation activities have no national borders. Without the help of Prof. Dr. Fischer, this project would have never existed. I should also be very much grateful that Prof. Shujiro Yazawa agreed to take the position of the second reviewer of this dissertation, despite of a quite short notice which was given by me. Conversations with him in Japan inspired me to move forward during the project period.

There are colleagues around the world who participated in a series of World Social Sciences and Humanities Network (World SSH Net) Thinkshop meetings. Their thoughts and discussions motivated me to write this dissertation, especially because their academic concerns are also closely related to academic dialogues for knowledge generation in various international contexts. I hope that my piece of work would be able to contribute to ongoing discussions of international knowledge generation practices. Further, I must express my gratitude to the organizers of the above-mentioned academic meetings and of other academic conferences in which I had great opportunities to present some parts of my doctoral project. Participation in such events gave me chances to refine and reconsider my work.

Needless to say, this work would not have been completed without help and support from people who kindly offer their participation in the empirical part of this study in Japan. Despite of the novelty of the study, the research participants tried to understand the essence of the study, and they provided really valuable comments and thoughts. The narratives of their working life as academics will certainly be contributions not only to this study but also to future studies I am going to continue. Thank you so much.

Since the empirical study was carried out in Japan, I expected some financial difficulties at the beginning of the project. In this respect, my sincere gratitude goes to The Konosuke Matsushita Memorial Foundation, Japan, for funding this project. Most of the cost which the empirical study required to be fulfilled was covered by the fund from this funding organization. Without their support, I might have had to give up some empirical parts, therefore, they played an essential role to make this study as it is.

I should not forget people who helped me achieve the final form of this dissertation. The invaluable comments from and the stimulating discussions throughout these four years with Michael Kuhn surely improved the contents of the dissertation a lot. Besides, Jack Rummel helped to make my humble English that has a strong influence of the Japanese language more sound academic English as a language editor. There are other people who provided me rather critical views about what I wrote. I should also appreciate their contesting comments and views, because they made me realize that those contesting views were exactly the main point that I tried to tackle through the dissertation. No matter how positive or negative the comments were, all the comments which reached me were good food for developing my thought.

Although it is rather indirect to this project, there have been some organizational cooperations. The World SSH Net as the main place of my academic activities provided me a lot of opportunities for academic interactions and observations of international academic activities with its network members who are located around the world. The International Federation of Social Science Organizations (IFSSO) also gave me the opportunity of encounters with academics from various parts of the world, and through the annual conferences of the Japan Society for Multicultural Relations I had valuable opportunities to meet academics in Japan, which allowed me to casually observe how academics in Japan interacted with each other on academic events. I am also thankful to the Center for Glocal Studies at Seijo University, Tokyo, for giving me time for presentations twice during the doctoral project period.

There must be more anonymous people who inspired, helped, and encouraged me during these years, but my final big thanks should go to my friends and family members, above all, lovable Lena and Chika. Without their voiceless but firm encouragement, I could not have achieved the completion of this project.

Table of Contents

Acknowledgements 5
1. **Introduction** 9
   1.1 Background of the Study 9
   1.2 Rationale of the Study 14
2. **Research Question** 23
   2.1 Grounds for the Research Question 23
   2.2 Setting the Research Question:
       Components of Academic Culture 23
   2.3 Relationship between Academic Culture and
       International Academic Activities / Collaborations 26
3. **Literature Review** 31
   3.1 The Discourse about
       How to Measure International Collaborations 33
   3.2 The Discourse about the International Structure
       of Knowledge Production in SSH 42
   3.3 Science Policies in Japan on Internationalization 44
4. **Conceptual Framework towards
   Constructing Academic Culture** 51
   4.1 Holliday's "Small Cultures" 52
   4.2 Application of "Small Cultures"
       to the Construction of Academic Culture 57
   4.3 Epistemic Culture:
       Culture in Science with No National Boundaries 62
   4.4 SSH Academics in Japan as a Pilot Case 68
   4.5 Construct of Academic Culture 72
   4.6 Academic Culture and International Collaborations 81

5. **Methodological Operationalization** **85**
    5.1   Research Design 86
    5.2   Research Methods 95
    5.3   Ethical Consideration for the Empirical Research 125
    5.4   Data Analysis Method: Grounded Theory (GT) 127

6. **Findings of the Case Study** **145**
    6.1   Academic Environment 145
    6.2   Academic Practices 185

7. **Discussion of the Case Study** **211**
    7.1   Japanese Universities and
           Higher Education Policies in Japan 211
    7.2   Self-Perception of Academics in Japan 221
    7.3   Academic Knowledge: For What? 238
    7.4   Towards International Collaborations 248

8. **Discussion of the Concept of Academic Culture
    in the Light of the Case Study** **267**
    8.1   Relevance of the Implemented Research Methods 269
    8.2   Scrutinizing the Construct of Academic Culture 273
    8.3   Contribution of Academic Culture towards Future
           Academic Debates on International
           Collaboration in SSH 275

9. **Concluding Remarks** **279**
    9.1   What Is Achieved in This Study? 279
    9.2   For Future Studies 284

10. **References** **291**

1. Introduction

1.1 Background of the Study

Internationalization has long been a challenging topic in fields of social sciences and humanities (hereafter SSH) not only in advanced countries but also in developing countries.[1] Over the past several decades, interactions among academics, such as co-authoring books and journal articles, participating in international conferences and meetings, taking sabbatical leaves or study visits in a foreign country, and planning and organizing international research projects, have increased. One of the reasons why academics, regardless where they are based, have been drawn into more international academic activities can certainly be the phenomenon of globalization in the world system.

Although there has been a great number of debates about globalization, it seems that there is no consensus on what globalization is, and scholars and critics see globalization in various ways and from various points of views (Al-Rodhan and Stoudmann, 2006). Therefore, what I briefly explain here about globalization might not satisfy all readers' view on it. Nevertheless, since it is crucial to understand globalization in order to understand the above-mentioned international academic activities and / or internationalization of SSH, I will summarise what globalization is, according to what I read from some literature on this topic.

Globalization is not necessarily a recent phenomenon. It has long existed in different ways. For instance, trading as a phenomenon of globalized economy, in which European merchants bought spices, silk, ivory, and other products that did not exist in Europe from the Middle East, Africa, India, China and other parts of Asia, has existed for hundreds of years. After such a trading period, gradually modern capitalism replaced earlier merchant

---

[1] There are different views about how and why each discipline classifies itself. Humanities, instead of human science, may be more common, since the notion of science would make some readers uncomfortable, because of that they, like Japanese academics in this study also point out, would have closer orientation to the natural science when they see the term "science."

capitalism as the organizing principle of international trade. Until the Second World War, some suzerain countries like the United Kingdom and France monopolized selling-buying activities with their colonies, which meant that these suzerains restricted the selling-buying activities within the suzerain-colony relation in order to exploit and monopolize the goods of their colonies. This peculiar type of capitalism was abolished in the post-war period as former colonies became independent nations, while another system, namely socialism, had already been introduced in the early twentieth century by the Soviet Union. Since after the end of the Cold War, structures and frameworks in which human life is organized have been dramatically unified towards capitalism all over the world, and thus people across the globe have started to use the same structures / frameworks to lead their lives with regard to economy, business, trade, politics, education, and other essential aspects of the human life. Simultaneously, scientific knowledge became one of the most important commodities (e.g. Gibbons & Wittrock, 1985) in order to create world-wide competitive goods in terms of both quality and price, and thus science also launched into the world market of knowledge under the capitalism system.

Using the same capitalistic structures has also brought numerous competitions to the world of science, because competition is a part of the nature of capitalism. Originally, the education system and academic activities of a country were nationally confined structures before globalization started influencing them. They still are, to some extent. However, when we look at the European Union (EU) countries' education reforms resulting from the Bologna Declaration in 1999 as an example, it is apparent that the higher education (HE) and academic traditions of individual countries were drastically changed, if not abandoned, in order to create a bigger education system for the EU countries. This reform was enacted to increase the mobility of students and academics so that the EU countries could strengthen their citizen's intellectual and / or professional ability, which would lead to a more competitive Europe not only in education but in economy (see EENEE and NESSE networks of experts, 2008). This reform of higher education in the EU countries is part and parcel of the internationalization policy in the region. The aim of this internationalization in the EU is obviously to increase the competitiveness of the region by unifying the education and training system, based on the concepts of the knowledge-based economy. The Organisation for Economic Cooperation and Development (OECD) explained the connection between knowledge and economy as follows: "The term "*knowledge-based economy*" results from a fuller recognition of the role of knowledge and technology in economic growth. Knowledge, as embodied in human beings (as "*human capital*") and in technology, has always been central to economic development" (emphasis in original, OECD, 1996: 9). What we can conclude from the example of the EU higher education reform and the concept of knowledge-based economy is that knowledge is a means for economic growth in the context of world-wide competition. In order to strengthen the education and research sections in HE, where knowledge is strongly related to, the EU took an action to unify the member states' HE systems. Aiming to acquire world-wide competitiveness is a consequence of globalized capitalism as mentioned earlier. In the case of the EU, this goal is not contained within a single country, but similar attempts can be witnessed in any other individual countries of other global regions. Thus internationalization of HE and / or of academic activities is often seen as a part of governmental policy in a country to increase and enforce the presence of the country in the world in respect of economy.[2]

Needless to say, national and international institutions do not always overtly state that the internationalization of HE and academe is a means for a nation state's economic growth to be more competitive in the world. Rather, the internationalization of academic activities is often posited as a way to exchange and share different academic knowledge to advance knowledge. Indeed, as in the discussion on globalization, internationalization of HE and academic activities implies various interests, dependent on its

---

[2] Germany released a report on the governmental strategy for internationalization of science. There are various foci in the report to explain why German academe, higher education, and research fields should be more internationalized apart from economic foci. Nevertheless, it is obvious from the title of report, "Reinforcement of roles of Germany in the world knowledge-based society" (Botschaft von Japan in Deutschland, n.d. The title is translated by the author), that Germany attempts to indicate its presence by internationalizing German academe and higher education to the world. This report is found in Japanese: http://www.de.emb-japan.go.jp/nihongo/kenkyusha/kokusaikasenryaku.pdf

advocates' positions and viewpoints. These diverse interests seem to have caused scattered discussions, in which little substantial coherency and interrelationship can be found.

The same is true about discussions on international and / or interdisciplinary collaborations in SSH. Even the term *collaboration* seems to be very loosely defined (Kaz and Martin, 1997) and is used to express a broad range of academic activities from co-authoring articles to implementing a research project as project partners. Therefore, various people call various academic activities collaborations, and such so-called academic collaborations in SSH have rarely been investigated to examine how collaborations are organized and performed, what challenging aspects SSH academics tend to encounter, and why they attempt to collaborate with their counterparts.[3] Rather, if one tries to find such a study, one tends to end up with finding reports that were published under or with the help and supervision of a political body or a nation state. A good example in the European context is the Monitoring European Trends in Social Sciences and Humanities (METRIS) project funded by the European Commission, which "aims to support the European Research Area (ERA) in the social sciences and the humanities by increasing awareness of the structures, resources and ways of functioning of different national systems in SSH and new developments in these systems. The aim is not only to support international collaboration in SSH but also to support national level research decisions in awareness of the broader European context" (METRIS website, n.d.). This project releases country-specific reports on 42 countries, in which the EU member states are 27, and non-EU countries are 15.[4] Although a part of its aim is "to support international collaboration in SSH" (ibid.), the reports released by METRIS do not go beyond a description of science policy, the national funding system, and the nationally prioritised research theme in SSH of countries, which could be found in websites of ministries, science councils and funding organizations of respective countries. There is no doubt that such information and statistics are useful when one

---

[3] Collective work in Kuhn and Romoe (2005) analyses modes of collaboration, methodological and conceptual challenges in carrying out cross-national research projects under the European Commission Framework Programme.
[4] On the website, it states that this project covers 43 countries, but only 42 countries are found in the "countries" section on the website.

tries to see differences between countries and to compare different systems. Nevertheless, looking at differences is less helpful in overcoming these differences, because it is still an open question *how* SSH academics could then have fruitful international collaborations at more practical level of joint academic work with all those political differences.

As previously seen, international academic activities are considered from a nation state's perspective as part of national competition in the world of globalization. Therefore, a nation state or a regional politically united body like the EU is interested in collecting the above-mentioned information about other countries in order to be prepared to compete with them. However, they are not interested in ways in which such international activities are respectively organized and performed, what SSH academics, who are the main players of the activities, think about the activities, and why academics are interested in international collaborations. It is, in this sense, a very top-down approach to reflect on internationalizing countries' academe. As a result of this approach, the authorities such as the Ministry of Science / Education would be able to know a lot about their competitors' science policies, funding systems, and their current situations of HE and research fields, but would have little knowledge about or interest in the practices of international academic activities.

This is, however, not to blame this top-down approach in relation to internationalization of SSH in respective countries. The more important point here is why SSH academics as the main practitioners of the activities have not shown much interest in investigating what is happening to themselves under the internationalization policy in their own countries. Certainly, they must have been influenced under the internationalization policy to plan their middle- or long-term academic activities. Due to the internationalization policy, internationalization as a research topic has become a buzz word in fields of SSH, but is rarely investigating the international activities of academics. If we look at a study field of HE, we can find various topics relating to internationalization, such as concerns about international students (Chalmers & Volet, 1997; Thorstensson, 2001; Major, 2005), how to internationalize faculties (Altbach & Teichler, 2001; Knight, 2004), curriculum reforms to internationalize universities (Rizvi & Walsh, 1998; Leask, 2001; Haigh, 2002), international mobility of students and

/ or faculties (Teichler, 2004; Jöns, 2007; Kim, 2009; Teichler, 2009), and other numerous topics. However, international academic activities are rarely investigated, if not totally ignored, as if there was no problem to carry out international academic activities no matter where academics are located and work.

In reality, there have been sporadic attempts at discussions about how to internationalize SSH at more world-wide level. A typical example for such discussions is the World Social Science Report (2010), in which international collaborations in social sciences are widely discussed. Although it is a positive move that some academics do discuss international collaborations, such discussions do not yet go beyond the views on countries' competitions in social sciences. That is, discussions about which country's academics published how much, and which language is dominant as a publication language, and so on are often the main internationalization topics of these discourses. Of course, these form a part of internationalization issues in social sciences, and are relevant for discussions as well, but such ranking-orientated discussions about who is bigger than whom in the world are concerned with the competitiveness of a country in the globalized social science world and tend to pay little attention to what academics practically do and how this affects their joint work when they collaborate.

1.2 Rationale of the Study

As outlined by the background of this study given above, there is a strong tendency for topics of internationalization and academic collaboration to be viewed and discussed from the point of view of a nation state, which is interested in winning a global competition. As long as the discourses including those among academics only discuss the issues from this perspective, neither any relevant analysis nor more individual perspectives of SSH academics nor how they perform their work can emerge, and consequently, the entire discussions focusing on this very political perspective will tend to be superficial regarding the practices of academic work. This is not to totally deny the wider / broader, nation state perspective to understanding internationalization of SSH, because, on one hand, this is obviously one of the topics that a great number of governments set up as a prioritized science policy nowadays, and it seems quite natural that academics discuss the topic from the same or similar perspectives, granting that such perspectives are influential to their academic work. Nevertheless, on the other hand, it is surprising that there are few academic discussions emancipated from this very political view of internationalization of SSH by people who are most concerned with the topic, namely SSH academics. Compared with numerous studies on internationalization of HE and university students,[5] the topic of internationalization of SSH which especially tries to understand and analyse current situations and conditions of SSH academics in relation to internationalization / international collaborations seems sparse. Even those who are interested in discussions of this topic tend to focus on rather country or regional-specific issues and emphasize how *our* science community would be more visible in the world or stronger than the science communities in other countries. Such discussions could only be, as they have already been, repetitive, and would not be able to reveal much more than where "*our country*" is situated in the SSH world ranking.

In order for the topic to evolve from different perspectives, it is crucial to establish other frameworks for and approaches to analyses what SSH academics currently experience in their work in the era of internationalization. There should be many different approaches / frameworks, dependent on researchers' own particular interests, and such approaches and frameworks should be explored in order to scrutinize and properly capture the current situation in which SSH academics are placed. By establishing new frameworks and approaches to more broadly discuss the issues, the discussions of the topic could, then, involve diverse directions and

---

[5] A great number of academics, especially in the field of education, investigate detailed and individual cases of university students who study abroad, for instance, to understand difficulties of both students and teaching staff who have rarely encountered students with different styles of learning, communication, and other academic conventions. These studies seem to seek how to merge different education styles in a certain country setting. However, we should note that it is often discussed how teaching staff, who are often researchers themselves of such studies, could make foreign students accommodate more into their own education style and framework. In this sense, internationalization of students at universities could be deemed as adjusting the students to a country's education. Thus, strictly speaking, such studies could also be said that they are investigated from a country specific perspective.

perspectives as well as more depth in terms of non-political but genuine academic debates.

Currently, in the fields of SSH, a bibliometric approach to gauging internationality of SSH academics and respective countries' academe seems the main approach for discussing internationalization of SSH. This approach, originally an imitation of the Science Citation Index used by the natural sciences, not only indicates the world ranking of academics and of countries but also has sparked debates among academics about whether it is appropriate for benchmarking academic work in the fields of SSH. Considering the different nature of the natural sciences and SSH, it is understandable that SSH academics feel rather uncomfortable about being evaluated simply by the number of citations of their work in the limited number of academic journals. Therefore, there certainly is a call for another evaluation framework as well as the analytical framework for international activities of social science academics.

This study suggests a new approach based on a more individual level of SSH academics' working life in relation to mainly their research activities. To be more precise, this study attempts to listen to individual SSH academics' voices, regardless of their age, gender, status, and disciplines, about some selected aspects of their academic working life that could be considered relevant when discussing issues concerning internationalization even with different country settings. Since there is almost no other existing similar study with the similar intention to this study, the research framework of this study is new.

In constructing the research framework, first it is crucial that the study tries not to contain country-specific directions. As explained earlier, extracting country-specific aspects would simply result in a description highlighting a country's academic work as being different from that of other countries. What is aimed at in this study is not finding differences of academic work between countries, but trying to discover common backgrounds / settings / structures and conceptual aspects that are closely related to each other and influence academic research work in *any* countries. Of course, peculiarity of one country's HE system and of practices in each academic discipline do exist; however, if we imagine a situation in which academics from different countries / regions and from different disciplines carry out a research project together, we would rather not think about peculiarities of each party but about how to finally reach a good, fruitful academic collaboration. In this sense, therefore, it would be better to focus on looking at aspects that could be shared among SSH academics, regardless where they come from.

1.2.1 Culture and Academic Activities— National Culture or Academic Culture?

When a certain group of people from different parts of the world is investigated, the concept of intercultural communication study is commonly used to understand and analyse where difficulties in their activities originate from, and how people can avoid such difficulties and misunderstandings. For instance, studies about students studying abroad, in many cases in English-speaking countries, can be classified as a typical part of intercultural communication studies. Indeed, globalization has brought numerous encounters between students with diverse backgrounds in terms of nationality, style of education, and native language, as well as between international students, who are often referred to as Asian students, and teaching and / or administrative staff in higher education institutions (HEIs) (e.g. Cadman, 2000; Wong, 2004; Major, 2005; Andrade, 2006; Brown, 2008; Ryan & Viete, 2009). According to such studies, the aforementioned diverse backgrounds that each person carries into universities of English-speaking countries clash, and as a consequence, those who are involved in educational / academic activities tend to experience difficulties / challenges in academic activities. Such diversity is often accounted for and analysed by inherent qualities of national cultures such as collectivism versus individualism.[6] When asking why Asian students perform poorly in Western HEIs and why it is difficult to teach Asian students in Western universities (Nisbett,

---

[6] Although analyses heavily relying on inherency of national culture is mainstream, there are academics who question this type of analyses and disagree with stereotyping people simply by their national cultures. For instance, those who teach Asian students English language find it irrelevant to apply national cultural characteristics to analyse / understand learning styles and attitudes of Asian students (e.g. Littlewood, 1999; Guest, 2002; Stapleton, 2002). Thus, intercultural communication analyses based on national cultures is not the only way, by any means, to investigate interaction between people from different countries.

2005), researchers often focus on characteristics of national educational / academic culture in which critical thinking is seen as a construct of Western academic activities (Egege & Kutieleh, 2004; Nisbett, 2005; Durkin, 2008).

Similarly, studies of international corporations in regard to human resource management analyse intercultural issues by characteristics of national cultures and / or patterns of national communication styles (e.g., Goldman, 1992; Fink & Meierewert, 2004; Möller & Svahn, 2004; Peltokorpi, 2007; Scollon, Scollon, & Jones, 2011; Kim & Meyers, 2012; Kobayashi & Viswat, 2014). Geert Hofstede can be mentioned as one of the most prominent protagonists of this type of intercultural analysis in international business settings, and his work *Culture's Consequences: International Differences in Work-Related Values* (1984) has been heavily quoted in intercultural studies. Based on surveys in forty countries, four dimensions that differ in each country culture, Power Distance, Uncertainty Avoidance, Individualism, and Masculinity (ibid.: 11), are revealed, and his findings are supposed to be "interpreted on behalf of policy makers in national but especially in international and multinational organizations who are confronted daily with the problems of collaboration of members of their staff carrying different culturally influenced mental programs" (ibid.: 12). This statement makes the exact point as the above-mentioned studies of international students, namely, that owing to cultural differences there are problems when different nationalities meet and interact each other.

Thus this approach to analysing such international / intercultural issues seems plausible, if one believes that difficulties in interactions between people from different origins occur only because of their different national cultures. Nevertheless, this approach does not seem always to match with the reality, at least not in the case of academic encounters. Previously, I implemented research investigating how Japanese SSH scholars deal with situations when they encounter disagreements from their foreign counterparts in international academic collaborations (Okamoto 2010a). This research was based on a hypothesis, which is widely studied and theorised in the field of intercultural study, that Japanese people have difficulties expressing opposition to others' opinions. The study particularly focused on theories of Hall's high and low context cultures (1976) and of Hofstede's five dimensions of national cultural differences (1994). If these theories had been applicable to an analysis of the above situation that Japanese scholars could encounter, the outcome of the research would have been that Japanese SSH scholars had difficulties expressing opposed opinions to others in the international academic collaborations. However, in fact, the outcome was the reverse of the hypothesis. What is learnt from this study is that such intercultural theories are not necessarily appropriate for an analysis and for understanding *any* encounters between people from different countries. To a certain extent, intercultural theories might be useful to describe diverse national cultural inherency in general. Nevertheless, they seem only to aim at describing cultural and / or communication style differences, which could lead to nationally confined views that distinguish one national culture from another. At least, in my previous study, the communication style of Japanese SSH academics does not seem much different from other, particularly Western, academics. Therefore, it turned out that any total dependence on intercultural theories to investigate international academic activities of SSH academics should be avoided, because, as far as activities of SSH academics are concerned, they share academic practices and conventions across countries, and the so-called national culture does not play a great role to characterise their activities.

Thus, in this study, nationally confined cultural aspects are considered as much less relevant in the investigation of SSH academics' work. Instead, it is assumed that SSH academics have their own 'professional culture'—I call it 'academic culture' in this study—which could influence their work.

1.2.2 Aims of the Study

Considering all aspects mentioned above, this study attempts to achieve the following aims:

First, it aims at creating a non-country specific approach, and rather looks at academic work as a common entity for academics in any country. If international academic activities are to be more encouraged and be increased, discussing the issue of internationalization only from a nation state's perspective would be less helpful in understanding the substance of such activities and in evolving discussions and theorization on this topic.[7] Often, science is considered as a means of reinforcing a nation state power in the world, and some academics seem to be dragged too much toward this political direction when they try to think of and discuss science, academe, and academic work in relation to internationalization. Certainly, such policy-relevant discussions are appreciated by some people who are very much interested in the position and power of a country in the world; however, on the other hand, scrutinizing the relevance of such policy-centred discussions for academics themselves is also important, because motivations for academic research can be more diverse than the ones which the existing discussions assume.[8] Then, academic work is not necessarily seen as a country-specific activity but could be an activity which has more common settings, backgrounds, and structures broadly shared by academics around the world. This study has, therefore, no intention of comparing which country is higher / lower in any ranking systems, which country is more privileged than others, and so forth. This is rather a look at shared aspects of their academic work. In this study, these shared aspects would be called "academic culture," in order to replace nationally confined characteristics, which are often exploited to analyse and explain activities among people with different nationality. By excluding the above-mentioned political and intercultural discussions, this study can better focus on the structure and the contents of academic work, which seem to consequently influence debates of international academic activities, particularly of international collaborative knowledge generation practices. Thus this study is a starting point to build up a new approach to academic discussions on topics of

---

[7] Nishihara understands that globalization since the 1990s is not only economic globalization but also globalization of society. He, as a sociologist, claims that a society should be perceived as a place for interaction between diverse people rather than considering a society as a framework of a nation state (2010: 17-18). I share his point of view that academic discussions should be emancipated from nationalistic perspectives when discussing globalization.

[8] In a research project "Global SSH" funded by the European Commission, a questionnaire study was implemented in Russia, Belarus, China, and Japan to investigate SSH scholars' international academic activities. Regarding motivations for their international academic activities, respondents of the questionnaire raised "learning from others" and "intellectual curiosity" as their motivation most frequently (Kuhn & Okamoto, 2008).

academic work in relation to knowledge generation practices that is one of the core activities in international academic collaboration.

Second, emancipated from the existing country-specific approaches, this study attempts to examine academic work from more individual, scientific academics' perspectives. Since topics on internationalization of SSH have only been discussed and dealt from macro / nation states' perspectives, existing analyses have naturally been made from viewpoints of science policy of a country and / or perspectives of advocates with rather nationalistic views. Both of these are very keen on competitions that assay which country is bigger and powerful than others. Scientific academic work in practice has been ignored in the analyses from national perspectives, and therefore, what constitutes academic work that could impact international academic activities has never been clarified. Similar to the previous point, looking at more individual and scientific perspectives of academic work could develop a new approach to analyses of the aforementioned aspects in relation to international academic activities, and could shed some light on more detailed issues which are relevant for the discussion of the scientific aspects of internationalized academic work. As a result of the implementation of the new approach, this study could suggest new fields of study of academic work that would be closely related to knowledge generation practices that could form one of the central parts of international academic collaborations in SSH.

Since little interest in investigating the scientific contents of academic work in SSH has been indicated among academics so far, launching this new approach would be able to contribute to clarifying academic work at individual and scientific perspectives from scholars, to finding challenges which could not have been noticed by the existing approaches, and to advancing debates and academic knowledge on the topic.[9] Moreover, it would make academic debates on the related issues broaden, deepen, and go

---

[9] Some exceptions are the work in Kuhn and Remoe (2005), which exhibit in-depth investigations of SSH scholars who worked in research projects under the European Commission 4th and 5th Framework Programmes. Similarly, under the 6th Framework Programme, a project "Research Collaboration in the Social and Human Sciences between Europe, Russia, other CIS countries and China" (Global SSH) also investigated SSH researchers in relation to international collaborations.

beyond the existing national frameworks in science to discuss international academic work.

2. Research Question

2.1 Grounds for the Research Question

To find out the scientific structure and components of academic work, the social environments and conditions for work are the major issues studying academic culture. Certainly, political and cultural differences between research participants cannot be entirely denied, however; rather than focusing on mainly nationally constructed differences, looking at common factors shaping academic work are the main focus of this study about academic culture, a culture academics share. By observing academic work on the individual rather than the national level of academic work this study of academic culture aims to be able to depict what the major components shaping academic work are as well as to reveal the interrelationship between each component of academic work. Considering the role the joint creation of knowledge plays in international collaborations, knowledge generation practices are considered in the context of this study as the core academic practices not only in individual academic life but also in international academic collaborations.

Indeed, such observations of the components shaping the scientific aspects of individual academic work have been widely unnoticed, if not ignored, and, therefore, it has been totally under-studied. In this sense, there is a call for a study like this one, and if one would like to go beyond the existing style of analyses based on nationally confined frameworks, the search for different orientations / positions which are neither nationally nor culturally confined by nationalities of academics, but which focus on the components crafting the working life practices of academics studying what I call academic culture is inevitable.

2.2 Setting the Research Question: Components of Academic Culture

In order to construct such an alternative framework for analysis of academic work in connection with knowledge generation practices, the research question would have to include the aspects and the concerns mentioned above. That is, the research question should not refer to any political / national perspectives to avoid repeating the same discussions as the existing studies on the related topic. Second, any emphasis of national cultural characteristics that have been believed to exist and influence human behaviour and interaction between people should be avoided, owing to the fact that the intercultural approach seems much less relevant in studying academic work (Okamoto, 2010a). Third, the study is not to analyse academic work on the basis of productivity of outcomes quantitatively, but by scrutinizing the detailed scientific elements shaping academic work. Finally, by answering the research question, the study would show the relationship between the detailed contents of academic work and the knowledge generation practices, which could be closely related to academic collaborations both nationally and internationally.

Based on the research criteria mentioned above, the following research question will be raised in this study:

How do social and human science academics carry out their work towards knowledge generation practices based on the following elements?

The elements of individual academic work that are adopted in this study are:

1. Scientific discourse practices

2. Publication practices

3. Managing academic activities

4. Disciplinary practices

5. Interpersonal relations (e.g., hierarchy, status, gender, etc.)

These five domains focus on dimensions of academic activities that play a role in international academic collaborations. They, therefore, do not include teaching practices, since they do not occur in the international academic encounters. Weidemann (2010) has similar interests to this study in international collaborations and "academic culture," and she suggests the above elements together with some others as components of academic work, which are assumed to have connection with international academic collaboration. Although elements 3 and 5 are borrowed from the suggestion of Weidemann (ibid.), elements 1, 2 and 4 are devised by myself to supplement other aspects of academic work.[10] Exploiting these five elements to investigate individual academic work would enable this study to acquire in-depth description and understanding of academic practices that take place on a regular basis in academics' working life.

It is, however, not sufficient to look only at individual academic work to understand academic work as a whole, because it can be assumed that the individual academic work has something to do with environment around such work. Since academic work is normally located in the HE system in a country, observing the location of work seems necessary. Further, the HE system is often influenced by the science / education policy of the country, therefore, some political aspects relating to academic work should also be examined. That is to say, in order to answer the research question, academic work will have to be clarified and analysed by not only looking at scientific academic practices but also at the academic environment. Then, as a result, it will be possible to outline academic work as a whole to understand the relationship between academic work and knowledge generation practices.

The following components constituting the academic environment and shaping academic culture are analysed in the study :

1. National science policies
2. Higher Education and institutional research policies
3. Mission of academics in society
4. Academic knowledge in society

---

[10] Weidemann (2010) suggests some aspects which form academic work in social sciences in relation to international collaboration. Since her discussion is structured from intercultural perspectives, it does not cover all possible aspects in academic work in general. She refers to academic writing style, but it is not the same meaning as the publication practices as the element 2 suggests.

2.3 Relationship between Academic Culture and International Academic Activities / Collaborations

The study of academic culture is the close observation of how academic work is carried out and influenced by an academic environment. It focuses on issues related to knowledge generation, knowledge management and on the publication practices and on the environment in which these pursuits are embedded.

Due to the novelty of the concept of academic culture and of the style of study, a pilot case study to develop the concept of academic culture as an analytical tool is set up. In the case of this pilot study, studying academics in Japan were selected for this purpose. The selection was not simply because the author of this study is a Japanese national, but mainly because Japan is a worldwide unique case regarding the ways it has historically established social sciences, unlike in Europe where they have been created, and unlike in the colonized world where they have been imposed to. Japan experienced a unique establishment and development of the social sciences in relation to internationalization, which involve much less aspects of a suzerain-colony relationships in the history of social science in Japan. If there is any other suitable case for this study, it could have been academics in any other country. Unfortunately, if one studies any situation of one certain country, it is often misunderstood that the researcher of the study is only interested in studying this certain country to depict particular characteristics of the country. Although this study describes and analyses the situation of academic work in Japan, this approach should not be understood as a single-country approach studying the peculiarities of a country.

2.3.1 Academic Culture Is Not a Study of 'National' Academic Culture

Studying academic culture aims at developing an analytical tool and goes thus beyond studying the peculiarities of a country. The case study about Japan is rather an attempt to study this analytical tool. More important than this case study is therefore to create a new path of academic debates on international collaborations and internationalization of SSH and to create a theoretical instrument that allows to understand how academics perform genuine academic activities, embedded in and influenced by an academic working environment. In order to create such a path for future reflections, focusing on the genuine academic work, rather than all those above debates discussed from a national perspective on internationalization, academic culture is an attempt for developing a new analytical framework studying how academics interpret their work, an interpretation of academic work with which they enter international collaborations . Thus, this study has two layers: The outer layer is to form a new analytical framework called academic culture as a contribution to the field of study. The inner layer is the description and analysis of a case study about academic work in Japanese SSH. That is, the outer layer embraces the inner one, and the distinction between them should be neither mixed up nor overlooked to fully understand this study.

Although this study can be perceived as a study of academic work in Japan (and, in a certain sense, it is), the study as a whole is not interested in classifying academic work by different nationalities or any national peculiarities. As seen earlier, my previous study about the disagreement discourse of Japanese SSH scholars in international academic collaboration failed to confirm that academic work including communication and behaviour in international academic activities is structured and framed by characteristics of a national culture. Furthermore, a taken-for-granted view that there must be differences in academic work in different geographical / national settings is only an assumption which many people seem to uncritically believe, applying such national concepts of culture to the world of academe. By contrast, Shin refers to the commonality of HE and research between the West and the non-West:

> Even though there has been an indigenous development of education and research in each country in the non-West, the model of sciences developed in the West, mostly in the United States of America, dominates the idea of sciences and its institutional configuration in the non-West, that is, as hegemony of scientific education and research among universities in the non-West. (Shin, Forthcoming: 34–35)

Albeit the various developments of education and research in the non-Western countries is recognized in the above statement, he understands that the Western style of science and scientific / academic institutions is widely shared in parts of the world other than Europe and the United States. Why, then, are always differences in academic environment and / or academic work rather than commonality emphasized?

As numerous existing studies demonstrate (e.g., World Social Science Report, 2010 published by UNESCO & International Social Science Council), there are differences of working conditions in academic work in different countries such as usage of languages, flow of research fund, and various other different conditions of academic infrastructure. This study also touches upon the academic environment as a possible influential factor in academic work shaping academic work in different ways in different national academic environments. However, as seen earlier in this study, those different academic environments do not seem to define the essential nature of academic work in relation to knowledge generations, especially as a 'national' academic culture *per se*. In other words, those different work environments can be influential to academic work to a certain extent, but it is not the whole that represents the entire academic work in one country, and it is not the essential genuine nature of what academic work is about, if one looks at academic work in international collaborations from a less political and instead more from a scientific perspective. Thus, to perceive this study as a kind of country case study to investigate particularity of academic work in a single country does not do justice to this study as a whole. Without this understanding, one will not be able to understand the relationship between academic culture and international academic activities / collaborations, which this study focuses on.

2.3.2 Can Studying One Country Relate to 'International' Matters?

Following the aforementioned statement by Shin (ibid.), we can notice that the fundamental system and structure around academic work such as the meaning of science and institutional structures are widely similar around the world due to the extensive import of the Western style of science and education in the non-West. It is the hypothesis here that by analysing how academics work we would be able to discover the common aspects in academic work of one national setting, if such systems and structures originated from the West are the fundament of other countries' academe and science.

Academic culture, which employs the basic concept of Holliday's small cultures (see chapter 4 section 2 for a more detailed discussion), perceives academic work as the activities of a certain group (in this study, academics), essentially regardless of nationalities of the group members. That is to say, it does not originally aim at making distinctions between different national academic communities, but at observing dynamic activities of the group of academics as a whole. Therefore, in this context, there is no concept of 'national', but academics are perceived as the observed object in this study, a group of people creating their own culture. Consequently, studying academics in Japan is not perceived as a study of Japan, but a study of one subgroup within the whole group that consists of the entire academic culture.

As seen earlier, it is possible to understand that not only a group of academics in the identical national setting but also an individual academic person brings a certain diversity of academic culture into international academic collaboration. Even academics working in the same country do not carry the identical academic culture, because they could also carry diverse academic backgrounds even though they work in the same country setting. Then, strictly speaking, the classification by the unit of country to judge academic culture makes little sense. A country (Japan) was selected as a matter of convenience to structure and organize the empirical research, but academics in Japan can simply be considered as people with diverse academic backgrounds who happen to work as academics in the same country.

Further, since this study is interested in what each of them may bring as academic culture to international academic scenes, the importance is placed only in ordinary daily academic work. Some may wonder how studying academic work carried out domestically relates to international activities; however, international academic experiences in this study are not understood as something exceptional that are separated from the daily work of academics but as something ongoing as a part of daily academic work. With this understanding, then, we understand that ordinary (domestic) academic work will reflect international academic work, because the way they normally work in the ordinary work environment will not suddenly change in international settings. Except for a few academics, the majority of academic work as a whole involves mainly domestic activities, and it is this domestic academic experiences which constructs the basis of academic work in general and thus it is also this domestic experiences that shapes the work of academics when they work internationally.

Unlike all those comparative studies, mainly focusing on students, trying to find differences in how different nationalities work in international settings, it seems to make more sense to study the daily domestic work of academics, and to assume that the way daily domestic academic work is carried out will appear in and influence the way academics work with foreign counterparts. In discussions of international academic activities, an emphasis of international experiences seems always to be foregrounded. However, this is merely one option to see international activities by experiences within international settings, and it is neither necessary nor the only way. International academic work is normally based on domestic academic work, therefore, understanding domestic academic work (academic culture) will be more meaningful towards the reflections on international academic work than looking at only international academic experiences, without knowing what the collaborators carry from their domestic routine work into these international collaborations.

By posing the above sketched research question, I expect this study to reveal rarely documented ways in which academic work operates. These observations should allow us to analyse the interrelation between routine domestic academic work and international academic collaborations.

3. Literature Review

Locating a new piece of research into the existing knowledge of research fields is a convention of academic research practice, since the existing research fields are the place where the new research would make an academic contribution to build up further knowledge in the field. In other words, the existing research field and the new research reciprocally exist for advancement of the academic knowledge field(s). Literature review has a significance in that it can indicate how thoroughly the author understands the academic field(s) he / she is going to contribute to by introducing and discussing the existing research topics and themes. Identifying appropriate research fields and locating the new study in them is not normally a difficult task, as long as the new study discusses within one disciplinary and / or a thematic area that has been established for some length of period. There would be a storage of related literature, be it new or old.

However, studies which deal with inter- / multi-disciplinary topics as this study does have struggles locating themselves in only one disciplinarily defined place. This is not to say that it is impossible to do it. For instance, some might try to discuss the same topic as this study from a certain disciplinary perspective such as sociology of knowledge, higher education studies focusing on internationalization of academic work, ethnography of academic working life as cultural anthropology, and so forth. Nevertheless, such attempts would only be able to depict a small part of the entire picture. This is exactly the biggest limitation for this study to synthetically understand academic work in relation to international academic activities. Therefore, in this section, some thematic topics are chosen, regardless of the classification of academic disciplines that the literature belongs to, so that the rather scattered literature in various disciplines could draw a preliminary broad picture beyond the disciplinary borders.

Additionally, there is another reason to do this: In all academic disciplines, there are very few, if not none, exact academic literatures that deals with the topic of this study. This does not imply that this study is academically irrelevant, but rather indicates the intricacy that the topics of this study comprehends.

The thematic topics of literature that can be basis and background of this study will be introduced as follows:

First, the topic will be moved to the aforementioned current 'tensions' among academics in the social science, which reviews literature discussing current structures of knowledge creation in the social science. Despite that styles and process of scientific knowledge generation seem to be shared throughout the world, today's social science academics confront diametrical structural relationships in various processes of knowledge generation. The diametrical structural relationships refer to imbalanced conditions in which social science academics carry out academic activities in International contexts. Such conditions are often expressed as centre-periphery, North-South, hegemony of Western science / scientific communities, dependence, and other different notions. Such debates are frequently seen in internationalization of HE / HEIs, and, therefore, are a central issue. It is central because internationalization in this context means world academic competitions. More details of this nature will be identified in the next section.

Second, due to internationalization, new phenomena appear in HE and social science academics. World university rankings among HEIs is one thing, and evaluation of academic work is another. Both ranking and evaluation indicate their competitive nature, and both rely on a common system that exploits well-known citation indices to rank / evaluate academic institutes and people. The extent of academic collaborations is also gauged by the same mechanism. Judging from this, bibliometric studies in relation to international academic activities certainly has a significance, and discussing it cannot be avoided. In relation to academic ranking / evaluation and academic collaborative activities that are often considered as co-authorship, literature of bibliometric studies will be introduced.

Third, the science policies on internationalization in Japan will be reviewed in this section. As this study investigates academic work in Japan as a case in relation to international academic activities, it is assumed that looking at science policies on internationalization in Japan would be helpful to summarize what kinds of discussions on this issue have taken place until now. It should also be beneficial to know the past discussion as background information, in order to better understand the analysis of the empirical study at the later stage of the this study. Besides, science policy of a country seems to greatly frame its HE system, HEIs, and people working in such systems of the country. In this sense, it is crucial to understand the development of science policies in Japan in relation to internationalization.

Thus literature on the related thematic topics to this study will be reviewed from a perspective of the academic environment, which includes scientific knowledge and knowledge creation structure in general, to a more narrowed-down perspective, which focuses on Japanese science policies regarding to internationalization. Although no exact literature that has the same focus as this study can be introduced, gathering literature with these thematic topics could provide us with an overview what has been discussed on the related issues in different academic fields.

3.1 The Discourse about How to Measure International Collaborations

Literature on international collaboration in the social sciences is difficult to identify. There are a number of studies on international collaborations in the natural sciences, however; despite the different natures of natural science and social science, some commonalities between the natural and the social sciences in respect of international collaborations could be found. The most obvious commonality is that scientific collaborations are very closely related with the publication of scientific articles / books. Luukkonen et al. (1992) study scientific productivity by exploiting co-authorship patterns in international collaborations. Katz and Martin (1997) as well as Glänzel and Schubert (2005) confirm that co-authorship could be used to gauge collaborative activities. Thus the major interest of academics in international collaborations seems to be the relationship between co-authorship and collaborations.

Considering the way academics understand international collaborations, it is easy to imagine why the role of citation indices has become so crucial in order to gauge international collaborations. Katz (1999) states that "bibliometric indicators can provide a reasonable measure of the publishing size and impact of these research communities" in fields of economics and psychology which, according to him, are more internationally orientated than the other social science fields, which are supposedly more bound to national contexts. On the other hand, he also admits that the use of the bibliometric approach in the social sciences is somewhat problematic compared to its use in the natural sciences (ibid.). In the same light, Hicks (2005) shares the concern of Katz on the use of the bibliometric approach to gauge academic activities in the social sciences by indicating other types of publication pattern in the social sciences and humanities than publishing in academic disciplinary journals. According to her, books, national literature, and non-scholarly literature coexist with academic journals in English that are listed in the Social Science Citation Index (SSCI) for the fields of social science. As a consequence, "a core literature is less clearly delineated" (ibid.: 474), because the SSCI does not mention these other non-journal publications.

Although the bibliometric approach is considered problematic especially in the fields of SSH to measure the achievements of academic researchers, its use persists within the SSH fields. As a corpus of studies that deal with world structure of knowledge creation, World Social Science Report (WSSR) published by UNESCO and International Social Science Council (ISSC) in 2010 widely involves studies exploiting various bibliometric studies that indicate how knowledge in the social sciences is created and evaluated in an unbalanced manner.[11] Exemplifying a few, Frenken and his colleagues study research collaborations between nine geographical regions by exploiting the SSCI and the Art and Humanities Citation Index (AHCI) to identify which global regions are centres of and therefore dominant in social science research collaborations. They conclude that North America and Western Europe dominate in such collaborations, and that centre-periphery structure of knowledge generation and dissemination has persisted for more than two decades (Frenken, Hoekman, & Hardeman, 2010). That means that regions other than the two dominant regions are marginalized in knowledge generation and dissemination activities in the social science. Gingras and Mosbah-Natanson arrive at the same conclusion as Frenken and his

---

[11] Especially chapter 4, titled "Uneven Internationalization," discusses where and in which language social scientific knowledge is created, based on data retrieved from the SSCI and the AHCI.

colleagues (ibid.) that North America and Europe are the most favoured global regions in social science research. This situation, they continue, questions other regions' autonomy, and other regions consequently tend to be dependent on the dominant regions (Gingras & Mosbah-Natanson, 2010). Ammon is more interested in languages for scientific communication and asserts that English is a hegemonic language in scientific activities and that Anglophone researchers / research institutions benefit from the use of English language in terms of funding, flow of information, and attractiveness of Anglophone universities (Ammon, 2010). Thus the SSCI and the AHCI are exploited to confirm inequality in social science knowledge generation and dissemination in the world.[12]

Although the aforementioned studies in the WSSR (UNESCO, 2010) all indicate rather negative aspects in the structure of knowledge generation and dissemination in the social science by the bibliometric approach exploiting the SSCI and the AHCI, the authors do not question much about the usage of such citation indices to measure academic activities. Rather, they believe that those citation indices can be very useful to map the current social science world, co-authorship between countries / regions, and proportion of respective publication language (English, German, French, etc.) by looking at a number of citations (personally, nationally, and regionally). This is, in fact, a typical usage of the citation indices in SSH to gauge today's international academic activities. As an example of this trend, Ayata and Erdemir (2010) exploit the SSCI and AHCI to gauge the extent to which scholars working in Turkey in SSH fields collaborate with scholars outside Turkey.[13] They claim that their study indicates the growth of internationalized scholars based in Turkey in terms of co-authorship, the number of publication, the number of citation, and

---

[12] For further detailed discussion about hegemony, domination, and inequality in social science research activities, referring to the WSSR (UNESCO, 2010), see "What is Hegemonic Science? Power in Scientific Activities in Social Sciences in International Contexts" (Okamoto, 2013).

[13] Ayata and Erdemir do not mean the nationality of scholars in this context, but those who work in Turkish organizations. As they explain, academic outputs of Turkish nationals working at a German university are excluded in their study, while those of German nationals working at Turkish universities are included (2010: 269).

impact of their publication. In keeping with the authors in the WSSR, Ayata and Erdemir do not show any methodological concern with the usage of the citation indices for evaluating academic activities in SSH.

On the other hand, some scholars show their scepticism about this approach for the aforementioned purpose. Lariviere, Gingras, and Archambault (2006) state that the bibliometric approach poses three major problems: Firstly, knowledge dissemination practices in SSH are more various than ones in the natural sciences. Second, subjects of research in SSH are often more locally (or nationally) orientated and, therefore, these research articles are typically published in the mother tongue, not necessarily in English, unlike the natural sciences. Third, disciplines in SSH have more paradigms than in natural sciences, and as a result, publications in SSH is more fragmented. Therefore, they suggest that such citation indices cannot be relied on to produce research impact indicators and to rank individual HEIs' research performance (ibid.: 521). These points are mostly in concert with Hicks's view about the problems inherent in relying on the SSCI and the AHCI database to measure academic activities (Hicks, 2005). By contrast, Lariviere et al. (2006) suggest that such mechanism could be useful to "map SSH scholars' collaborative activities by measuring joint publication of articles and highlighting differences among disciplines." Often, SSH scholars exhibit their doubts about the usage of the citation indices, compared with usage of the Science Citation Index (SCI) in the natural science and engineering fields, as though the bibliometric approach perfectly fits in order to measure achievement of natural scientists, unlike in SSH. However, contra their assumption, Seglen (1997) suggests that it is not feasible to evaluate the quality of scientific work in natural sciences by totally relying on the SCI database. He starts the discussion by stating as follows:

> Ideally, published scientific result should be scrutinised by true experts in the field and given scores for quality and quantity according to established rules. In practice, however, what is called peer review is usually performed by committees with general competence rather than with the specialist's insight that is needed to assess primary research data. (ibid.: 498)

His critique on evaluating published scientific work is that people who evaluate such work do not necessarily obtain expertise in fields which they evaluate as committee members of scientific journals. Consequently, their evaluation tends to rely on "secondary criteria like crude publication counts, journal prestige, the reputation of authors and institutions" (ibid.). This statement can be interpreted to mean that published scientific work is evaluated by committees who are not particularly specialists in what they judge, therefore, they inevitably rely on the above-mentioned "secondary criteria" to evaluate scientific work rather than quality of contents that can only be scrutinised by "true experts in the field" (ibid.). Editorial board members of academic journals are believed to be chosen because of their excellent scholarly records, therefore, are considered as experts / specialists of relevant field(s) that a journal deals with. Based on this assumption, however, Bedeian, Van Fleet and Hyman (2009) find that it is not necessarily the case that editorial board membership is a result of and / or reward for excellence of their scholarly work. Thus not only is judging the quality of scientific work a difficult task, but also there is an important issue who is going to judge the quality.

Moreover, it has been widely believed among SSH scholars that natural science and engineering fields are much more properly evaluated by exploiting the SCI, due to the fact that work in those fields are more commonly published in English (van Leeuwen, Moed, Tussen, Visser, & van Raan, 2001), that knowledge created is less national / local context-bound than SSH (Hicks, 2005), and that natural scientists tend to publish more in scientific journals than other dissemination channels (Glänzel & Schoepflin, 1999). It might not be, to some extent, a totally wrong observation about the evaluation system in natural science and engineering; nevertheless, Seglen, whose study focus is impact factor of journals in the context of evaluation of published work in natural sciences, reveals that "a substantial fraction of scientific output is published in the form of books, which are not included as source items in the database" (1997: 500) in many fields of natural science. He assumes that this omission results in serious bias in evaluations if one relies on only such a database. Additionally, he refers to publication language bias in using the SCI as a means of evaluation, because of the SCI database prefers to English language journals. As a result, non-English journals that are included in the database will get low impact factor. This point of the language bias is agreed by van Leeuwen et al. (2001). They investigated the language bias in the coverage of the SCI that could impact international comparisons of national research performance by focusing on comparative aspects among five Western countries (the US, the UK, France, Germany, and Switzerland), and found out that non-English language journal articles have "a considerably lower impact than those in the English language journals" (ibid.: 345). Therefore, France, Germany, and Switzerland in their study tend to be underrepresented in the SCI database. Such issues of overrepresentation of English language journals and of non-coverage of books and other types of publication by, for instance, the Thomson ISI database, are also discussed in natural science and engineering fields in exactly the same way as this issue is discussed in SSH. Academics discuss these various biases in the databases as well as the subtleties in selection procedures of articles (Bedeian, Van Fleet, & Hyman, 2009) and of journals which are adopted in the SSCI (Klein & Chiang, 2004).

Thus, researchers into this bias, on one hand, indicate quite serious scepticism about the bibliometric approach to benchmark academic work, but continue to use the approach, on the other hand. In this contradictory situation, we sense a need for another concrete evaluation system that could judge not only quantity but quality of academic work. One consequence of quantitative-based evaluation is the severe worldwide competition on the institutional level in the ranking systems such as the Times Higher Education world university rankings and Academic Ranking of World Universities published by Shanghai Jiao Tong University.[14] On the individual level, a consequence is the aspiration towards recognition of scientists / scholars. The evaluation system and the

---

[14] Despite its popularity, the relevance of Shanghai Ranking in measuring academic performance of HEIs is sometimes questioned (Liu & Cheng, 2005; Billaut, Bouyssou & Vincke, 2010). Liu and Cheng, who are actually working for the Ranking Group in Shanghai Jiao Tong University, state that those who are interested in such a measurement "should be cautious about any ranking and should not rely on any ranking exclusively, and make their own judgement regarding ranking results and indeed ranking methodologies." (2005: 132) Because they admit that there are some methodological and technical problems that are pointed out elsewhere, they indicate their awareness of those problems and suggest solutions and future improvement of this ranking system, while some scholars like Billaut and the colleagues (2010) strongly reject and seek alternatives to Shanghai ranking.

worldwide academic competition both at the institutional and the individual levels are closely interrelated. Particularly, when the trend of internationalization is considered, a great attention and interest of HEIs and people working there is geared towards how they become recognised and become prominent, within such a competitive mechanism (e.g. Weingart, 2005; Hazelkorn, 2009).[15] In other words, bibliometric study has acquired importance in the world of academe, due to the fact that performance of respective HEIs and academics has to be measured with scores for indicating their productivity and impact of their academic work. Furthermore, the evaluation result would consequently influence enrolment of students, especially of postgraduate / doctoral students, recruitment of faculty, and external funding at the institutional level. On the individual level, this system affects the process of acquiring a tenured position, promotion, and obtaining membership in highly recognized academic society / societies (for the discussion at the individual level, see Cole & Cole, 1967; Merton, 1968; Merton, 1988). This correlation between the ranking / evaluation system and academic fame / benefit is, thus, obvious. The better the ranking / evaluation is, the better and the more privileged conditions both individual academics and academic institutes can achieve. Therefore, as an important source of judgement of 'quality of academic work', the bibliometric approach carries great weight with the academics, administrators, and institutes. Since academic collaboration, which is almost synonymous to co-authoring, nowadays is also a decisive component of such rankings, it is, therefore, not surprising that academics view co-authoring as a way to assert their excellence of their work and / or of the country their institutes are located in.

Recognizing the limitation of the bibliometric approach to gauge individual academic achievement and outcomes of international collaborations, some academics attempt to go beyond this approach and to analyse academic work more qualitatively, for instance, in order to understand the motivations for collaborations. Katz and Martin (1997) are interested in economic aspects that could influence academics' motivations for academic

---

[15] Background of this competitive mechanism relating to internationalization / globalization and scientific knowledge is briefly discussed in the introduction under background of the study of the thesis.

collaborations. They cite the sharing of instruments and facilities and the falling price of travel and communication as influential aspects for academics to be motivated to participate in collaborative academic work, while Melin (2000) doubts whether cheaper travel and communication costs really contribute to the increase of international collaborations. Welsh and Maloney (2007) raise an issue of challenges that academics encounter in international research teams such as group diversity, communication, physical proximity, and task interdependence. Some others are also interested in the proximity of collaboration partners, and Lariviere, Gingras, and Archambault (2006) state that using the same language and physical proximity can be decisive factors in choosing collaboration partners. However, physical proximity does not seem to be a major challenge in international collaborations, since international inevitably implies being remote to each other, and, after all, academics could "collaborate over distance" (Kraut et al. 2002) with the kinds of communication technologies that are available today.

From the above technical / pragmatic perspectives on international collaborations, some academics shift discussions to more individual perspectives that try to look into experiences of individual collaborative research. Melin (2000) seeks more individual motivations for international collaborations and the process of actual activities. He reviews existing literature relating to the topic and finds that micro (individual) level of analysis on the topics such as motivation and reasons for collaboration, what benefits academics expect from collaborations, how they found collaboration partners, and how collaborative work was organized have not yet been well-explored. Kuhn and Weidemann (2005) carried out a study that depicts how research collaborations in the European Commission's Framework Programme were undertaken and what methodological, conceptual, and managerial challenges academics encountered in the research projects. Although the participants of their study are confined to European researchers, the study manages to extract that there are diverse ways of perceiving concepts and terminologies, different understanding on research methods, and challenges in using the English language as a mutual communication language throughout research projects. This profound study contributes to further studies: Weidemann and Kuhn (2005) investigate the role of English as a lingua franca in European social science research collaborations. Although, as they state, it is the reality that English is widely used for academic publications and communication between academics who do not share their mother tongues, implications behind the use of English for academic purposes, particularly in the context of international collaborations, are not yet much explored. Weidemann and Kuhn (ibid.) shed some light on other elements of the use of English than individual English language proficiency, which could often be a main topic for discussions on international collaborations. Furthermore, Weidemann (2010) points out some elements that might cause misunderstanding and miscommunications in international collaborations and suggests a "polycentric social science" approach (ibid.: 371) to overcome challenges based on the assumption of a shared Western style of academic work, which could hinder mutual academic discourses and smooth collaborations.

From the literature reviewed above, one must conclude that studies that look at the contents of academic work in the context of international collaboration are still scarce. The reason why this type of study has not been well-developed until now might be the domination of evaluation / ranking based style of academic work. As I previously noted about the relationship between globalization and the social system in the framework of capitalism, competition has become an inevitable structure of any social life including academic life. Since this competition requires an evaluation about which party has more than the others, it requires a comparison of one party with another. In this way, a systematic and 'objective' evaluation mechanism, represented by the citation indices in respective science fields, is introduced and exploited. Then, some academics who focused on this particular aspect of academic work started to form a field of study in relation to internationalization of academic work and / or HE. This is how and why the bibliometric approach gained such popularity as the legitimate approach to analysing academic work. Despite some disagreement with this approach from some academics, the bibliometric approach seems to be the only approach that can be understood as a theoretical and methodological approach in discussions of international collaborations and / or internationalized academic work. However, it is quite apparent that the bibliometric approach cannot cover all aspects of academic work, as the aforementioned literature indicates. Therefore, further research, including scrutinizing the validity of the bibliometric approach, should be built up on the existing qualitative research.

3.2 The Discourse about the International Structure of Knowledge Production in SSH

After about some decades of observation on international collaborations, patterns of collaboration have been identified by a number of academics. Such analyses of international collaborations are, however, just confirming the world map of academic power / hierarchy, which was already obvious before such analyses. For instance, discussions on academic centre versus periphery, North versus South, West versus non-West are at the centre of the topic of such studies. Whichever terms are used, they all highlight the skewed power balance structure in the world of academe between so-called developed and developing countries (e.g. Gaillard, 1994; Cano, 1996; Canto & Hannah, 2001; Jentsch & Pilley, 2003; Boshoff, 2009).

Connell (2007) challenges the North-centred structure of the social science by claiming that metropolitan theories which were generated in the global North are neither placeless nor universal, because they ignore the diverse social world of the South. Altbach (2002) uses the term centre-periphery to explain the above-mentioned structure. He starts his discussion from admitting that "the conditions of academic profession and of academic work in developing countries is not positive" (ibid.: 3) and clearly states that some elite universities in the North set the standards of academic work everywhere, even across the developed countries. He also notes that European countries imposed their own academic models to their colonies, and that the influence remained even though these imposed countries could have got rid of the European model in their societies and replaced it with their own after their independence. Not only are the peripheries dependent on the institutional model of the centre but also on funds, resources, and facilities for research. According to him, being periphery is related to dependency (ibid.: 5).

With regard to dependency, Syed Farid Alatas is one of the most renowned advocates of this concept. In his work, Alatas analyses dimensions in which these periphery countries are dependent on the centres in the North. He exhibits the dimensions of dependency as follows: ideas, media of ideas, technology of education, aid for research and teaching, investment in education, and demand in the West for Third World social scientists' skills (2003: 604). He also refers to the relationship between colonialism / imperialism and the current structure of academic knowledge production, which seems similar to the aforementioned argument of Altbach (2003), referring to the colonial influences that still persist in the former colonies of the West. Nevertheless, Alatas claims that "academic neo-imperialism or academic neo-colonialism as the West's monopolistic control of and influence over the nature and flows of social scientific knowledge remain intact even though political independence has been achieved" (ibid.: 602). What he means is that the current structure of the world academe is not based on colonial power of the West but on the condition of academic dependency "of Third World scholars and intellectuals on western social science in a variety of ways" (ibid.).

Whether or not developing countries / South / periphery are dependent on the developed / North / centre social science academe, this power structure is widely recognized and has also been analysed by numerous academics. Indeed, it is not a new field of interest due to the more recent phases of internationalization / globalization of HE and the academe. For instance, in 1978 Edward Said criticized Western scholars for looking at and judging people, culture, and life in the East from Western perspectives, although his work about 'Orientalism' (2003, [1978]) received as much criticism as support.

As the above-mentioned literature shows, the structures of academe, of academic knowledge generation, and of academic life in the world are influenced by the political and economic power of certain countries. Such discussions are certainly helpful when drawing a world map of academe in respect of inequality / skewed balance of man-power, materials, funding, and the like; however, there is little discussion about how academics can move forward to build up alternative structures in relation to international collaborations and internationalized academic work. It is certainly not easy, though, to build up such structures, and analyses on the topic will stagnate if any attempt to move out of the current situation is not made. As seen, most of the academics who are enthusiastic to discuss the international structure of knowledge production use contrastive terms such as North / South, centre / periphery, powerful / dependent, dominant / dominated, and so on (Kuhn, 2013: 41). These contrastive terms tend to create an image that the powerful party rules the international knowledge generation system and ignores the less powerful one(s), and therefore, the powerful one is referred to as the hegemon (as its rule as "hegemony") in the world academe. This adversary relationship seems to be rooted in the competitive system that is supported by the world ranking of HEIs and various level of rewards / fame for individual academicians, [16] as reviewed previously about the bibliometric approach. The discussion on this adversary relationship is more related to conditions in which academics all over the world carry out academic work, as Kuhn rightly points out (ibid.). In other words, those advocates of the adversary relationship in the international knowledge generation do not pay much attention to ways in which academic knowledge is generated in practice but to ways academic knowledge is disseminated and valued internationally. Consequently, very similar to the discussions around the bibliometric approach and evaluation of academic collaboration, it can be concluded that existing literature on the structure of international knowledge generation reveals that the whole discussion on this issue is from the result of the competitive nature of scientific fields in the era of globalization / internationalization, and that there are very few discussions that focus more on what academics could do to overcome this skewed structure.

3.3 Science Policies in Japan on Internationalization

In the previous section, it seems clear that the international structure of knowledge creation in SSH is divided into two polarised parts, no matter how one expresses it. Japan, however, has not been clearly defined as the either part in this structure. As a

---

[16] For more detailed discussion about hegemony in social science and recognition, see Okamoto (2013). It is stated, "notions of hegemony, power, and dominance could merely be a way to disguise the losers' irritation and frustration toward winners" (ibid.: 59).

developed country, it can belong to the "North" from economic and materialistic perspectives, but if the country is observed in terms of its international role in academic knowledge creation activities, one would certainly hesitate to call Japan a "centre" of world knowledge creation.[17] Thus, it is quite hard to understand the situation of Japanese SSH in relation to internationalization from the overview of a world map onto which a great number of scholars try to draw by the bibliometric approach and the conceptual framework of world knowledge system. The aim of this section is to view the internationalization of Japanese SSH from literature that introduces political attempts to internationalize the Japanese HE / HEIs. By looking at such internal discussions and political decisions, the position of the Japanese academe in relation to internationalization, and what it tries to achieve by internationalization, becomes clearer.

Historically, it is recognized that there were a number of scholarly exchanges between Europe and Japan during the nineteenth century just after the establishment of the University of Tokyo, originally Tokyo Imperial University (Ishida 1984). Simultaneously, European mainstream theories in social sciences (mainly law, politics, and economics, later sociology) at the time were translated into Japanese and taught in Japan (ibid.). This trend to import and acculturate one could call "intercultural translations of knowledge" from Western social sciences and still

---

[17] Kuwayama (2004) sees Japanese anthropology as rather peripheral, compared to Anglo-American anthropology. Alatas (2003) refers to the case of Japan in the similar context that it is not so clear where Japanese social science is located in the world social science. His discussion about academic dependency is quite closely interrelated to respective nation states' political and economic power in the world. If we strictly follow his argument, Japan can be qualified as a dominant country in social sciences. However, he continues, some cases such as Japan and Germany have different styles to practice academic activities in social sciences. That is, in Japan and Germany "great prestige is to be derived from publishing in the national language in nationally recognized periodicals." (ibid.:606) What he means by this statement is that these countries are the politically and economically developed countries, but they do not take the typical Anglo-American style of publication as a means of knowledge dissemination in social sciences. Consequently, such countries opt "out of that game" (ibid.). He has difficulty categorizing such countries neither as a scientific power nor as being dependent, and after all, gives a name for them as the "semi-peripheral social science power" (ibid.).

continues to a great extent in the today's Japanese social sciences (Machimura, 2010), although, unlike in the nineteenth century and the beginning of the twentieth century, this process is no longer strongly politically initiated.

Although the Western social sciences were imported by such intercultural translations of Western academic publications and via the exchange of scholars between Japan and the West, this does not mean that the Western social sciences totally penetrated the scientific knowledge in Japan or Japanese culture as a whole.[18] Rather, the imported Western social sciences were and are modified so that these theories fit into the framework of Japanese society and its cultural settings. Ishida (1984) takes an example of absorbing the German national politics into the Japanese politics. He explains that Japanese scholars had to exclude some liberalistic aspects in the German theories of nation state and to add, moreover, some mysterious and patrimonial elements that appear in ancient documents such as the *Chronicle of Japan* (ibid.: 40). This is because the introduction of Western social sciences was major part of the Meiji government's goal of making Japan an international player on par with the Western imperial powers. *Fukokukyouhei* (富国強兵), which literally means enriching the country and intensification of the army, and *datsua'nyuou* (脱亜入欧), which means getting out of Asia and joining Europe, are the well-known political slogans of this period in Japan. In order to achieve such status of the nation state, the Japanese government prioritised learning from the mainstream knowledge in the West, especially from Germany, France, and Great Britain, in order to build a successful nation state like those European countries.

The relationship between the national policies and the internationalization of the academe in Japan is thus obvious.

---

[18] Nakayama (1989) suggests two different modes in the development of Japanese HE: First was a "window shopping" mode in which Western (in this particular period of the late nineteenth century, it was European) models were observed and partly adopted, and second was an "involvement" mode that largely appeared in the post-Second World War period in Japan to adopt particularly the U.S model of HE system. Although the "involvement" mode shows the strong influence of the U.S occupation in Japan just after the Second World War, Nakayama points out that the Japanese HE is a unique case in the world that had almost no imposition of any Western country on its educational and academic system.

However, a great number of academics, discussing internationalization of HE and academe today seems to believe that the policy on internationalization of HE and the academe is a rather new issue in Japan and has only become popular since late 1980s. Umakoshi (1997), for example, is one of those who advocates that the policy on internationalization of HE and HEIs is new, and he exemplifies what kind of activities have been implemented for internationalization of the academe in Japan. Among the issues Umakoshi has raised, one of the most frequented topics is increasing the number of foreign students in the Japanese universities. Ishikawa (2009) clearly mentions that internationalization is a politically prioritised issue in Japan, and consequently Japanese universities aim at recruiting more international students as well as foreign faculty members. Similarly, Horie (2002) takes the so-called Nakasone plan, which was set by the Prime Minister Yasuhiro Nakasone to increase the number of foreign students in Japan by 100,000 by the year of 2000, to exhibit the political trend on internationalization of HE in Japan, and deploys the argument while discussing what should be done by the Japanese government to increase the number of international students as well as suggesting challenges which are involved in an increasing number of foreign students. There are further discussions about how these international students could be accommodated themselves into Japanese HEIs. In this context, Lassegard (2006) investigates the obstacles and requirements for international students, starting his study from this very governmental policy to increase the number of international students in Japanese HEIs. Tanaka and her colleagues study international students in Japan in respect of adjustment that the international students might experience during their stay in Japan (Tanaka, Takai, Kohyama & Fujihara, 1994). Murphy-Shigematsu (2002) explores psychological aspects of international students in Japan, as a response to the ongoing policy since 1983 by the Japanese government to increase international students. A work of Shao (2008) that compares the Japanese education policies released in 1983 and in 2008,[19] has more political implications,

---

[19] The policy released in 1983 is the Nakasone plan as shown in the main text, while the one in 2008 was released under Fukuda Administration. This new plan was supposed to be continuous from the Nakasone plan and aims at increasing international students in Japan by 300,000 as of the year 2020.

and exhibits situational changes for HEIs and international students in Japan during the period between 1983 and 2008 as well as changes in political aims to increase international students. Indeed, most of studies relating to the topic of internationalization of HE and HEIs discuss this governmental policy as a starting point of their studies and attempt to suggest solutions towards obstacles and challenges that are identified in these studies.

Similarly, increasing the number of foreign scholars in Japanese HEIs is also mentioned as another aim of the Japanese science policies regarding internationalization. However, few studies of foreign scholars teaching in Japan have been carried out. Huang (2009) admits that research concerned with the internationalization of academic life such as research activities carried out by Japanese academics is rarely reflected on. Huang (ibid.), therefore, analyses the current situations of Japanese HEIs as well as of academic profession in Japan quantitatively by exploiting surveys which were implemented in 1992 and in 2007. The result of his research shows that in the 1990s and 2000s, faculty members at Japanese HEIs became less enthusiastic about exchanging scholars and any other kinds of efforts to make Japanese scholars more international (ibid.: 157).

On the contrary, despite of the HE internationalization policy to encourage Japanese scholars and students to go abroad to enhance international academic competitiveness of the Japanese academe as a whole, the topic investigating academic activities of Japanese scholars and students abroad generally seems very much under-researched. The topic of studying abroad is, thus, considered to be connected to studies on foreign language learning problems (e.g. Morita 2010; Mimura et al. 2003), which are emphasized by Japanese academics, while studies and analyses of Japanese (or Asian) students studying at Western HEIs seems to be a job of Western scholars. Thus, the foci of research on internationalization of the Japanese academe is still rather import orientated, that is, a great number of research focuses on how to acquire and obtain international students and to make them comfortable with Japanese HEIs, while what happens to Japanese students and / or academics when they encounter different academic environment abroad does not raise rescrarch interests.

It seems that the national research institutes in Japan mainly carry out research on international collaboration between Japanese and foreign academics. However, the contents of such research are reduced to counts of which Japanese academics have co-authored studies with foreign academics, and with which countries Japanese academics collaborated, and / or would like to collaborate, in the future, and in which academic fields collaborations are frequent and reasons why this is the case (Ebihara & Kuwabara, 2009; Usami, Hara, & Takasugi, 2010). Thinking about what actually happens in such collaborations, how they are carried out, who is doing what, what the challenges are, or where such challenges originate from is not a topic for those national research institutes, because they are more interested in the status and rankings of Japanese academics. One could, therefore, say that science policies on internationalization of the academe in Japan in principle remains as was in the Meiji period, in which import of Western social sciences was the major interest of the Japanese government (Okamoto 2010b: 63). While the principle approach is the same, today's Japanese science policy seeks to compliment the strategy of importing sciences with ways to also support the export of knowledge created within Japan via either increasing the number of international students or publishing Japanese academics' work in English via supporting more co-authoring with foreign scholars.

4. Conceptual Framework towards Constructing Academic Culture

The concept of academic culture is neither known nor well-established. Even though the term can be sometimes witnessed in academic writings, it refers to various meanings and covers a wide range of activities not only in work carried out by academics as this study attempts to investigate, but institutional aspects and activities as HEIs (Jensen, 1982; Altbach, 2004), and activities at schools, colleges and universities carried out by pupils and students (McCabe, Trevino, & Butterfield, 2001; Broeckelman-Post, 2008). Thus it can be said that academic culture has been expressed differently dependent on its authors' interests. Therefore, there is a necessity that meaning of academic culture in this study is clarified before we start looking at any details of academic culture in this study.

As a starting point, a conceptual framework which structures academic culture of this study will be introduced. This framework is based on the concept of "small cultures" advocated by a British linguist, Adrian Holliday, who is a strong protagonist of the non-essentialist approach of studying cultures. In general, people's perception of cultures is often based on and inclined to concepts of 'large' (or 'big') culture that is strongly interconnected with ethnicity / nationality. Despite its popularity in academic research, adopting the concept of 'large' culture for studying academic activities seemed quite problematic, because it is more likely that some other factors could influence academic activities than mere national cultural traits of academics.[20] In this light, Holliday's non-essentialist orientation well matches the interest of this study.

Therefore, in the section, Holliday's "small cultures" will be firstly introduced and explained in order to support the construct of academic culture. Then, how the concept of small cultures is applied to construction of academic culture will be explored. The

---

[20] It refers to my previous study on SSH scholars' disagreement discourse in international collaborations (Okamoto, 2010a).

construct of academic culture will be followed by explanatory statements indicating relationship between academic culture and international academic collaborations.

Additionally, relating the alternative understanding of culture to national culture / large culture, Karin Knorr Cetina's "epistemic culture" will be briefly introduced and discussed in relation to conceptualizing culture in science / academic work. Although the structure and concept of academic culture is strongly influenced by the concept of small culture advocated by Holliday, Knorr Cetina's epistemic culture has a great relevance in this study to the extent that it pursues the relationship between culture and knowledge without involving nationality / ethnicity of practitioners in order to discuss culture. While agreeing with the fundamental structure of epistemic culture, there is also disagreement with and unsuitability of application of epistemic culture to this study. Therefore, aspects of epistemic culture that conceptually clash with fundaments of this study will be examined and explained.

4.1 Holliday's "Small Cultures"

Among the other linguists with teaching experiences of English language in non-English speaking countries (e.g. Littlewood, 1999; Guest, 2002; Stapleton, 2002), Adrian Holliday is the linguist who felt uncomfortable about essentialist approach to investigating learning attitudes of students who study English as a foreign language, because using stereotypical national cultural traits only generates "reductive statements" (Holliday, 2000: 40) that is already known before any research activity starts. This means, since the national cultural traits are already defined and fixed by theories, research findings would only confirm that their research samples / participants *do* have the very cultural traits that are already known. That is to say, a researcher set up a hypothesis that behaviours which is problematized in his / her research are caused and appeared, due to national cultural traits of research object(s). Findings of the research, then, simply confirm that the hypothesis which is based on predefined national cultural traits is applicable to the researched case. While one could claim that it is because the theory describes national cultural traits so well and precisely that it could be applicable to such studies of human's behaviour, others like Holliday would find it reductive and feel uncomfortable that all human's behaviour is verified only by this nationally confined fixed cultural traits, as if there was no complexity in explaining human's behaviour but only differences in cultural traits defined by nationalities of people.

Holliday also points out that often cited cultural traits within the essentialist approach to cultures such as individualism versus collectivism, masculinity versus femininity, and all other contrastive descriptions of cultural traits "supports various spheres of political interest" (1999: 243), and they can allude that one culture is right and other is wrong. In a great number of cultural studies, Western culture and / or views seem to be considered positive, good, and therefore right, while those of non-Western are reverse to the Western ones. As the renowned work of Said (2003 [1978]), *Orientalism* expresses, one cannot escape from his / her own Western norms when a Western Self sees Others, and they almost unconsciously and uncritically analyse something new and / or different for them based on their norms and conventions in their Western life. This is how people are led to contrastive descriptions of culture and human beings, which imply and judge what is right or wrong.[21] Holliday exhibits some types of discourse of culture, and regarding to this above contrastive aspect in cultural studies, he classifies this as 'West as steward' discourse that contains "the notion that non-Western cultures are deficient and lack characteristics which can only be learnt in the West." (2014: 3) According to him, those who believe in this type of discourse think that "they are well-wishing and provide genuine support" (ibid.) for non-Western people, but such a belief can also indicate superiority and justification of Western culture[22] to non-Western ones. Therefore, it can be understood as that they say that our culture is better and correct, and that is why we should lead people from other cultures to better ways of life by making them learn our better culture. Thus, 'culture A versus culture B' type of

---

[21] For instance, Said states on the Orientalist approach as follows: "The West is the actor, the Orient a passive reactor. The West is the spectator, the judge and jury, of every facet of Oriental behaviour" (2003, [1978]: 109). The statement implies and describes that the West is active, good, and correct substance compared to the Orient.

[22] Holliday considers that this 'West as steward' discourse can be seen also in political scenes as military actions against non-Western countries in order to save people there and 'War on terror' situations (2014:3).

discussion and analysis seems to involve a great risk to define and judge not only culture as such but also people who are considered as practitioners of a certain (national / regional) culture as either positive or negative substance. [23] As seen in the work of *Orientalism* by Said (2003 [1978]), positive one is, needless to say, the Western, and the negative one is non-Western culture. Therefore, no matter how many times such a type of essentialist approach to studying cultures is implemented, it can always only draw the same conclusion, which is how different non-Western culture is from the Western culture, and how we can adjust the non-Western people to the Western ways of life and behaviour.

In order to avoid mixing up (national) political interests with academic interests and repeating the same statement about people studied, Holliday takes another approach to understanding people's behaviour and culture, which is non-essentialist approach. For Holliday (2000), culture can be "discovered" by non-essentialist approach because it "can help us to unlock *any* form of social behaviour by helping us to see how it operates as culture per se" (emphasis in original). His intention is not to define culture as "X rather than Y, but to clarify what we mean when we use the word in different ways for different purposes" (1999: 238). Hence, Holliday does not claim that non-essentialist approach, which is later introduced as "small cultures," is correct and the only one to analyse people's behaviour, rather he introduces an alternative way to understand people's behaviour that is more an exploration than confirmation of predefined ethnic / national cultural traits in people.

From the aforementioned conceptual standpoint, Holliday distinguishes culture as two forms: One is large cultures and the other is small cultures. The distinction of these is not exclusively Holliday's own; the meaning of small cultures, advocated by him could be different from others. Large cultures mean cultures that are classified by geographical region / country such as Asian and

---

[23] Holliday (2014; 1999) also refers to the "centre-periphery" discourse as a related example of the contrastive type of discussion on culture. This centre-periphery relation, at a glance, seems to be often claimed by people in the periphery side how hegemonic the centre, in other words, the West is. Although this claim seems valid to point out the Western cultural hegemony and to liberate the culture and people in the periphery, they are practicing the same essentialism as the so-called centre / West does.

Japanese, which is the foundation of essentialist approach. On the other hand, small cultures are seen differently: Some people might see small cultures as a matter of size, and therefore, might understand them as subculture. Simultaneously, subculture is considered as a deviant form of large culture. Then, subculture, as Holliday points out, is "essentially a large culture concept" (ibid.: 238–9). That is to say, subculture is only small due to its size compared to large culture, but it belongs to large culture as its fundamental concept. Holliday calls this structure and relationship between large and subcultures as "Russian doll or onion-skin" to visualize it, and what he advocates as small culture is not subculture. Rather,

> The idea of small cultures . . . is non-essentialist in that it does not relate to the essence of ethnic, national, or international entities. Instead it relates to any cohesive social grouping with no necessary subordination to large cultures (ibid.: 240).

Thus, in his concept, small culture has little to do with size, and is different from so-called "subculture" which is a component of large cultures that are categorized under ethnicity / nationality. To explain small culture a bit more in detail, Holliday (ibid.) refers to a study of a secondary school in Cairo, implemented by Herrera (1992), which informs us that Herrera found the secondary school in Cairo very similar to Herrera's own experiences at "the parochial school in downtown San Francisco" (ibid.: 80–1, cited in Holliday, 1999: 239) despite of the superficial difference between two schools in different countries. That is, what Holliday attempts to show readers is how culture can be dealt with without touching on essence of the national / ethnic, crossing freely "the boundaries of larger cultures" (ibid.), and therefore small cultures "constitute a seamless melange which stretches across national boundaries" (ibid.: 240).

It seems quite obvious that his emphasis on small cultures is based on a strong disagreement with the idea of 'culture' as something predefined, fixed, and oversimplified into a stereotypical categorization by mere ethnicity / nationality. This categorization stemmed from the large culture concept results in "otherisation," and according to Holliday, otherisation is the process in which "the 'foreign' is reduced to a simplistic, easily digestible, exotic or degrading stereotype. The 'foreign' thus becomes a degraded or exotic 'them' or safely categorized 'other'" (ibid.: 245). That is to say, in the process of otherisation, 'foreign' (to the Western) would not be observed in details, but rather, would be simplified and minimized as totally exotic substance to 'us'. The separation between 'us' and 'them' and indicating superiority of one party to the other yield discussions on culture inevitably reductive and repetitive, since the message in such discussions is firmly fixed and directed to the same conclusion as advocates of it intend. Therefore, Holliday's concept of "small cultures" can be assumed as a new concept of cultures that would attempt not to bind people's behaviour by nationality / ethnicity but to understand it by looking at them as a unit of cohesive social groups. Indeed, small culture does not mean to generate different type of definitions of cultures, but more to observe "a dynamic, ongoing process which operates in changing circumstances to enable group members to make sense of and operate meaningfully within those circumstances" (ibid.: 248). In this process, Holliday does not deny that group members of a small culture would bring any other small cultural residues from other settings, environments, and experiences, even the residues can be from their large culture. However, those residues are not deemed, in the context of small culture, as 'differences' that would or might cause tensions in behaviour of the group members. Instead, commonalities of settings and experiences are appreciated more than differences as elements forming the new small culture. Thus the concept and meaning of small culture may be novel to many of us; nonetheless, it has a certain potential for deploying a new type of discussion on culture that can be more explorative and flexible to investigate people's activities and behaviour without relying on overgeneralized national cultural traits.

As a summary of the above discussion, the two paradigms of small and large cultures are briefly explained and characterized.

	Small cultures	Large cultures
Character	**Non-essentialist, non-culturist** Relating to cohesive behaviour in activities within any social grouping	**Essentialist, culturist** 'culture' as essential features of ethnic national or international group
Relations	No necessary subordination to or containment within large cultures, therefore no onion-skin	Small (sub)cultures are contained within and subordinate to large cultures through onion-skin relationship
Research orientation	**Interpretive, process** Interpreting, emergent behaviour within any social grouping Heuristic model to aid the process of researching the cohesive process of any social grouping	**Prescriptive, normative** Beginning with the idea that specific ethnic, national and international groups have different 'cultures' and then searching for the details (e.g. what is polite in Japanese culture)

Table1: Two Paradigms of Culture (Source: Holliday, 1999: 241)

4.2 Application of "Small Cultures" to the Construction of Academic Culture

It is neither easy nor straightforward to discuss people's behaviour and activities by using the term *culture*, since the notion of (large) culture involves the inevitability of differentiation of people (otherisation) and implication of superiority of a particular culture (often the Western culture). The serious concern is not only that large culture- oriented discussions would put great emphasis on stereotypical national / ethnic cultural traits but also that they introduce the hierarchy between those national / ethnic cultures that could be unnoticeably exploited in political debates. It is, then, no wonder that a considerable number of studies dealing with intercultural issues always reaches the same conclusion that culture of nation A and that of nation B are different each other by the nature of otherisation in such discussions. At the same time, there would be an unstated message in the declaration of that culture A and B are different. That is, it is not a mere classification but the judgement of which culture is better than the other (c.f. Holliday, 2014). Further, due to the popularity of this type of intercultural study and its frequent use among the academic researchers,[24] the majority of them do not seem to notice that one particular culture is considered superior to the others in this conceptual framework. [25] Although there could be regional / national cultural traits in people's behaviour and mind, there certainly is a risk of simplification and overgeneralization on people under study when the concept of large cultures is the only one that is available as the conceptual framework to study diverse people's behaviour and activities.

There is a good example of this simplified and overgeneralized intercultural approach which was not workable to analyse people's behaviour in international settings. My previous study exploiting the large culture concepts such as "collectivism," "uncertainty avoidance" (Hofstede, 1984) and "high-context culture" (Hall, 1976) failed to *confirm*[26] that the so-called Japanese national cultural traits existed in work of Japanese academics when they encountered disagreement discourses with their foreign counterparts in international academic collaborations. This research outcome simply made me question the sole and total reliance on essentialist intercultural theories, which very roughly classify ways of people's behaviour around the world, for analyses

---

[24] It is quite evident that popularity of certain types of studies, theories, and methodologies justifies their correctness in quality in the field of social sciences. Citation indices are greatly appreciated and heavily relied on to benchmark the quality of scholarly work. I call it as the "democratic approach / majority rule" (Okamoto, 2013: 66) in social sciences to explain why the role of citation indices in social sciences (and humanities) is so significant. That is, the more cited, the more credibility of work is given, and it leads to the evaluation that such work is excellent. In this sense, popularity means high quality, excellence of work, and credibility of contents of work.

[25] It is not only Western but also non-Western academics that are keen to analyse people's behaviour by the large culture concepts. Obviously, in the large culture context, non-Western culture is considered as less superior (or, even worse, inferior) to Western culture in most cases. This implies that non-Western people / culture subordinate to Western counterparts, and such an implication will only be able to generate vertical structure of discussions about cultures.

[26] Confirming that it is how they are because of their national cultural trait is a typical analytical style of intercultural studies. It is the essentialist / culturist approach exploiting the concept of large cultures.

of academic work which involves international elements. In other words, there should be another approach than this conventional approach in order to study academics as a unit of group regardless the places they are located in the world.

I, therefore, paid great attention to the concept of small cultures advocated by Holliday, because I noticed that SSH academics around the world practice similar, if not the same, contents and aspects of academic work. In terms of generating academic knowledge, there is not a Japanese, American, or African academic work, but fundamental academic work which can be shared its concept and practices around the world such as acquiring the existing knowledge,[27] planning and carrying out a research project, and publishing research findings. Then SSH academics around the world can be assumed that they form a certain culture around academic work, regardless of their individual nationalities (See the illustration A below). Borrowing Holliday's notions, SSH academics around the world could be a unit of "social group" and academic work could be "cohesive process of any social grouping" (ibid.: 241). It is, then, possible that the study of academic work in whichever countries would be emancipated from analyses bound by national cultural traits by application of the concept of small culture.

---

[27] In Holliday (1999), something similar is mentioned with an example of university students from different parts of the world to establish their own small culture.

60 Conceptual Framework towards Constructing Academic Culture

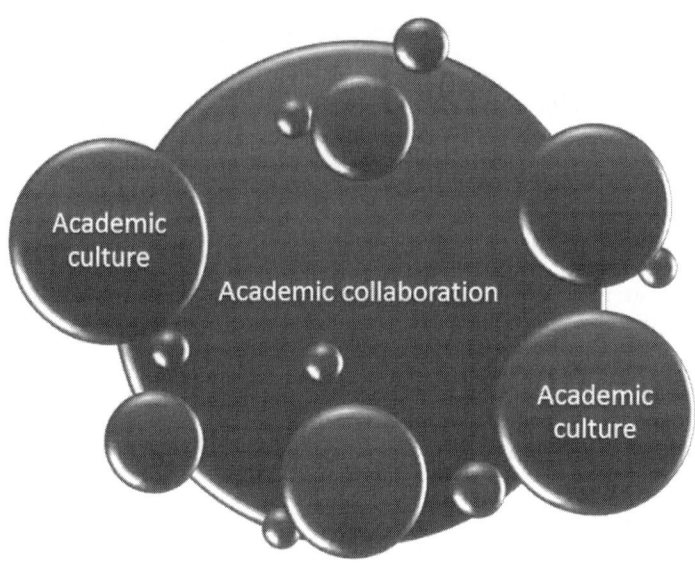

Illustration A: Individual Academic Culture and Academic Collaboration

Moreover, small culture is "more to do with activities taking place within a group than with the nature of the group itself" (ibid.: 250). In other words, it is possible to understand contents of activities in details rather than defining what the group under study is. If academic work is to be understood as a flux, dynamic activity rather than still and unchanging one, it would be less meaningful to fix it in one place with a definition. Holliday suggests that small culture is "a means to investigation rather than an end in itself" (ibid.: 255), and it seems to be an appropriate approach to study a certain group of people, whose work tend to face up ongoing changes and new aspects. Academic work in the globalised academic world can be claimed as such type of work. Especially, talking of international academic knowledge generation practices, academics would encounter various situations and challenges which they have never experienced before.[28]

---

[28] As work of Kuhn and Weidemann (2005) and Weidemann and Kuhn (2005) suggest, what academics took for granted in their own academic conventions could turn out to be quite different from the academic conventions in other countries. International academic collaborations could, therefore, imply

The concept of small culture could, therefore, be favourable to establish a concept of academic culture. Academic culture is intended to have no subordination of national / regional culture and is liberated from the fixed framework as studies exploiting large culture concepts often end up with. There would be no hierarchy, no segregation of people with different nationalities / ethnicities, and no fixed definition of people's activities by the application of a small culture concept to establishing academic culture. As a result, the study would be more explorative, heuristic, and qualitative than the existing studies on people of different nationalities.

By setting up the framework of academic culture, not only could we closely observe academic work in a confined setting[29] but also we could exploit the observation for future similar studies to clarify and confirm elements and factors in academic work which could influence international academic activities. An ultimate aim of establishing academic culture is to achieve mutual discussions among scholars on academic work in SSH without the "battlefield"[30] nature of discussion by understanding what aspects and practices effect on activities of generating academic knowledge. I expect that this new type of discussion could be deployed with

---

generating a new way of academic work. Judging from the work of the above, there does not seem to be the only one correct way to work in international collaborations, but there could be many patterns. In this sense, academic work in international collaborations can particularly be deemed as flux and dynamic type of work.

[29] In this research project, the setting is the SSH academics / academe in Japan. It often tends to be interpreted that the study seeks 'Japanese' particularities in academic work if one has an image of conventional cultural / intercultural studies. This study, however, has little intention of finding 'Japaneseness' in academic work, but to exploit the academics and academe in Japan as a case, in order to obtain broader views that are applicable to other similar settings, which, in the context of this study, would be other countries' academics and academe.

[30] The notion of "battlefield" refers to Kuhn's critique on the current status of globalized knowledge generation practice as following: "Are they seriously thinking an internationally acting academic is a kind of intellectual soldier gathered and organised in national science entity fighting a battle between national science organisations from different countries?" (Kuhn, 2013: 43). He refers to how the current discussion on international knowledge generation practices, and describes that it is as if they were on the international battlefield to fight for their own nation states with academic knowledge generation practices.

more qualitative nature of research that would look into details of academic work rather than conventional quantitative analyses of academic work. It is not to reject quantitative analysis on this issue, but would suggest introducing an alternative way to analyse and discuss it, so that SSH academics could see their own work from various angles,[31] especially when their work is located in a global setting.

4.3 Epistemic Culture: Culture in Science with No National Boundaries

In the discussion of small culture, a great emphasis was put on the aspect that the concept of small culture does not involve any analysis of stereotypical national / ethnic cultures, since national cultural traits do not seem to necessarily influence academic work (Okamoto, 2010a). Although the term *academic culture* and similar notions of culture in settings of universities can be found in some studies (e.g., Tierney, 1988; Epps, 1989; Darder, 1991; Siepmann, 2006), they tend to discuss culture more in teaching and learning settings rather than academic activities of scholars / scientists focusing on knowledge generation. Even though there are studies focusing on the life of academics or the academic profession (Bourdieu, 1988; Yamanoi, 2007; Arimoto, 2008), their interests are scattered in various aspects of academic life, and they do not seem to focus particularly on knowledge generation practices.

Under the aforementioned circumstances of studies dealing with culture in relation to knowledge / knowledge generation practices, Karin Knorr Cetina's work of epistemic culture is outstanding. With regard to the relationship with this study, the approach of Knorr Cetina to construction of culture in science is worth noting, because the concept of epistemic culture does not put emphasis on national cultures in scientific activities. This is, in the context of this study, significant, since it is rare to find academic discussions and theories that are related to a term *culture* without a notion of nationality / ethnicity as the core element of discussion. Emancipation from the notion of national

---

[31] Currently, academic work can be only evaluated quantitatively by number of citations, as discussed earlier.

culture when discussing science and / or knowledge implies that the discussion which Knorr Cetina developed, and her use of the term *culture*, focuses on science and scientific activities, not on differences rising from national culture. This point is the fundamental commonality between her study and this study to approach to analysis of academic work. Therefore, the development of epistemic culture seems meaningful to look at in the context of this study.

Second, Knorr Cetina paid close attention to scientific practices rather than "the history of scientific ideas, the logic of scientific discovery, or the analysis of scientists' writings." (Knorr Cetina & Reichmann, 2015: 18) Placing the focus on scientific / academic practices in order to understand and analyse scientific / academic work is an uncommon approach, and the majority of scholars who are interested in 'cultures' of scientific / academic work tend to look at current situations in which such work is placed, outcomes of work, and development of scientific work from the past to the present, as Knorr Cetina and Reichamnn have pointed out. In other words, these conventional approaches to studying science and / or knowledge are often only interested in the status of science / scientific knowledge as well as academic work / persons / profession and the development of such status by observing them chronologically. That is to say, these analyses are outcome-based and use academic publications as the source of their discussion of how science / scientific knowledge is and was produced. Although this kind of analysis may be understood as a study of scientific practice, due to the understanding that the academic publications are a means of recording of scientific / academic work, it is not the same as observing what is actually done during the process of achieving scientific knowledge as an outcome of scientific work. Indeed, the process and the practice of scientific knowledge generation has widely remained unknown, if not ignored, in studies of science / knowledge, noted as "black box" (Knorr Cetina, 2007: 363; Knorr Cetina & Reichmann, 2015: 18) to indicate how much it is unknown to scientists and scholars. As a point of departure to study science / academic work, the approach that looks at work practices is common in both Knorr Cetina's epistemic cultures and in this study.

Thus, the way to relate culture to science / academic work and the approach to studying scientific / academic activities are shared between Knorr Cetina's epistemic cultures and academic culture of this study. Therefore, this study seems to be able to relate to the approach from which epistemic cultures are constructed and developed, and the conceptual framework of epistemic cultures seems to be relevant and applicable to construct academic culture in this study. However, despite some commonalities and similarities between these studies on science and on academic work, there are also some unignorable points that are incompatible with each other. In the following part, I give reasons why the conceptual framework of epistemic cultures cannot be adopted in the study of academic culture.

Disagreements with Epistemic Cultures as the Conceptual Framework

First of all, the emphasis put on epistemic cultures by Knorr Cetina is quite different from the one in academic culture. The main interest that epistemic cultures hold is studying and understanding "amalgams of arrangements and mechanisms . . . which . . . make up *how we know what we know*" (emphasis in original, Knorr Cetina, 1999: 1) in scientific work. As briefly introduced in the previous part, Knorr Cetina is concerned with the fact that no one seems to pay much attention to how scientists accomplish scientific knowledge through their work. Instead, science has been considered as a unified entity, which can imply that once scientific work achieved a form of 'knowledge', such knowledge is all labelled as science. At this point, Knorr Cetina had a strong opposition towards the taken-for-granted view of "unity of science" (Knorr Cetina, 1999: 3), therefore, attempted to disunify the science by exhibiting "*diversity* of epistemic cultures" (emphasis in original, ibid.). Obviously, her assumption and belief is that science is not a simple single entity, and she states, "[T]he background assumption which motivates the concept is the idea that science and knowledge may not be as unitary as has been thought" (Knorr Cetina, 2007: 364). In order to disunify the science, Knorr Cetina saw the necessity of closely observing practices in scientific work which is to accomplish scientific knowledge as outcomes of such work.

Although, as noted earlier, Knorr Cetina's approach is in agreement with the approach of this study, the main objective to achieve by the Knorr Cetina's approach is dissimilar from the one of academic culture. Knorr Cetina clearly expresses, "I am interested not in the construction of knowledge but in the construction of machineries of knowledge construction" (Knorr Cetina, 1999: 3). While this study of academic culture is interested in elements and factors surrounding and consisting of academic work to understand effect(s) towards knowledge generation practice, Knorr Cetina's emphasis is more put on the "machineries of knowledge construction" (ibid.) to understand and clarify the diversity of science. This means that Knorr Cetina seeks more diverse aspects within science / scientific work by identifying the machineries. The following statement is revealing this point:

> Magnifying this aspect of science—not its production of knowledge but its epistemic machinery—reveals the fragmentation of contemporary science; it displays different architectures of empirical approaches, specific constructions of the referent, particular ontologies of instruments, and different social machines. (ibid.)

Then, second, Knorr Cetina's perception of *culture* turns out to be different from the one in academic culture. That is to say, as the term *epistemic cultures* indicates, "sciences are in fact differenciated into cultures of knowledge that are characteristic of scientific fields or research areas" (Knorr Cetina & Reichamnn, 2015: 18). It is indisputable that Knorr Cetina hoped to find different characteristics between different scientific fields, if the main objective of her study was disunifying science. This results in the term *epistemic cultures* with the plural form, since, in her view, there are diverse cultures in science. On the other hand, as explained in the previous part about small culture, culture in this study is understood as a means of investigation for ongoing activities within a group, rather than a fixed definition / characteristics of a group. Since this study attempts to look at commonalities rather than differences in academic work towards knowledge generation, the perception of culture in epistemic cultures, which seek diversity and differences in science / scientific work, seems simply contradictive as the conceptual framework of this study.

Third and finally, although more minor compared to the two previous points, difficulties in applying study examples taken from the natural sciences to studies of SSH constitute another reason why Knorr Cetina's epistemic cultures cannot form the framework of this study. Although it is claimed that epistemic cultures can be discussed in other contexts than discussions of science (e.g., Knorr Cetina & Reichmann, 2015), it is difficult to apply various aspects Knorr Cetina explores in the study of epistemic cultures. For instance, as Cronin (2003: 6) rightly points out, "the epistemic culture of the high-energy physics community is far removed from the world of humanities scholarship". Further, Cronin (ibid.) refers to issues of co-authorship and of the role of individuals in a big scale of scientific collaborations in the context of epistemic cultures, and these are also not issues for humanity scholars, as their work is much more individual based. Indeed, Knorr Cetina's epistemic cultures are based on scientific practices in laboratories for experimental work, which involve machines and other facilities for experimental work. Besides, they are not considered as mere locational settings where science / scientific knowledge is generated but are given significant roles to identify characteristics of epistemic culture in each studied field (Knorr Cetina, 1999).[32] The emphasis is put on analysis and interpretation of non-human objects to discuss epistemic cultures:

> One of the characteristic features of research in the natural sciences is that it brings together the world of non-human objects with human contexts and processes. . . . The underlying idea here is that the human environment and the object world are two separate spheres, which need to be brought into some sort of an alignment, for science to discover how the strange objects tick. The practices of creating this alignment, and of working with strange effects and behaviors, are *a core component of epistemic cultures*. (emphasis of my own, Knorr Cetina & Reichmann, 2015: 19–20)

At this point, it is obvious that epistemic cultures are constructed to study so-called hard science, which involves non-human objects in research. If the aspect of bridging non-human objects and human contexts is the core component, epistemic cultures cannot be a candidate to study academic work in SSH, where the emphasis of non-human objects can hardly be found.

To summarize, as an approach to study science / academic work, epistemic cultures and academic culture have commonalities. Despite of the notion of culture, both are not

---

[32] As examples, chapter 2 discusses laboratories under the chapter title "What Is a Laboratory?", and chapter 5 deals with the roles of machines (detectors) under the title "From Machines to Organisms: Detectors as Behavioral and Social Beings". (Knorr Cetina, 1999)

interested in analysing scientific / academic work by units of nationalities of practitioners and by units of locations where such work takes place. This can avoid a trap of viewing academic / scientific work from any perspectives based on nationalities. Although it is not clear whether or not Knorr Cetina's epistemic cultures had a certain intention to avoid analysing culture in science by a unit of nation / nationality, excluding this aspect is one of the most important criteria on establishing the analytical and conceptual framework of studying academic work in this study. In this light, epistemic cultures is worth noting as a reference to structuring a study of culture and science / scientific work, since studies involving culture tend to prefer analysing phenomena under study by culture of a country / nationality.

Another outstanding aspect in the work of epistemic cultures, which is shared with the approach of this study, is that it attempts to closely observe scientific practices at work. It may sound natural that a scholar observes practices of his / her research object, but it is not very usual to witness it in studies relating to science / academic work and other topics around academic knowledge. In other words, academic / scientific work and academic people are unlikely to be an object of empirical study in research. Probably, there might be an assumption that scholars / scientists know about how their work is and how they work, and this assumption could lead them not to carry out empirical study. Knorr Cetina, however, clearly states about the relation between culture and practice as follows: "*Culture*, . . . refers to the aggregate patterns and dynamics that are on display in expert practice and that vary in different settings of expertise. Culture, then, refers back to practice in a specific way" (emphasis in original, Knorr Cetina, 1999: 8). In this statement, the importance of practice in her study related to culture can be seen. Understanding culture by observing practices is exactly what this study aims at.

Thus some conceptual and methodological approaches in Knorr Cetina's work seem to be very similar to the ones of this study. Nonetheless, it turned out that more fundamental aspects are in disagreement each other. While the main focus of Knorr Cetina's work is finding out differences in scientific work by understanding machineries of knowledge construction, this study will focus more on looking at and / or finding out common grounds in academic work in order to further discussions of international academic activities with regard to knowledge generation, which have been only looking at differences in them. With this regard, the perceptions of culture between this study and hers are totally different. Since the perception of culture in a study play a great role in defining the orientation of the study, this disagreement lies in not being able to adopt epistemic cultures as the conceptual and analytical framework of this study. Were it possible to introduce the framework of epistemic cultures, there would be other difficulties that the study of natural science should be transformed into the study of SSH, both of which have incomparable work settings, styles of work, and aspects of work. This means that the fundamental structure of epistemic cultures is unlikely to be adopted in this study.

As discussed, Knorr Cetina's epistemic cultures has some noteworthy aspects as a study of science which refers to culture. However, due to the fundamental differences in the focus and the orientation, exploiting the conceptual and methodological framework of epistemic cultures does not seem feasible in this study. Therefore, academic culture is structured according to the aim and interest that this study holds. In the following section, a detailed construct of academic culture will be introduced.

4.4   SSH Academics in Japan[33] as a Pilot Case

SSH academics in Japan are exploited in this study as a pilot case in order to establish and to develop an analytical framework of academic culture. Although selecting academics in one particular country might seem to contradict the non-nationally confined approach as suggested earlier, this is not to investigate characteristics / peculiarity of academics in Japan. A country

---

[33]   Please note that the notion of "academics in Japan" does not have exactly the same meaning as the notion of "the Japanese academics". "Academics in Japan" includes scholars of any nationalities working in Japanese universities, while "the Japanese academics" implies academics whose nationality is Japanese. This difference in this study is significant, because it informs us that academics in Japan in the context of this study are understood as heterogeneous in terms of nationality, but they simply work in the same geographical space, which is Japan, regardless of individual nationalities. It seems to be oversimplified if one national science community is perceived as a group of one nationality. Thus, the above two notions looks similar, but have such different and important implications.

which is exploited as a case in this study can be any other country than Japan in the world, and if one country was selected, there may be a misunderstanding by readers that the study attempts to pursue descriptions of the object as a country-specific study of a certain topic. Nevertheless, the main aim of this study is not depicting situations of academic work in one country, but establishing the new analytical framework to better understand how academic work in SSH fields is carried out, in order to enable to this study to contribute to future academic debate on international academic activities from a different perspective than existing debates. In this sense, academics in any countries could be a case for this study; nevertheless, the intention of exploiting a case of academics in Japan is the following:

First, unlike many other countries, Japan is a country that is much less affected by the history of being either a suzerain or a colony. Such a suzerain-colony relationship has great impacts on how science in a country has been developed, as well as on other social, political, and economic aspects, and the impacts from their suzerain country / countries quite often remain even after the independence of the colonies. It can be witnessed that former French colonies, as an example, have strong French influences in their education and science, not only which language they use for academic debates but also what literature should be referred to, how to construct academic articles, and so on. This suzerain-colony relation in science should not be overlooked, since it could easily lead the entire discussion in this study to the postcolonial debates. Certainly, the postcolonial debate is one of the most essential issues and should not be ignored in discussions on internationalization of SSH in a broader sense, however, post-colonialism does not necessarily form a part of academic activities in all countries. From this viewpoint, and as a starting point of building a new framework for analysing academic work, the possible best first case for the study would be a country that has less influence of a suzerain-colony relation. In this sense, Japan is one of the rarest cases in the world because it has had much less impact in this respect. Although this does not mean that Japan is totally neutral in this respect, at least, it is assumed that academics in Japan have very little influence of suzerain-colony relation in their academic activities. Then, the study is emancipated from post-colonialist debates, which is rather unsuitable for the context of this study.

Second, internationalization is not a newly emerged phenomenon for the Japanese academe. The origins of Japanese social sciences were already very international. Some disciplines of social sciences were imported and introduced from European countries, which were then the most advanced countries in social sciences, particularly from Germany, France, and the United Kingdom, until the Second World War, and from the United States after the war (Ishida, 1984). Unlike the above-mentioned suzerain-colony influences that forced one country (colony) to accept another (suzerain) country's science, Japan purposefully chose to learn from social sciences of the above countries, because these countries were economically and politically the most powerful countries in the world at the time. When Japan's national seclusion ended in the nineteenth century, the Meiji government took a political decision to learn from these powerful countries in order to become similarly powerful country. The science policy of the Japanese government then, therefore, was a part of the political aim to become a world-wide power (Okamoto, 2010b). Japan invited scholars from these European countries, especially from Germany, which seemed the most suitable country from which to learn.[34] Thus German influenced social sciences were taught at the first imperial university, currently the University of Tokyo, many foreign books were translated into Japanese to acquire the social science knowledge generated in those countries, and the Japanese government sent students and scholars to these countries and paid for their expenses (Ishida, 1984). In such ways, the Japanese social sciences started and absorbed the foreign social sciences in order to achieve the political ambition of the government. Interestingly, the knowledge acquired through this process was not a simple imitation of the European social scientific knowledge. Since no other power ever imposed European knowledge on Japan, Japanese scholars adapted European knowledge to better match the Japanese societal reality in various ways. By doing so, gradually the Japanese social sciences found its own way for further

---

[34] Prussia was the most favoured model for a nation state building for Japanese elites at that time. The first Japanese constitution was established with help of some German scholars.

development. It is, indeed, very unique that the social science of one country emerged and developed in this way, without insisting on their own scientific tradition and thoughts or having another country's science imposed on it. In other words, the fields of social science in Japan has been voluntarily developed in a very international and collaborative context since the nineteenth century at a time in which internationalization was not yet an important issue for many other countries.

It seems worthwhile to study today's cases of academic work in Japan, since, as the above-mentioned history of the Japanese social sciences informs us, the case of the Japanese social sciences is much less influenced, unlike other non-Western countries, by any imposition of social sciences of the suzerains (Nakayama, 1989). Under these circumstances, all the above-mentioned debates concerning the history of political power which could influence academic work / academic life becomes much less relevant in the case of Japan and therefore more fundamental issues focusing on the aspects of acculturations in the realm of academic work could be studied in the case of the Japanese academe, while cases of the former colonized countries inevitably focus on impacts of their suzerains' imperialism in their academe.

To summarize, the social sciences in Japan could be seen as a unique entity in terms of studying the contents of academic work (academic culture). Considering the numerous debates about how academic activities are influenced by suzerains such as the United States, Great Britain, France, and other Western countries, Japan is a rare case among non-Western countries, which has evolved its own knowledge, concepts, and theories in the social sciences out of Western social science knowledge without being forced to do so, as well as being unique in that the incunabula of social sciences already had international aims and means. The field of social science in Japan, therefore, could stand for a model of an inherently internationalized science community with little influence of scientific power on them. It is also not unimportant to notice that some fields of studies to have emerged from Japan such as managerial theories (e.g., Nonaka 1994) have been influential in the world of academe, despite of the fact that it is normally only these former suzerains that rule and influence the entire world of academe. Thus the way Japanese social science has been developed to include international perspectives, and the outcomes of its internationally well-regarded science community, are unprecedented. Hence, studying the academic culture of SSH in Japan allows for a distinct approach to and analysis of academic work, unlike the ones in most other countries in which the social sciences tend to be the product of a suzerain-colony relationship, resulting in a more imitation of the Western science and structure of academe.

4.5 Construct of Academic Culture

Academic culture in this study is constructed in order to investigate and analyse aspects of academic work that could be related to and therefore influence activities of international collaborations, which is, in this research context, considered as collaborative activities of academic knowledge generation. In other words, academic work is defined in this research as generating academic knowledge. Therefore, even though most of academics are based in universities and are committed to teaching and supervising students as well as their own research activities, teaching work is scarcely counted as academic work in this study. Moreover, any aspects which are specific to a particular country, discipline, and university would not be explored, because it is presupposed that collaborations can be international, inter / cross-disciplinary, and / or across diverse universities even within a country. If any specific aspects are taken into account, the research outcome would put more emphasis on differences rather than shared aspects of academic work. It is true that individual country, discipline,[35] and university may have its uniqueness, however; the uniqueness is out of this research context.[36]

---

[35] Holliday states that academic disciplines can be assumed to have small culture (1999: 250). In this sense, academic disciplines can also form academic culture, although it would a different research contents from this study.

[36] Needless to say, in other research contexts / settings, it would be possible to include the specific aspects. For instance, researching a particular discipline's academic culture would be possible. What I emphasize here about the specific aspects is to clarify the construct of academic culture for this particular study on academic work with regard to international academic collaborations.

Academic culture in this research is divided by two aspects:[37] Academic environment and academic practice. The following section gives the details of the respective aspects:

4.5.1 Academic Environment

Academic environment is largely a situation where academic work is located. Although the main focus of this study is to investigate academic work itself, the backgrounds, settings, and locations of academic work cannot be ignored, since they could also influence ways academic work is structured and carried out. In order to investigate such background aspects, the following factors are identified:

- National science policy

    Such as funding system / programmes and nationally prioritized research topics / fields could directly influence ways in which academic work—in other words, research activity—is structured. This does not mean that academic work is controlled by national science policy, and that therefore academics have no autonomy in carrying out their academic activities. Though some might feel uneasy about discussing the relationship between national political agenda and academic activities, it is naïve to consider that they have nothing to do with each other. Certainly, science policy in each country exists, and the policy is passed to national science / research councils for implementation of research that is required by the nation state, then finally it reaches at respective universities, other research institutes, and academics. It is also

---

[37] The two aspects and individual factors in them are identified and set up, according to a variety of literature on structure of Higher Education (HE) system, roles of HE institutes, and other numerous studies on HE in general. Strictly speaking, they are too broad to identify and define academic work at more individual and practical level, since interests of above literature do not necessarily share the interest of this study. However, since there are few studies which have similar orientations to this study, and consequently, no clear identity and definition of academic work in this context could be found in the existing literature, these levels and factors had to be newly identified and devised by myself.

apparent that there always are research trends for research topics / themes, and societal and / or national demands for academic research, which are largely defined and decided by national science policies. Additionally, national science policy also has an impact on funding programmes / topics of private funding agencies to some or great extent. In this sense, academic work is largely framed by national science policy and is influenced by research stakeholders' interests. Therefore, taking aspects of national science policy into consideration in forming academic culture is of importance, since national science policy is one of the most significant environmental factors for individual academic work.

Relating to national science policy, the topic of university governance should be mentioned. Studies of university governance are very closely related to university reforms from around the 1980s to the early 2000s, which could be seen around the world with the introduction of New Public Management (NPM) into public sectors such as universities, together with a notion of knowledge-based society / economy (Schimank, 2005; de Boer, Enders & Schimank, 2008; Hayashi, 2009; Christensen, 2011; Oba, 2011; Langemeyer & Martin, 2015). This attempt to apply corporate management approaches to management in universities greatly impacts roles of HE, forms of university management, and academic practices. As a result, universities are obliged to become organizations that clearly demonstrate their productivity, efficiency, and accountability to society. Discussions of university governance are very broad and complex, and they are often discussed from macro / institutional perspectives rather than perspectives relating to individual academic work. Therefore, in this study, topics of university governance are not exclusively discussed, though some related issues of university governance will be discussed when applicable in the context of the study.

- Institutional infrastructure: Roles of Higher Education

  Universities as educational and research institutions are framed and regulated by national science / education policies, while universities are the place for academic work at the individual level. Although universities are considered as the place where various forms and process of knowledge generation take place in this research context, it might not be the main and / or only role of university institutions in reality (e.g., Kitamura, 1999: 16). Diverse roles of universities are likely to be easily overlooked, since universities are considered as institutions which obtain universally shared concepts, roles, and systems across the world. It might be true to a certain extent, nevertheless, roles of universities might not be totally identical throughout the world. For instance, universities in Japan are expected to contribute to research, education, and cooperation with society / social contribution through academic activities. As suggested in the previous point on the science policy, these three expectations towards universities in Japan are defined in the School Education Law (MEXT, 2008: 34), and it can be stated that the role of universities in Japan is obviously decided by the science policy. Related to the science policy, university governance that has led to university reforms in many countries can be one of the most significant and influential aspects to discuss. A great number of studies discuss relationships between the university governance and autonomy of universities. Similarly, then, how university governance relates to academic work and autonomy of academics can be discussed in the context of this study. Accordingly, academic work can be assumed to be influenced by this framework, which is set by science policy of a country. In this sense, it can be also imagined that science policies in other countries may give universities in their countries different roles than the ones in Japan. It is not the diverse role of universities in different countries but understanding of the working environment of academics in which they carry out academic work that interests us in the context of this research. The working environment could impact their academic work, since it could also be an important element that defines what work they are expected to do at their work places.

- Mission of academics in society

  The focus here is further narrowed down to looking at academics with relation to the outside of academic world, which is society. Connected to the above roles of universities, missions of academics in society is explored. That is: How are academics are seen / understood in society? What do lay persons in society expect academics to do / be in society? These questions are raised to unfold how academics are perceived by the public. When academics are defined as people who generate academic knowledge, these questions ask what position academics are placed in society. It might seem less relevant, at a glance, to investigate such aspects, but, considering that academic work and academics do not exist only in the academic environments such as universities and other academic societies / institutions, they are certainly connected to the public world, which is non-academic society. Investigating the position and perception of academic people in society would clarify the relationship between the academics, who are people generate academic knowledge, and society. It could also reveal the kind of society[38] in which they generate academic knowledge.

- Academic knowledge in society

  Similar to the factor of 'academics in society', roles of academic knowledge and the relationship between

---

[38] Such a question is raised because societal demands have influence on academic work. Although the societal demands do not directly come to academics, what the society requires can often be top priorities as today's research agenda (e.g. poverty, aging population, unemployment, etc.). Under such circumstances, it is not ignorable to understand what the public society think about academics as people generating knowledge.

academic knowledge and society should be closely investigated. Although it looks quite identical to the previous factor which examines the roles and missions of academics as people who generate academic knowledge, the interest here is the academic knowledge itself. Granted that societal demand could influence, and, to some extent, form demand for research topics and activities, it would not be unimportant to see how academic knowledge is perceived and expected in society. Same as the perception and missions of academics in society, it seems to be taken for granted that what academic knowledge means is obvious to everyone. It might be obvious to those who work for academic knowledge generation to define what it is. However, it does not necessarily match academics' perception / definition of academic knowledge with ones of lay persons in the public society. Therefore, it is worth touching on this factor in order to clarify its perceptions and meanings in society as one of those factors that could influence ways in which academic work is perpetually carried out.

To sum, the academic environment of academic culture mainly refers to the location and the environment in which academic work takes place. Though such background factors might easily be overlooked, taken for granted, and consequently are not considered as significant components of academic work, it is very crucial to look at them, since they are the grand framework of academic work. Academic work cannot exist by itself: It requires the place, fundamental institutional and financial infrastructures, and the rationale for the activities. Especially after HEIs and HE in the world received a great impact of globalization, the archaic, traditional, and original concepts of universities and of academic researchers should be of less use to understand today's academic culture. Thus, this level can be assumed as a place for investigation to the precondition of academic work.

4.5.2 Academic Practice

In contrast with the academic environment, more practical academic work will be explored in the aspect of academic practice. The factors at this level focus on daily activities / aspects concerning with academic knowledge generation. As relevant factors in this aspect, the following five factors are identified:

- Academic discourse practices
- Publication practices
- Managing academic activities
- Knowledge acquisition practices
- Disciplinary practices

By investigating these academic practices, a closer look at academic work is possible. The above factors inquire of ways of communication with their colleagues; topics they discuss with their colleagues; where, how and why they acquire academic knowledge; what, where, and why they publish their academic work; and other aspects in their daily working life. The study of what academic people actually do in their working life has been ignored, [39] probably because observing what happens in their working life seems to have been considered as unnecessary and irrelevant. However, it is not irrelevant to look at something that seems normal, usual, and known to confirm that all these conventional

---

[39] The work of Clark (1987), *The Academic Life: Small Worlds, Different Worlds*, might be recalled to by some of the readers. This work is based on a large scale research project funded by the Carnegie Foundation to investigate the academic profession and academic life in the United States. Also, a similar work, exploiting the same framework as the Carnegie project in the U.S was carried out by Arimoto (ed. 2008) and published in Japan. Such work seems to have commonalities with this study; however, they tend to outline academic work / profession in the U.S / Japan by depicting diversity in academic work / profession as well as commonalities in them among academic workers in those countries. For instance, in the Japanese case, the chapter authors write about income, stress, working condition, productivity, gender bias etc. Some of them have relevance to this study, but others don't. It is probably because their intention was more to generate a kind of country report on this topic in a more general sense.

activities are surely carried out for certain purposes and in certain ways.

The factors of this aspect are related not to general academic daily work but the academic work practices which have close relations with academic knowledge generation activities. Academic discourse practices refer to discourses with their colleagues in the same academic / disciplinary fields, which could influence their knowledge generation practices. Publication practices are considered as outcomes of knowledge generation practices. Motivations for and supposed significance of publishing their academic work, types of publication, and experience and frequency of publication are explored. If the output is the publication, the input is defined as knowledge acquisition practices. Such research is interested in the origin of knowledge that academic acquires, the use of acquired knowledge, and the motivation for knowledge acquisition activities. Disciplinary practices focus on activities within disciplinary fields as the main location for knowledge generation practices. This level also refers to management of academic work, which could involve other aspects than research / academic activities such as administrative work, teaching, and other obligations and commitments required by universities they work for. It might seem less related to the knowledge generation practices, and they are actually not related to knowledge generation directly. Nonetheless, if these activities are expected of university employees, it would mean that they do not spend the whole time in carrying out their own research activities, since universities have different missions and functions in and for society, as previously pointed out. This is not to expand the scope of the study from the aspects of academic work in terms of knowledge generation practices to the other aspects such as teaching and administrative work. The reason why I refer to importance of touching on the ordinary working life of academics in universities is that the structure and the components of their general working life could influence each other. Indeed, it is assumed that respective work component such as research, teaching, and other commitments in the work place is not an independent being, but they are interwoven and operated in the complexity of the entire academic work. In this respect, looking at their ordinary working life can be considered as an activity to look at the interwoven relationship between the working life as a whole and the knowledge generation practices.

In aspects of academic practice, it can be said that we would look at not only the individual work factors, but also interrelationship of these factors to each other. Even though the main focus of this study is knowledge generation practices, it does not necessarily mean that we should only focus and investigate knowledge generation practice itself. As with other societal situations (e.g. school education, working life in a commercial company, family life, etc.), any social life is situated among other situations in the wider settings that seem unrelated to them. In this sense, the respective factors in academic environment also relate to each other, and should not be seen as separate and independent being as a component of academic work.

Just as working life at non-academic sites are impacted by social relations, we can presume that academic working life is also not an exception to this. Therefore, the below three factors are identified, which could influence academic work, are following:

- Hierarchy / Status

- Gender

- Nationality / Ethnicity

These factors often tend to be considered as components of national cultural characteristics, or be seen as results of influence from national culture.[40] Nonetheless, including them does not emphasize national culture *per se* but carries the intension of simply exploring these factors at work. That means whether or not such social relations influence implementation of academic work. Furthermore, even if it turns out in the empirical study that all or some of the above factors influence academic work, this would not directly relate to influence of national cultural traits, because the same result might be seen in other countries on these factors.[41]

---

[40] In the large culture concept, for instance, hierarchy and gender are often discussed in relation to the Japanese and / or Asian culture (e.g. Hofstede, 1984). Consequently, it is not rare to find statements that the Japanese society is hierarchical and paternal due to its national cultural traits.

[41] At this moment, we cannot know whether or not it is the case, since the article is based on the study on academic culture focusing on the SSH scholars in

Then, it would be rather considered as a part of shared academic culture across countries / regions. Additionally, there could be more other social relation factors at this level; however, I try to limit the factors which could be related to knowledge generation activities.

Thus academic culture is constructed from the foregoing aspects. There are many other possibilities of constructing academic culture, as suggested earlier. Nevertheless, the construct of aforementioned academic culture is strictly focused on academic work, particularly on academic knowledge generation that is a core of not only individual academic work but also of collaborative work. The two aspects are not hierarchical but different scopes in which academic work takes place, and they are interrelated with each other to form the academic work as a whole. So is each factor at one level. Although each of them looks unrelated and independent of each other, all of them are essential to act together so that one could achieve a form of knowledge generation practice. In other words, academic work in the context of this study does not mean only work (activity) itself such as a various level and phase of research activities, but it is an accumulation of a numerous academic, societal, and political elements around academic work. Academic culture, therefore, is a synthesis of all those above elements which involve different processes towards academic knowledge generation.

4.6 Academic Culture and International Collaborations

Since this study attempts to better understand academic work in relation with international collaboration, the relationship between them needs a clarification. Having understood academic culture—its conceptual framework, meaning, intention, and structure—the relationship between academic culture and international collaborations will be explained.

Japan as a case. Therefore, it would be clearer about this point when the same / similar studies are implemented in other countries. This entire research project does not yet aim at making a grand generalization on academic culture worldwide, but attempts to suggest other approach to discussion on globalized academic work as such.

Understanding academic culture is necessary for an understanding of international academic collaboration. It has almost never been attempted to establish a conceptual and analytical framework to investigate academic work, especially, in order to go beyond the nationally confined views which can be only used for comparative, country-specific studies. As discussed earlier, international collaboration means, for academic practitioners, satisfying their intellectual curiosity by working together with their foreign counterparts. They are not individually motivated to compete against each other with their national flags, as the existing studies related to international collaboration seem to insinuate. Further, such studies give us a strong impression that international academic activities including collaborations are a means for competing to establish which country's science is more prominent and strong. In this light, the existing discussions and analyses contradict the viewpoint of academics towards international academic collaboration that indicates little competitive nature. In other words, the existing studies have been conducted from the perspective of the nation state, and such perspectives are disguised as if they represented academics' own perspectives that all academics also consider academic work as a means for competitions. If we think of reasons why we carry out academic work as an occupation, it is certainly not because we would like to beat someone else from other countries. Of course, the reasons for this vary from one person to another, but it can be assumed that SSH academics are interested in knowing and understanding what makes up the world around them. Simultaneously, it is supposed that a number of academics are interested in how their foreign counterparts generate knowledge. A possible motivation for academic collaboration can be as simple as this. Thus, it is better to leave the existing framework and discussions about academic competitions, but to consider academics as people who share aims and motivations for joining academic collaborations with their foreign colleagues, as a unit of social group.

Academic culture would be more helpful to observe and analyse academic work, which is carried out even within a country, because in such everyday work is the foundation of all work, whether it is carried out nationally or internationally. In this study, the academics in Japan are studied by the framework of academic culture. I do not have an intention of studying the "Japanese" academic culture, but to set up the academic culture whose construct would be applicable to academic work in any countries for the same purpose as this study. Japan is a case for the first attempt to apply academic culture. Of course, contents of each factors above described might be diverse from one setting to another, nevertheless, academic culture is not interested in descriptions of each country's case and differences between countries, rather, is more focused on how those factors would influence academic work in global settings such as international academic collaborations.

Understanding of academic work through academic culture would lead us to better analyses on academic work which is carried out in international settings. Using the concept of academic culture allows us to show ways in which academic work is carried out and broader background in which academic work takes place, and it explains and analyses activities that could impact and influence on international collaborations. Academic culture does not provide any fixed definitions of academic work; instead, it provides a broad framework in which diverse activities and phenomena could be observed to analyse academic work, in relation to knowledge generation practices, in the context of this study. Since each scholar carries academic culture, this framework would be useful to explain and analyse academic activities when they meet their counterparts, may they be foreign or the same nationality.

Hence, academic culture could provide a different analytical framework for discussion of international academic activities beyond the national cultural framework and competitive nature of discussions on the issue.

Academic culture is established in order to create a new analytical framework for discussing international academic activities. The motivation for setting up the academic culture came from dissatisfaction with the existing discussions of international academic work: First, the existing discussions, which are all based on quantitative analyses that exploit a various science citation indices, manage to generate the same statement that there are certain dominant countries / regions, and that it is rather unfair to exploit the aforementioned science citation indices due to some biases in their database. Second, such quantitative analyses would lead us to a fixed contrastive picture of the winner-loser relation in international academic work. Third, this contrastive picture would fire into the competitive natured discussions as the existing discussions indicate, and consequently, much more attention to the competitions in academic work has been paid by academics participating in such discussions than to issues which attempt to discuss and to understand the current academic knowledge generation practice in international academic scenes. It means that the current discussions vastly ignore other aspects of international academic work by looking at the above-mentioned nature of academic work. As seen, on the other hand, the perception of international collaborations varies depending on people's positions. For academic practitioners (scholars, researchers), international collaboration is a broad range of academic activities with their foreign counterparts, which is not limited to publication activities. However, it seems conventional in the existing discussion of international collaboration to consider international collaboration as synonym to international co-authoring. Thus the discrepancy can be seen in use of the term *international collaboration*, and the current discussion does not deal with the most components of international collaboration, such as motivations, its process, and evaluation of contents of international joint knowledge generation practices. Therefore, establishing the framework of academic culture aims at filling the long missing gap between the existing discussions and actual academic practices on the basis of not the outcomes of such activity (publications), but of the contents of it. Without this new type of discussion / conceptual framework, the topic of international collaboration will end up with repetition of old discussions, and as a result, this field of study stagnates.

5. Methodological Operationalization

On implementing academic research and writing up one's analysis and findings, it is necessary to clarify how the entire research project is structured, why it has to be structured as it is, and what epistemological standpoint the researcher is based on to structure the research project, in order to answer research questions he / she posed. Research methodology may be understood as a mere mechanism of the research project; however, it is not just a mechanism but quite complex manifestations in which every individual element and part of the research is closely interwoven towards the research findings. Therefore, the researcher should explain where he / she disciplinarily and epistemologically stands, and which research strategy, paradigm, and approach are adopted based on his / her disciplinary and epistemological background so that readers of the research could also follow his / her logical constructions. Moreover, each methodological and epistemological element should be consistent to each other in order for the findings and research procedures to acquire relevance, persuasiveness, and validity.

Naturally, the research methods are also consistent with and are reflected by the aforementioned elements of the research design. Consequently, readers would find it easier to follow the analysis and discussions that emerge out of the empirical part of the project after having read the methodology section, for the empirical and analytical parts are also underlain by the following methodological elements.

Bearing the above in mind, I will introduce, firstly, design of the research, which includes: disciplinary field of the study, research strategy, paradigm, and approach. These elements explain the overall standpoint of the researcher that is the base on which knowledge is created in this thesis. Then, I will move onto the research methods, which consist of practical details of in-depth, face-to-face interviews, open-ended questionnaire, and focus group discussion.

5.1 Research Design

5.1.1 Disciplinary Field of the Study

It is very normal that a research project is proceeded and framed within a particular academic discipline,[42] therefore, is analysed from a perspective of that certain discipline. The same could be said about a researcher. That means that he / she comes from a particular discipline and exploits knowledge of the discipline to investigate and analyse objectives of the research. The objectives and / or the major topic of the research can be shared between disciplines; nevertheless, respective research projects are classified as sociological, educational, psychological, linguistic, political, and other disciplinary studies. It is, on one hand, beneficial to develop specialized knowledge in respective disciplines about a certain topic in such a conventional way of research / academic practices. On the other hand, however, there could be a great risk that such specialized knowledge in different disciplines under the same topic could be very scattered, and, as a result, would not be systemic when one tries to grasp an overview of the objectives under study. This is the background of the current urge for interdisciplinary research projects, because objectives / phenomena in society are complex and cannot be entirely understood by knowledge of one single discipline.[43] Indeed, this urge for interdisciplinary research

---

[42] When classification of academic disciplines is discussed in the international research context, one should note that there seems no clear and definite consensus among academics about how they define disciplines. For instance, when one talked about education, other might think that it should be sociology, or more precisely, sociology of education. The classification of academic disciplines varies from one country to another. In this study, needless to say, the classification is based on the comprehension of academic disciplines by myself, who has Japanese and British educational and academic backgrounds.

[43] In the case of Japan, specialized disciplinary knowledge in SSH has been questioned, and consequently, as a part of science policy in Japan, the funding agency in Japan which is an independent administrative agency established a funding programme to promote more interdisciplinary research projects in SSH (JSPS, n.d. "Programme for Promoting Methodological Innovation in Humanities and Social Sciences by Cross-Disciplinary Fusing" http://www.jsps.go.jp/j-ibunya/index.html only available in Japanese) . A similar intention was widely expressed also by the Science Council of Japan, regarding to academic research activities on the unprecedented earthquake

activities is not only the academic trend in Japan but also in other countries. For instance, if we observe an introductory document issued by the European Commission as a part of call for "Horizon 2020," research on cross-cutting issues is one of "the key concerns" (European Commission, 2013: 16) of the work programme, and this document states that "in many cases interdisciplinary solutions are needed, cutting across multiple specific objectives of Horizon 2020" (ibid.). Thus, an interdisciplinary approach to studying social issues is no longer rare, and rather, it is more and more appreciated in research fields of SSH.

Taking appreciation for this research approach into an account, this study also has an interdisciplinary orientation. Because academic work in any research field is largely framed and constructed by national science policies of a country, a number of researchers have attempted to analyse life of academic people in relation to national science policies of their countries (e.g., Inoki, 2009; Arimoto (ed.), 2008; Yamanoi (ed.), 2007; Ehara and Umakoshi (eds.), 2004), and they are most likely to be classified as a field of educational studies, particularly focusing on the Higher Education (HE) system. Certainly, such educational studies play a significant role for this study; however, as it is pointed out earlier, educational studies in this research context is rather insufficient and imperfect, since they inevitably put emphases on national perspectives on HE policies of a country. In other words, educational studies have a certain limitation that hinders them from going beyond the analyses from the national perspectives. Therefore, this study should not be only classified as educational studies although it includes much of such type of studies and analyses from the field of HE study, but also involves other fields of study in order to study more on individual aspects of academic work.

The other field of study that I will draw on is anthropology. It might sound surprising that this study is classified as anthropology, due to general images of this discipline, which has been active under colonial regimes in the past centuries. Among the classics of anthropological work is Clifford Geertz, well-known for the

---

disaster "Great East Japan Earthquake" on 11th March 2011. In a report published by the Science Council of Japan, needs for more collaborative interdisciplinary research by SSH and life science, science and engineering are emphasized (Science Council of Japan, 2013: 5).

expression of "thick description." Geertz, an American anthropologist, was heavily involved in research on Bali, Java, Indonesia (see Geertz, 1973) and, at the later stage of his career, Morocco (Geertz, 1971), relying on extensive fieldwork in these countries / regions. Bronisław Malinowski was also a pioneer of ethnographic study that requires staying a lengthy period of time in a research setting to observe and record how people live, how they make sense of things, what are rules to carry out certain activities, and other life aspects of local people, which is known as participant observation. Especially, Malinowski's great contribution to anthropological studies is known by the fieldwork in Trobriand Islands, Papua New Guinea (Malinowski, 1922). In relation to Japan, "The Chrysanthemum and the Sword" by Ruth Benedict (1967), an American anthropologist, should be mentioned. This work is nowadays considered as an academic anthropological work, although it was also exploited by the U.S. authority and played an important role after the Second World War in order to better govern Japanese people. All these studies certainly give us an impression that anthropology is a field of study in which the civilized person visits and studies a place / places where they find people and life there exotic. The implication of 'exotic' is not restricted to a reference to indigenous people in unknown lands, but, as the study of Benedict about Japanese people, it includes studies about different races of human from the race of a person who studies them.

However, anthropology does not only deal with those cultures, peoples, and lifestyles deemed as exotic to Westerns, but also with current Western people's life, culture, and behaviour. A good example of this is a book entitled "Watching the English," written by an English social anthropologist, Kate Fox (2004). Fox's work is about investigating rules of English people's behaviour, which is described as, in her terms, "rules of Englishness" (ibid.), by exploiting participant observation, one of the research methodologies that anthropological studies often employ. The book consists of two parts: conversational rules and behavioural ones in the day-to-day life of the English. By describing certain common behaviours in various life situations such as at home, in workplaces, in pubs, and even on the roads, Fox tries to find out commonalities, that is, what she calls "rules" among people in England. The commonalities she finds through her research would finally be labelled as Englishness to depict and as well as to help better understand how English people live and behave.

One of the unique points of this study is that the way in which it illustrates how today a researcher can study her own country, which is neither exotic nor unknown from Western perspectives. Ribeiro (2006) neatly describes status and developments of anthropology as an academic discipline chronologically, and his work indicates that anthropology was a discipline which studied mankind that was strange and exotic to scholars from the Anglo-Saxon world until the late twentieth century. The discipline was strongly connected to political interests of a nation state / government in relation to uncivilized / colonial / Third World countries on which the country was willing to, or in many cases did, control. On the other hand, Ribeiro points out:

> For hegemonic anthropologists,[44] natives were no longer those exotic people living thousands of kilometres from their homes; they became neighbors. . . . The lines between natives and non-natives were blurred, and the structures of sociocultural otherness (Krotz, 1997) in global and national contexts increased in complexity (ibid.: 371).

Thus, due to the influence of globalization, which has created conditions for greater mobility of people around the globe and resulted in a massive transnational flow of information, it is inevitable for the discipline to change the views on its 'objectives.' In light of such a change in the discipline, Fox's work can be classified as a recent type of anthropology, and this study on academic work in Japan shares a number of methodological and epistemological points with the work of Fox on Englishness.[45]

This study is, therefore, classified as an interdisciplinary study of educational studies and anthropology which forms the core of the study. Nevertheless, some other disciplinary work that has already been implemented with similar interests to this study

---

[44] The meaning of "hegemonic anthropologists" is anthropologists mainly operating in Anglo-Saxon countries in this context. This is not to state that scholars from such countries as individuals are hegemonic, but Ribeiro discusses more about academic power structure / academic world system as such.

[45] Unlike Fox's study of Englishness, however, this study does not intend to depict Japaneseness in academic work. The referred similarity of this study to Fox's is confined to the methodological and epistemological points, as mentioned.

would also be exploited, since there are a lot of overlaps of discussions between respective disciplines and the topic includes many aspects that are not discussed and analysed systemically because of disciplinary borders. Therefore, disciplines such as sociology, intercultural studies, history, and philosophy of science could be also exploited in order to create a wider and deeper overview on the topics under the study.

5.1.2 Research Strategy, Paradigm, and Approach

In order to structure a research paper, it is necessary to clarify the epistemological standpoint of the researcher, the relationship between aims of research and the logical structure of research, and any other aspects that influence ways that the researcher deploys his / her discussion. Even if the exact same topic is studied, ways he / she approaches and builds up the research project would be varied, dependent on his / her ontological and epistemological point of view. Thus, one should consider that not everyone would see, and therefore, investigate things in the same way that one might take for granted. The purpose of this section is to explain to readers how the author of the thesis tries to see, understand, and analyse the world.

First, abductive research strategy will be introduced and discussed to indicate an approach of logical construction to this study. It matches the aim of this study, which attempts to describe and analyse academic working life in relation to international knowledge production in order to have a broad overview.

Second, interpretivism, as the epistemological standpoint of the author, will be argued. Epistemology is defined as "the theory of knowledge, especially with regard to its methods, validity, and scope" by the *Concise Oxford Dictionary* (1999). In this section, however, a very philosophical in-depth discussion about epistemology as such is not possible. Instead, a brief description of interpretivism is made, and the interrelation between interpretivism and this study is examined. That is, a role of interpretivism in the context of this research project is explained.

Finally, a non-essentialist approach to topic analysis is briefly introduced via an explanation of how this study seeks to avoid a deep-rooted nationalistic analytical approach.

By exploring these methodological and epistemological aspects relating to the study, I hope to make clear to readers what the study mainly aims at and how this can be achieved. Albeit this section does not directly refer to the main contents of the study, understanding the methodological and epistemological orientation of the study will help readers obtain a better understanding not only of the main analytical contents but also about the connection between such contents and the structure / framework of thoughts in the study.

5.1.3 Abductive Research Strategy

Abductive logic / reasoning is introduced by an American philosopher, Charles Sanders Peirce (Reichertz, 2004; Gold et al., n.d.; Dubois & Gadde, 2002) as a method for hypotheses building in natural science (Blaikie, 2007: 88–89). According to Blaikie, abductive research strategy in today's social science is employed as a method of theory construction by exploiting "social actors' language, meanings and accounts in the context of everyday activities" (ibid.: 89). That is, it is based on a belief that the social world can be perceived through viewpoints of social members, not through researchers' views. A similar belief has been shared among sociologists such as Weber, Schütz, Douglas, and Giddens, although their individual scientific interests are not necessarily the same.[46]

The aim of this research strategy is, as briefly mentioned above, generating a theory by making sense of social life of the researched people through their point of view without imposing a researcher's own common sense and / or knowledge. This aim has commonality with the origin of Grounded Theory (GT) founded by Glaser and Strauss (1967). These sociologists also claimed the necessity of theory generation through iterative data collection and analysis, which mainly rely on people's accounts, world view, implicit knowledge shared among members of a certain group / society,

---

[46] Each of their scientific interests might be diverse, but their approach to generating scientific knowledge seems under the same framework and influences each other to some extent. For instance, Weber's work seems to have inspired Schütz's, and Douglas relied on Schütz's work. (See Blaikie, 2007)

etc.[47] Thus my research strategy has a similar orientation with the GT analytical framework.[48] Besides, abductive research strategy is, as seen from the way it attempts to generate a theory, closely associated with interpretivism, [49] which is the epistemological orientation of this study. This conformity is not unimportant to indicate coherency of the epistemological and methodological structure of the study, because every relevant study should be constructed in a consistent way, with interconnections between methodology, epistemology, and overall composition of the thesis to acquire persuasiveness as a whole.

Apart from the above-mentioned correlation, the main reason why this study is structured within the abductive research strategy is because of the nature of the study. Since no prior similar fundamental study exists, and, therefore, there is a lack of relevant theory on the main topic(s) of this study, deductive research strategy is obviously not feasible. Deductive research strategy, or rather better known as deductive reasoning / deducing, is normally used for theory / hypothesis testing by falsification in order to finally create a sound argument. To exploit this strategy, there should be an already known or proved statement that could be called a theory, then, a single case would be applied to the theory, and a conclusion could be drawn. If this flow of logic is consistent, it is logically considered as correct. On the other hand, inductive research strategy / reasoning has a reverse flow of logic to deductive one: Inductive reasoning starts from an observed fact such as "all the dogs I have seen are black." From this observed statement, it would be concluded that "therefore, all dogs are black." This strategy would be able to create a broad generalization. However, as seen in the above example about dogs, it could end up

---

[47] For further details and discussions on GT, see the later chapter of the thesis.
[48] Reichertz (2010) also admits the close relationship between abduction and GT.
[49] Blaikie (2007) states that abductive research strategy is "based on and *idealist* ontology and the epistemology of *constructionism*"(emphasis in original. P.90). Strictly speaking, it might be a better description of epistemological orientation of abductive research strategy, nevertheless, interpretivism is preferred in this thesis, due to different meanings and understandings in respective social science disciplines under the term of constructionism / constructivism (as a part of constructionism). This could only create confusion for readers, and, in a broader sense, interpretivism is sufficient to describe the epistemological orientation of this study.

with a mere description of what has been observed, and consequently, lead to a false conclusion, even though its logical construction is not false. More important, both deductive and inductive research strategies rather have more positivistic orientation than abductive one, considering the notion of "falsification" in deductive reasoning, and the way observed reality is deemed as a fact, therefore, it leads to truth in inductive one. This positivistic epistemological standpoint is very problematic for this study, as already explained earlier, and it would make the structure of the study extremely inconsistent. The main concern is this epistemological discrepancy between inductive / deductive reasoning and the nature of this study, which has little intention of seeking for "truth" in a positivistic sense. That is why inductive and deductive research strategies are eliminated as possibilities for the research strategy of the study, and the abductive research strategy is chosen as the most suitable one for this study.

5.1.4 Interpretivism

When we talk about social science research, often the question of whether or not the interpretive nature of research is scientific knowledge is raised. What lies behind this question is a bigger question about how scientific knowledge should be. To one side lies the claims that scientific knowledge should be generating law-like generalization, which would see social reality under investigation as something 'out there' and is separated from individuals (Cohen, Manion, & Morrison, 2007: 7). On the other side, lies an insistence that social reality is not something one can observe and judge but rather is a product created by individual minds (ibid.). The former is conceived as positivistic epistemological position and the latter is as interpretivistic one. There is no agreement about which one is better or more correct social scientific knowledge, because which stance one would take depends on how a researcher looks at the social world being studied. There have been intensive debates about positivism versus interpretivism in the social sciences; but as already mentioned, considering the relationship between the research questions and the research strategies, the research paradigm of this study stands in the field of interpretivism.

What interpretivism here means is that any studies of social phenomena should take into account the understanding of social participants' views of the social world which is constructed and reconstructed in their daily lives. Unlike the positivist views, the standpoint of interpretivism is that the understanding and interpretation of the social participants on their lives cannot be observed just through the human senses. Although there have been numerous debates about whether or not the interpretivist approach is really appropriate for scientific knowledge generation,[50] positivist and realist approaches do not seem to investigate the subject matter in depth. Since academic working life can be also a creation of a group of social participants, listening to their accounts and involving them into the scientific analysis towards theory development are crucial for this study. In light of the subject matter of this study, interpretivism seems well suited as the research paradigm for this study.

5.1.5 Non-Essentialist Approach

Holliday (2000) argues about the differences between the essentialist and the non-essentialist approach in dealing with culture. According to his argument, the essentialist view coincides with Hofstede's classification of national cultures (1984), and, therefore, might "be characterised as positivist, and non-essential as interpretive" (Holliday, 2000: 38). The major discussion here is that using predefined national cultural characters to analyse behaviour / activities of a group of people would only create "reductive statements" (ibid.: 40), that is, that the essentialist approach would prevent researchers from exploring other aspects than the aspects that are already predefined before the research activities commence. Moreover, such predefined views are often expressed "in a dichotomous way, with a positive and a negative pole, such as male and female, and black and white" (Chiapparino, n / d: 5). This dichotomous description would lead to a hierarchy between the positive and the negative poles, implying the positive one as the norm and the negative one as something "'lacking'" (Zanoni & Janssens, 2004, cited in Chiapparino, n / d: 5) against the one considered as the norm. Defining one culture as positive / correct or negative / wrong, according to Holliday (1999: 243),

---

[50] This type of debate is also related to qualitative research methods such as case study interview which this study employs. Further discussion would be introduced, therefore, in the research methods section.

"supports various spheres of political interest." This means that there is little room for an explorative type of study if essentialist approach was adopted, because research findings would always be same, reductive and politically embedded.

On the other hand, the non-essentialist approach would allow researchers to liberate reflections from the essentialist pre-conceptualized views to investigate behaviours of members in an entity. Holliday states (2000), "a non-essentialist approach can help us to unlock *any* form of social behaviour by helping us to see how it operates as culture per se" (emphasis in original). That is, culture can be "discovered" (ibid.) in the non-essentialist approach through an analysis rather than being constrained by the predefined and imposed national cultural characteristics. Since this study clearly denies the application of national cultural characters to analyse academic work, the non-essentialist approach matches its purposes.

Needless to say, non-essentialist approach is also in line with interpretivism as Holliday confirms (2000), as well as with the abductive research strategy discussed above. Now, it is evident that the strategy, paradigm, and approach of the study are in sync and will work together in this study in order to achieve the aim of research. This structural consistency is also interrelated with the means of investigation, that is, the research methods. In the next section, each method employed in the study will be closely looked at.

5.2   Research Methods

Among various ways of academic research, choosing right research method(s), in agreement with aims of research, is an important requirement. If appropriate employment of research strategy, paradigm, and approach enables us to structure an outline of research as we have just seen, research methods are the means to embody what a researcher would like to achieve by his / her research project. In order to achieve his / her own research aims, the means that are chosen should also be the right ones.

The purposes of this section are: First, introducing the research methods that are employed for this study. Second, explaining ways in which they are implemented in practical settings. And finally drawing attention to other methodological issues that each research method often confronts.

5.2.1 Interviews

5.2.1.1 Active Interview

The interview is probably the most frequently employed method in both quantitative and qualitative research. While in quantitative research interviews tend to be a form of structured and close-ended questions like questionnaire surveys, qualitative interviews consist of semi-structured (sometimes unstructured) and open-ended style questions. The former "can be used for the purpose of measurement" (Fontana & Frey, 2003: 62), and the latter can be exploited to understand and interpret a group of people's view, life, and thoughts. In this study, qualitative interviews are implemented, due to the aim of research and the researcher's epistemological orientation. As Fontana and Frey mention, qualitative interviews "are not neutral tools of data gathering but active interactions between two (or more) people leading to negotiated, contextually based results" (ibid.). That is, in other words, qualitative interviews do not attempt objective generalization by quantified data as if the world was a visible object in front of us, which could be understood by various numbers and formulae as quantitative researchers claim, but aim at grasping people's life in depth by mutual interactions between an interviewer and an interviewee, ideally without any hierarchical positioning between them.

This is, to a certain extent, what Holstein and Gubrium (1995) introduce as an "active interview." An active interview seems quite similar to Douglas's creative interview as Holstein and Gubrium (ibid.) refer to. Douglas's creative interview (1985, quoted in Holstein & Gubrium, 1995) suggests that an interviewer "must establish a climate for *mutual* disclosure" (Holstein & Gubrium, 1995: 12, emphasis in original). In order to achieve the mutual disclosure, firstly the interviewer should show his / her strong willingness to the respondent that he / she is prepared to share the respondent's thoughts, views, and so forth. Then, as the result of this committed attitude of the interviewer, the respondent would be assured that he / she could also disclose his / her deep feeling.

Consequently, this mutual disclosure would lead the interview to acquire the respondents' "deep experiences" (ibid.).

Although what Douglas suggests as the method of creative interview sounds too emotional and rather exaggerated as an academic research method, it implies a strong criticism of the conventional standardized structured interview method, which put a strong emphasis on neutrality of an interviewer towards interviewees. In such quantitative structured interviews, order of questions, wording, and the employment of certain phrasings are fixed and inflexible. As Holstein and Gubrium describe, respondents of quantitative interviews are often seen as "passive *vessels of answers*" (ibid.: 7, emphasis in original). This presents us with an image of respondents being like a box that contains what the interviewer wants to obtain. Therefore, any emotion towards and / or close mental relationship with respondents is rejected in quantitative interviews. Douglas's intention seems to clearly depict an antithesis between qualitative and quantitative interviews, and he tries to suggest another way escaping from the conventional standardized interview practice in order to methodologically establish an alternative to it in qualitative research.

The active interview takes a more developed form in the creative interview, [51] which has more involvement of respondents in interview practices, to establish not only mutual discourse but also mutual interpretation between the interviewer and respondents. This is quite unique to involve respondents in interpretation of their interactions. Normally, as seen so far, a main role of respondents in interview research is providing answers, description, and their own views on issues under study. Interpreting is a role of the researcher of the study, and has almost nothing to do with respondents. Although respondents never

---

[51] This creative interview remains, according to Holstein and Gubrium (1995), as a method which leaves the respondents as passive as in conventional standardized interviews, since Douglas (1985) focuses mainly on how an interviewer should behave towards respondents, and not on respondents' role in such an interview. In this sense, they point out, respondents are treated as vessels of answers, who just wait and provide what they have in a different atmosphere created by the interviewer from that in standardized interviews. This contradiction brings Holstein and Gubrium to suggest the active interview as an interpretive interview method.

participate in data analysis activities, interpretation in this context means that respondents do not only exist to provide what they know and feel, but through interaction with an interviewer what they think they know would be further "activated, stimulated, and cultivated" (ibid.: 17). Consequently, Holstein and Gubrium confirm:

> Respondents' answers and comments are not viewed as reality reports delivered from a fixed repository. Instead, they are considered for the ways that they construct aspects of reality in collaboration with the interviewer. (Holstein & Gubrium, 1997, 127)

This does not mean, however that the active interview is a simple personal interaction between interviewer and interviewee. The interviewer should create a friendly atmosphere so that respondents can feel more relaxed and are willing to talk with the interviewer than in conventional formal interview practices, but simultaneously, he / she should take a lead in the interaction and focus on the research topics.

With this active interview method, it is believed that a researcher could achieve not only information he / she seeks, but mean-making (ibid.) out of what is said together with respondents. In this respect, active interviewing seems profitable for this study, because it has a very exploratory nature that seeks things which have never been written down in any statistics and / or policy documents. Moreover, the study aims at observing the work of social science academics from their own perspectives. In order to achieve such aims, interviews for simple information gathering would be insufficient, and the study requires not descriptive reality but implication of working life led by social science academics in Japan in relation to international academic collaborations.

5.2.1.2 Samples

There are some ways to select interview samples, dependent on the purpose of research, and qualitative researchers often employ purposive sampling (Bryman, 2008: 375). Unlike quantitative research, qualitative research has much less intention for generalization and representation, therefore, drawing samples from a wide population by probability sampling is less used in qualitative research than in quantitative research. Purposive sampling is a sampling strategy in which a researcher selects samples, according to his / her research purpose(s), which would satisfy conditions, characteristics, and other elements that are sought for the purpose of study. In Cohen, Manion, and Morrison (2007), purposive sampling strategy is frequently employed to obtain those who are knowledgeable and have deep insights in the topics under study. Therefore, it could be someone that the researcher has already known rather than total strangers who would be selected from a list of roughly determined target population. Since purposive sampling is used in search of in-depth knowledge about certain issues, covering wider population, without knowing whether or not all members of the population are knowledgeable enough for the research purpose, makes little sense. Indeed, Cohen, Manion, and Morrison (ibid.) state that it is not a concern that people selected by purposive sampling may not be representative and that their comments may not be generalizable in this sampling. This is a particular characteristic of qualitative research which pursues in-depth analysis over breadth in number.

This study employs the purposive sampling for the above-mentioned reason. Seven academics who work for Japanese universities have been selected. They are, except one person, acquaintances and former colleagues with whom I have collaborated before. I selected them because they either had known my research interests earlier than this interview research or seem to share main points of this study, which emphasize significance of analysis of this research topics not from national perspectives but from individual ones. In order to collect a variety of different views, I paid attention to balances in gender, age, academic background / expertise / disciplines, affiliation / types of university to which they belong,[52] and other relevant academic experiences / background. As a consequence, five male and two female respondents, aging from in their forties to sixties were selected. Their disciplinary backgrounds are sociology, anthropology, linguistics, logic, English language, and cultural studies. They currently teach at private

---

[52] Japanese universities have various characteristics, roles, and missions in Japanese society, which could be surprising to non-Japanese readers. A question of in which university one works is of a great importance to understand interviewees' individual background for their working life. Further details will be discussed in the section that refers to analytical discussions based on the empirical data as well as in the findings section.

universities, but some of them used to work for national universities. Although interview questions are not related to any international academic experience and foreign language ability, their common background is that they have studied and / or worked abroad. This aspect is purposefully set as a sampling condition, for such academic experiences in foreign countries could be motivation for and interest in international academic collaborations in both direct and indirect ways. Besides, I presupposed that it might be easier for the interviewees to understand the fundamental purpose and background of the study with their international academic experiences. Thus the interviewees were identified and selected in order to accomplish the aim of research by implementation of active interviews.

5.2.1.3 Interview Questions

The interview questions are based on the research question: How do social science academics carry out their work towards knowledge generation practices based on the identified elements?

For generating the interview questions, I recognize that academic work can be distinguished between the academic environment, which consists of aspects that underlie and inevitably influence overall academic work, and the academic practice, which can be labelled as aspects that more closely related to individual activities in participants' daily academic work. Despite the aim of this study that analysis of academic work in relation to international academic collaborations should be generated from academics' individual perspectives, interview questions broadly include academic environment perspectives. Nevertheless, including aspects of the academic environment does not contradict the aim of the study. Rather, the academic environment aspects could corroborate ways in which academics carry out their work, since both aspects of academic environment and academic practice are inseparable in observing and analysing their working life, especially when considering that this study is not about academic work in general, but about academic work with regard to international collaborations that heavily involve aspects of academic environment such as national science policy. In other words, the academic environment aspects frame and embrace the academic practice aspects. It has been problematic that these two aspects are always discussed separately under the name of 'internationalization of academic work and / or HE', as if they had no interrelation at all. Combining the both aspects, therefore, could overcome this absence of either aspect to draw a much more complete picture of interrelationship between individual academic work and international academic activities. The academic environment aspects that form the interview questions are the following:

> A) National science policy
>
> National science policy determines quite directly academic work in any scientific disciplines as well as ways universities exist and operate. It is so determining and influential on practical academic work and academic life that quite a few scholars have attempted to approach various topics on internationalization of SSH.[53] Certainly, the importance of the role of national science policy in academic work is unquestionable, especially two aspects given below:
>
> 1. Funding[54]
>
> 2. Prioritized research topics / fields
>
> These two aspects seem relevant for academics in any disciplines and at any stage of an academic career when carrying out academic research. Therefore, they are put into the front. Further, dependent on interviewees' age, experiences, and career background, some additional questions are suggested to enquire further into details of national funding programmes, funding systems, and mechanism of such systems etc.

---

[53] See 'Science Policies in Japan on Internationalization' under the Literature Review section for detailed discussion.

[54] There are private funding organizations, but they do not play a central role to structure a wide range of academic research activities. Therefore, the interview question focuses on only the national research funding.

B) Institutional infrastructure

The second aspect of the academic environment is the higher education institutions (HEIs) for academic work. Rarely have we encountered a 'freelance scholar', and the majority of scholars belong to universities. Universities are the next biggest framework nesting in the national science policy framework. Needless to say, it is not hard to imagine that working environment, structure of workplace, and systems at work influence and shape individual work performance. In light of this, it is vital to enquire about infrastructure of interviewees' workplace in relation to their individual academic work. The following two aspects are foci of the interview questions as institutional infrastructural aspects:

1. Roles of HE (Undergraduate and Postgraduate education)

2. Institutional research policy

Although this study is indifferent to educational / teaching aspects in academic work, some questions will be asked about educational aspects with the understanding that teaching practices in undergraduate and postgraduate education, individual objectives in teaching at universities, and attitudes of students towards academic activities are helpful for acquiring an overview of institutional infrastructure. That is, we could better understand what universities in Japan generally aim at through teaching students via questioning the above point (1). This is not so apparent but important, because the university is a place where scientific knowledge is created and passed to the next generation through research and education. Then, the educational practices mentioned above should have another implication in a relationship between institutional infrastructure and scientific knowledge than asking about general teaching practices.

In regard to point (2), each university has different research orientations and policies. In the case of Japan, this point is quite prominent when discussing various issues about HE in general, because there are nearly 800 universities, according to the most updated data released by the Ministry of Education, Culture, Sports, Science and Technology (MEXT), Japan.[55] These universities have different characteristics, roles, and aims, which could influence the individual work of scholars to a great extent, because the majority of universities in Japan are private.[56] However, it is not to say that this is a particularity of Japanese HEIs. In non-Japanese contexts, different characteristics, roles, expertise, and aims certainly exist at each university in other countries. In this sense, there is no doubt that institutional research policy and general climate towards research activities at each university could impact individual academic work.

C) Mission of academics in society

1. Roles of and expectation towards academics (i.e., How are academics seen / understood in society? What do the public expect academics to do / be in society?)

2. What kind of roles do you think you, as an academic, play in society?

D) Academic knowledge in society

1. Roles of academic knowledge and / or relationship between academic knowledge and society

2. How is academic knowledge perceived in society?

---

[55] It can be found on: http://www.e-stat.go.jp/SG1/estat/List.do?bid=0000010 51733&cycode=0 (e-Stat, 20 December 2013, available only in Japanese.) in the table number 2. According to the table, in the academic year of 2013, there are 782 universities in Japan.

[56] This point would be further discussed in the analysis section with more details.

3. What is your perception of academic knowledge as an academic?

The question section (C) and (D) are interwoven, as they both enquire into the relationship between the general public society and academic knowledge / academics. An interest here is to understand ways in which interviewees perceive roles of academics / academic knowledge in society as well as perception by lay persons on academic knowledge and academic people. Since academic work and outcomes of it cannot exist only in ivory towers, it is assumed that the interviewees who are the practitioners of such activities should be conscious of society and lay persons. Moreover, these questions aim at clarifying who they are and what academic knowledge is in society where they are located.

Different from sections (A) and (B), the scope of academic environment shifts to non-academic, public world. This is because perception of academics and academic knowledge in society could also represent how they actually are in society. Such perceptions might not match academics' own perceptions of themselves and academic knowledge. Nevertheless, the important point is that they are conscious of perceptions of them from society and society members. This recognition, it is presupposed, could also be influential to their work as academics.[57] That is why the questions include interrelated aspects between society and academics / academic knowledge.

There was originally section (E), relating to an aspect of national culture and questions about academic practices, but it seemed excessive for the originally planned time frame of one and a half to two hours for the interview research, therefore I did not include them in the interview questions. Instead, they are asked in the follow-up

---

57 In Japan, academics are supposed to contribute to society in various ways. Although it may not influence their work to a great extent, academics are not to be unaware of the connection with society in the context of academic work.

questionnaire after the interview implementation to supplement the lack of time.

The interview questions are formulated for the above-mentioned aspects so that they could also be transferred to and exploited in different settings (i.e., in different countries) for future research. Because this study not only aims at analysing academic work exploiting the Japanese case but also creating a new strategy and a framework for more synthetic discussions about related topics, which are not so much bound to country-specific views, as discussed earlier. Thus the interview questions try not to include and ask particular to academe of Japan, but try to focus on and explore possible common aspects that are interrelated to each other in academic work anywhere in the world.

5.2.1.4 *Interview Practice*

Prior to the interview practice, the above interview topics were circulated to the interviewees. By doing so, the interviewees could roughly prepare beforehand for providing their views as well as trying to understand what this study is about. It is also helpful for the interviewer to save some time for explaining details, background, and foci of the study when an interview is carried out each time. This circulation of the interview topics was done via email correspondences with the interviewees. The interviewees were asked whether there was anything unclear to them in the provided document and were allowed to ask any questions on the research topics, albeit they are not familiar with the topics of this study. Normally, clarifying topics / questions and answering to their questions could take place during the interview practice as a part of probes and prompts (Brown & Dowling, 1998: 76; Bryman, 2008: 206–207), that is, activities that would help interviewees answer questions when they have difficulties to understand what is meant by a question in a way it is phrased. However, this study had quite a strong time restraint for carrying out face-to-face interviews, due to the interviewees' and the interviewer's schedule in Japan. Therefore, it was assumed that it would be better to reduce possible unclarity of the interview questions and any other general aspects of the study such as background of the study before the interview is implemented.

The interviews were carried out from the end of October to the beginning of November 2012. Due to heavy commitments to the interviewees' teaching and research activities, one and a half to two hours interview was originally suggested, and some could only spend for one and a half hours for the interview while others could share three to four hours. The place of interview was selected by each interviewee, according to their convenience, but it was their own office in most cases; otherwise, in any public space such as a common room for lecturers and a café. Each interview was electronically recorded by a MP3 device for documenting the entire interview in order to transcribe it at the later stage of the research for data analysis.

It is a frequent issue how to obtain rapport with interviewees in carrying out in-depth qualitative interviews (Payne & Payne, 2008: 142; Bryman, 2008: 201–202), because it is normal that an interviewer and interviewees have totally different background, job, social status, and so forth. Therefore, it is said that there tends to be a power relation between the interviewer and the interviewees (Luff, 1999; Kvale, 2006; Duncombe & Jessop, 2012). Besides, in such situations, it is not unnatural to assume that there might be diverse understanding and / or misunderstanding about phrasing, contents of questions, and even basic information of the research in general. Nevertheless, concerns about the relation between the interviewer and the interviewees and uncertainty whether both parties really share the same understanding during the interview are less evident in this study, for the both parties belong to the same sphere, i.e., the world of academe, particularly in fields of SSH, which is a unique case for social research. Regarding rapport, as is shown in the section about sampling, most of the interviewees knew the interviewer before the implementation of the study, and good, friendly atmosphere was seen during the interview. The same could be said about status difference between the two parties, in which the interviewer is a PhD candidate and the interviewee often is an experienced and established professor. Whatever academic position both have, there seemed no obvious power relation in which one that is in the higher academic status dominates and supresses the other in the interview.

With the strategy of active interview, the interview questions are all semi-structured, and the sequence of the questions were changed, dependent on interviewees' individual academic background and experiences. Although there was a framework of the interview, as mentioned earlier, each interview took place as if it was a free conversation on relating topics to the study. This interview practice was not intended to obtain fact / truth from the interviewees but rather to participate in sense-making activities by confronting with the interview questions with the interviewees. Sometimes, interviewees' interests deviated from the questions which they were asked; however; such interests which seem unrelated to the question posed at a glance could reveal not only their thoughts but also how they construct their thoughts, philosophy in their work as academics, fundamental information to enable me to better understand why it was meaningful for them to tell, or emphasize certain aspects, etc. Although some of the interviewees had a really tight schedule for participating the interview, the strategy of active interview generally worked well to allow a variety of topics and aspects with the interviewees which had not been originally included in the questions. All interviews were carried out in Japanese in order to create possible best flow of conversation between the interviewer and the interviewee, for both parties are native Japanese speakers. It can be a disadvantage to interview in Japanese when thinking of writing up the thesis, as it is written in English and requires translation for interviewees' accounts, nevertheless, it would have been difficult for the interviewees to express everything in English at the equal level of that they wished to express in Japanese. A risk that using English as the interview language might lose subtlety in their accounts seemed too big to fully explore their stories and experiences, which is one of the major points to employ active interview strategy.

5.2.1.5   Critiques of Qualitative Research

Despite the positive aspects of qualitative research, such as enabling in-depth accounts, as Geertz (1973) states as "thick description," to depict social phenomena in natural settings, and therefore being sensitive to contexts in which a study is implemented, this approach is criticized mainly from a viewpoint of researchers who has more quantitative orientation. The following are some issues which are frequently raised as critiques of qualitative research.

First, sceptics often ask whether qualitative research is objective enough as scientific research. In other words, qualitative research is considered as too subjective at any stage of research procedure. For instance, selecting samples can be dependent on the researcher's own connection / network, from which samples are drawn like this study does by purposive sampling. Within this type of sampling strategy, as the name literally indicates, samples are selected by a researcher him / herself intentionally. It may imply that the researcher's subjectivity sneaks into sample selection procedure. Nevertheless, as discussed earlier about sampling of the interview for this study, samples in qualitative research cannot necessarily be anyone drawn from a wider population by probability sampling, because of and dependent on what a qualitative research project aims at. Similar things are said about subjectivity in data analysis. In qualitative research, data are analysed based on a researcher's data interpretation. Even though qualitative researchers could also exploit computer-assisted / aided qualitative data analysis software (CAQDAS) such as NVivo, CAQDAS itself does not analyse and interpret whole data but helps coding and retrieving coded text (Bryman, 2008: 565), prior to data interpretation by a researcher / researchers. This means that interpretation of the researcher(s) still plays a main and significant role in qualitative research. Human's interpretation may be seen as subjective statements, but whether one sees such interpretation as subjective statements or elaborated descriptions and analyses of studied objects totally depends on individual ontological standpoints.[58] Normally, qualitative research is described as subjective and quantitative as objective; however, a question whether or not social research can totally escape from subjectivity should also be considered (see Sword, 1999 quoted in Horsburgh, 2003).

Second, connected to the issue of objectivity, a wide discussion on the generalizability of qualitative research (e.g. Firestone, 1993; Stake, 1995; Bassey, 1999; Hammersley, 2001; Larsson, 2009) must be mentioned. The origin of the critique that qualitative research cannot be generalizable seems to arise because of the incompatibility between natures of quantitative and qualitative

---

[58] This point is explained in the section of Research Strategy, Paradigm and Approach, particularly in the part on interpretivism.

research, and because of different aims that qualitative and quantitative research hold. If either of them insists that their approach to science is the only and true one, the other one would not fit into an approach that insists something else. In this sense, it is not so productive to defend one approach to science each other, as there would never be an agreeable solution for such discussions. From qualitative researchers' perspective, generalization in qualitative research does not mean a law-like generalization that is universally applicable to a wider population. Instead, qualitative research attempts to generate "naturalistic generalization," which Stake explains as a phenomenon that "can be made through vicarious experience [if it is] so well constructed that the person feels as if it happened to themselves" (Stake, 1995: 86). Thus naturalistic generalization heavily relies on readers' capacity to "feel" that what is written is their own experience, and therefore, it seems invisible but clear to those who read a research report in which they can find very similar experience of their own. [59] Similarly, Bassey (1999) distinguishes between different types of generalization, and generalization out of case studies is classified as "fuzzy generalization," which consists of more tentative and uncertain elements than other types of generalization that are understood as conventional scientific generalization. Williams (2000) introduces "moderatum generalisations" as a possible way of generalizing interpretive research:

> Moderatum generalisations: where aspects of S can be seen to be instances of a broader recognisable set of features. This is the form of generalisation made in interpretive research, either knowingly or unknowingly. Geertz's claim (in the quote above) that 'Every people . . . loves its own form of violence' is an example of such a general feature, which then is reworked and enriched through the specific inferences made about the 'cockfight'. (ibid.: 215)

Williams rejects the claim that generalization in interpretive research is impossible and points out that interpretivists do make generalization though they deny the possibility of it or ignore the issue of generalization (ibid.: 209). For Williams, quite similar to others who suggest a variety of alternative generalization to conventional statistic / positivistic generalization, interpretivists should also aim at generalization as long as they carry out research,

---

[59] Stake (1995) refers to case studies in particular to discuss naturalistic generalization.

and an important and common point on generalization in interpretive research among those advocates mentioned above seems that how researchers define generalization for their research projects beyond the generalization in positivistic approaches.

As a final remark in relation to some critiques on qualitative research, triangulation is often discussed as a way to overcome the above-mentioned critiques. The term of triangulation is used in social sciences as employment of two or more methods to collect data (Cohen, Manion, & Morrison, 2007: 141), and often synonymously referred to as a mixed method. Since there are inevitably advantages and disadvantages with using any research method, triangulation is suggested to reduce and supplement lacking methodological aspects as well as to cross-check findings (Bryman, 2008: 379) by using multiple methods, which enables researchers to increase confidence in research findings. From this viewpoint, triangulation often combines a qualitative method(s) with a quantitative method(s). However, this does not necessarily have to be a mix of qualitative and quantitative methods. As Bryman (ibid.) exemplifies, ethnographers exploit interviews to check whether or not their interpretations of observations are misunderstood.

Although it seems better to employ the technique of triangulation with mixed methods for enhancing confidence in research findings and to "overcome the problem of 'method-boundedness'" (Cohen, Manion, & Morrison, 2007: 142), this is not as easy or as straightforward as it looks. While some methodological concerns (e.g., that a single method is incapable of fully exploring an entire phenomenon under studied from all perspectives) may be overcome or be lessened, some other issues are raised and call into question whether triangulation is really useful and workable. Epistemologically, combining quantitative and qualitative methods could be seen as incoherent (Lincoln & Guba, 1985 quoted in Cohen, Manion, & Morrison, 2007: 144), and practically, such mixed methods require researchers' capability in and knowledge on both quantitative and qualitative research methods, as well as time and funding to fulfil such a research project (Bryman, 2008: 624).

This study employs several methods (interviews, questionnaire, and focus group), and they are intended to complement each other and enhance the possibility of a deep understanding of people's accounts in order to depict their world of academic work. In light of this purpose of employment of multiple methods in this study, triangulation seems suitable and appropriate for cross-checking and increasing confidence in collected data in each method. Epistemologically, inconsistency of using triangulation cannot be found in the context of this study, because each method is based on the qualitative nature and orientation of research.

5.2.2 Questionnaire

5.2.2.1 Samples

As shown above in the interview section, the samples for questionnaire research are the same as the samples for the interview, except two who did not participate in the questionnaire research. That is, five out of seven interviewees participated in the qualitative questionnaire for the study.

5.2.2.2. Questionnaire Foci and Questionnaire implementation

As the supplement to the interview, the questionnaire enquires about aspects of academic practice in Japan, which are closely related to the research participants' daily working life. This questionnaire has little intention to give this study a more quantitative touch, but simply attempts to continue the dialogues with the participants from a different perspective from the interviews. Since it seems that the enquiries put in the questionnaire are rather more descriptive and not as broad and abstract as the interview questions, it was assumed that asking the participants to write down the responses would be less complicated for them. As I wished that the participants would express their views more freely as if it was a continuation of the interview practice, the questionnaire was structured to be more open-ended, except a few yes / no questions. It includes four specified aspects of academic work shown earlier together with some other aspects which could influence their academic work:

1. Scientific discourse practices

2. Publication practices

3. Managing academic activities
4. Disciplinary practices
5. Knowledge acquisition
6. Social relations (e.g. hierarchy, status, gender, etc.)

First, scientific discourse practices enquire about whether there is academic discourse with their colleagues in academic affiliations (e.g., at the same department in the university, academic societies / association, and any other groups which they informally form, etc.), how often and in which style they communicate each other, and whether such discourses affect their own academic work.

Second, publication practices refer to publication as outcomes of research, i.e., knowledge generation practices. The questions consist of whether they have ever published academic publications, what kind(s) of publications they are (e.g., academic books, national / international academic journal articles, books for non-academic readers, etc.), and the importance of publication activities and the reasons why they think it is important (or unimportant).

Third, managing academic activities ask about their daily academic working life in the university, including aspects of teaching and other administrative activities. Although teaching and administration related activities are not the main foci of this study, they certainly shape daily academic working life of them. Moreover, they might have impacts on academic work as knowledge generation practices. Thus, this part includes what kind of work they classify as their typical daily work, proportion between research, teaching, and other activities in their daily working life, and how they were trained to carry out all the work they listed

Fourth, disciplinary practices focus on activities in their own disciplines, enquiring about differences between their own and other disciplines and the particularity of the discipline, and differences between national and international disciplinary associations in their activities. The main interest of this part is to understand whether the participants find any particularities in their disciplines, compared with other SSH disciplines, and the same disciplinary organization abroad. Given that the disciplinary fields are normally the main place for them to carry out their academic work, it is assumed to be important to understand how they perceive academic work in their own disciplines.

Fifth, knowledge acquisition relates to how the interviewees acquire academic knowledge, motivation for knowledge acquisition, and how to exploit such acquired knowledge. This part is interested in input activities of academic knowledge generated by others, because it surely forms a fundamental part of academic work, and, especially, in terms of knowledge generation practices, acquiring the existing knowledge is essential to develop their own research.

Sixth, they are asked about social relations as well as the influence of so-called national culture on their academic work. While other parts are enquiries about any activities closely related to academic aspects, this part tries to explore general interpersonal aspects that could be observed in other work settings, i.e., non-academic settings. As pointed out earlier, this aspect could be the main topic of study when people discuss activities of one certain nationality and / or a certain geographical setting (a country / a region). Since this study fundamentally disagrees with such an approach to analysing academic work, it is not interested in rooting out the existence of a national culture in academic work to analyse academic work as a whole. However, enquiring into this aspect is to make sure whether or not social (interpersonal) relations influence academic work.

The questionnaire was distributed by email with an attachment from March to May 2013. The interview participants were contacted individually to decide whether or not they would like to make a contribution to the questionnaire research as well. Same as with the interview, the research language was Japanese so that the participants could feel at ease and express their views in their mother tongue. On distribution, the participants were asked to enquire about any questions / expressions in the questionnaire whose meaning was unclear to reduce misunderstanding from their side as much as possible, although they should have been familiar with the topics after the participation in the interview research. At the end, five out of seven participants returned their full responses to the questionnaire.

5.2.2.3 Disadvantages of Questionnaire Research

It is certain that distributing the questionnaire as the supplemental research to the face-to-face active interview is beneficial to the study, but there are always pros and cons for any research methods. In this part I will briefly discuss some disadvantages of questionnaire research in the context of this study.

Generally, questionnaire research is often employed as a part of quantitative research with structured questions, because the main purpose of such a type of questionnaire research is to measure numbers and scale extents. Therefore, clarity of wording, caution for phrasing which might be understood as a leading phrasing / question, and proper consequences of questions are, for instance, very important in carrying out questionnaire research (Cohen, Manion, & Morrison, 2007; Bryman, 2008; Payne & Payne, 2008). Especially, since questionnaire research often takes as a self-completion style, avoiding misunderstanding of words / phrases and jargons that participants might not be familiar with is crucial to acquire sufficient and meaningful responses. Adding to this point, researchers employing questionnaire research are concerned with the response rate, which could be very low if it is a postal / online survey (Cohen, Manion, & Morrison, 2007; Bryman, 2008), because whether or not the questionnaire is fully and correctly responded and returned to them is totally dependent on decision made by recipients of the questionnaire (Bryman, 2008: 219). The low response rate negatively affects overall analysis and the results of research. Therefore, quantitative questionnaire researchers should attempt to make each question and a questionnaire as a whole as concise as possible (Bryman, 2008), although questions which sound too general such as "What do you think about this region?" should be avoided (Payne & Payne, 2008: 207).

Hence, quantitative questionnaire researchers' concerns seem mostly related to the status and / or nature of a self-completion questionnaire because there is no one to supervise and control how respondents would treat the questionnaire. This frustration of quantitative questionnaire researchers seems to result in listing disadvantages of self-completion questionnaire as follows:

> The down side . . . is that the researcher is not there to address any queries or problems that respondents may have, and they may omit items or give up rather than try to contact the researcher. Respondents may also wrongly interpret and, consequently, answer questions inaccurately. . . . Indeed, the researcher has no control over the environment in which questionnaire is completed, e.g. . . . seriousness given to the completion of the questionnaire, or even whether it is completed by the intended person. (Cohen, Manion, & Morrison, 2007: 344–45)

Similarly, Bryman (2008) points out that there would be lack of opportunities to obtain additional accounts / explanations from respondents when needed and uncertainty whether an appropriate person for the purpose of research would fill in the questionnaire.

In the case of a questionnaire for this study, situations and conditions are different from such quantitative questionnaire research. Albeit that it was the self-completion questionnaire, the respondents were not anonymous, as they were selected by the purposive sampling, and they already had ample information about the study, and are very knowledgeable as practitioners of what is studied. Therefore, the concern mentioned above about uncontrollability and uncertainty of the participants was not the case for this study. Yet, if a disadvantage of the questionnaire is to be suggested, as Bryman (ibid.) rightly states, lack of further accounts to what they write in the questionnaire is definitely one. Despite the fact that the responses are clear and not incomprehensible, had it been face-to-face interactions, there might have been more in-depth, detailed discussions about the accounts that they provided in the questionnaire. Further, regarding the risk of missing data (Bryman, 2008: 219), it is obvious that more responses would have been collected if all questions had been asked during the interview sessions. In this study's case, two people did not participate in the questionnaire research, in spite of some reminders. Although this study does not concern so much with the response rate and collecting more responses, because of the nature of this study being more descriptive and being in the process of development of analytical and methodological frameworks, it should be admitted that missing data occurred in this study because of absence of the researcher in front of the participants.

5.2.3 Focus Group Discussion

In this study, a focus group discussion was planned as response to individual interview data. Conventionally, focus groups and group interviews are perceived as different data collection methods (Kitzinger, 1994), though the style of both looks very similar. Before I go into details of focus group discussion for this study, I would like to introduce some general characteristics of focus groups.

Usage of focus groups was originated from marketing research (Morgan,1996; Kitzinger & Barbour, 1999), and Merton is said to have introduced focused interview with groups of people in the social sciences in 1950s (Kitzinger, 1994; Morgan, 1996; Bryman, 2008; Payne & Payne, 2008).[60] Focus group method has become more and more popular in qualitative research nowadays, although it was also used in quantitative research.[61] It is called "focus" groups, because "the group is 'focused' in that it involves some kind of collective activity" (Kitzinger & Barbour, 1999: 4), which takes a form of group discussion. Different from group interviews, an important emphasis on focus group is that it is an interaction between participants rather than simply responding to questions that are posed by a moderator / an interviewer individually in a group. In this light, researchers employing focus group expect to acquire views / accounts as a group, although it is pointed out by some methodologists (e.g., Morgan, 1996; Kitzinger & Barbour,1999) that researchers exploiting focus groups often do not pay enough attention to this very point and rather tend to follow an approach which is common in marketing research.

The focus group is a data collection activity in which a researcher provide certain topics to discuss. It can take a simple form of group discussion on the topics, but sometimes visual / reading materials can be provided to participants as a starting point of discussion to indicate participants the topics of discussion.

---

[60] According to Kitzinger (1994), Merton himself never used the term of *focus group* and wanted to distinguish what he carried out (focused interviews) from focus groups.

[61] Lunt and Livingstone (1996) refer to the work of Merton (1987 cited in Lunt & Livingstone, 1996) using focus interviews as "an addendum to the questionnaire or experimental study conducted with a random sample." (Lunt & Livingstone, 1996: 5), and qualitative use has been rather contemporary in the social sciences.

As mentioned above, it is not a group interview, and usually, a moderator is not dominant in discussions. Instead, the moderator concentrates on playing a role to make sure that the participants would not excessively deviate from the topics during their discussion. Discussions are often audio-recorded and will be transcribed. In some cases, fieldnotes are taken by a researcher when visual aspects such as body language, facial expression, and other activities that cannot be audially recorded are important for data analysis. Some researchers implement a number of focus groups, and others carry out a single focus group, dependent on aims of research. Sampling also depends on whether the research orientation is qualitative or quantitative, and it could take random sampling in quantitative research and purposive sampling in qualitative research.

To sum, focus groups are a particular type of group discussion in which topics are set by a researcher as a means of data collection. Definition of focus groups is broad and rather flexible, since it is a method that is often combined with other research method(s). In this sense, focus groups play a supplemental role as a research method that is rarely employed solely in a research project. The emphasis of employing focus groups is group interaction, which can provide researchers with collective views / accounts on the topics that would be difficult to acquire in individual interviews.

5.2.3.1 Discussion Foci

Focus group discussion in this study was planned in order to achieve the following two points:

1. Collecting further data in relation to individual interviews
2. Analysing some parts of individual interview data

Even though individual in-depth interviews can provide a number of various noteworthy accounts and comments, it seems that aspects with regard to "academic knowledge"[62] are supposed to be

---

[62] The term *academic knowledge* can be replaced with the term *scientific knowledge*. In a general sense, they can be used interchangeably. Nevertheless, "academic knowledge" is preferred here, since "scientific

one of the most relevant aspects in relation to debates on international collaborative activities, for academic knowledge is definitely one of the central elements that form knowledge encounters such as exchanging views with foreign counterparts in international research projects as well as academic activities within the country. While academic environment aspects as explained in the interview section can also be a big framework which would influence academic work, academic knowledge can be considered as the core of academic work. Until now, it has hardly ever been questioned whether academics in the world share the same perception of "academic knowledge," what they classify as academic knowledge, and what usage of academic knowledge could be. This viewpoint arises because academic knowledge is understood as substance of universally shared perception among academics, and consequently, there seem few studies, if any, that pay attention to such above questions in a context of international academic activities.[63]

Since some ambiguity on perception of academic knowledge through the individual interviews emerged, I felt that it was necessary to further investigate some perspectives of academic knowledge perceived by academics. Thus the issues around academic knowledge was set as a framework of this focus group discussion.

To establish the foci of focus group discussion, firstly preliminary analysis of individual interview question topics are reviewed:

D) Academic knowledge in society

1. Roles of scientific knowledge and / or relationship between academic knowledge and society

2. How is the academic knowledge perceived in society?

---

    knowledge" seems to imply to some Japanese people rather knowledge in natural sciences and technology than knowledge in SSH.

[63] It is not to state that there is no study about knowledge. Epistemology in philosophy obviously deals with such questions, but knowledge per se in the context of international / national academic activities seems to be perceived among academics as universal.

3. What is your perception of academic knowledge as an academic person?

Then, according to the interviewees' accounts on these questions, a further framework for the focus group discussion was formulated under three new topics:

- Origination of knowledge
- Methodology and approaches to knowledge
- Application of knowledge

The origination of knowledge refers to motivation for knowledge production, where knowledge that is a basis for new knowledge he / she is going to produce comes from, how research topics are chosen, and if there is any condition / criterion to choose research topics.

Second, methodology and approaches to knowledge inquires into how researchers approach their research topics (e.g., pragmatic or philosophical / fundamental), what research method(s) they tend to use, and why they employ such approaches and methodologies.

Third, as the topic of application of knowledge, the following questions are posed: How, where, and to whom knowledge they produced would be released and circulated, how people who receive the said knowledge would understand / perceive it as, whether the knowledge would be beneficial to them, and how such knowledge would be treated (e.g., used for future research?).

These questions are more related to contents of academic work with regard to academic knowledge, while the interview foci (D) above ask interrelationship between academic knowledge and society. This means that the foci are narrowed down from the perspectives of academic knowledge in society, which are dealt as academic environment, to the perspectives of it within academic practice. By doing so, broader aspects of academic knowledge could be explored and understood. Besides, since the both perspectives of academic knowledge are assumed to be closely connected each other, the aims of focus group discussion which bridges collecting further data and analysing some parts of interview data could be achieved.

5.2.3.2 Participants

Since more diverse views were sought after the individual, in-depth interviews, participants for this group discussion were selected from a member list of an academic society in Japan. Simultaneously, some of the interviewees were also asked whether they would be interested in participating such a group discussion. There is a fundamental difference between these two groups in nature: The former group of people did not know so much about contents of this research project, and the latter obviously knew what it is about. I tried to contact people from the former group, because one of the aims of the discussion is that discussants would, to some extent, analyse certain aspects of accounts that are made during the interview research. Although little problem was seen to involve some interviewees as the discussants, the former seemed to be a better choice, due to the tendency that they may have less bias / preconceived ideas about what they are going to discuss than the latter group. Accordingly, nine people from the former group were asked whether they could participate in the group discussion by email with some attachment documents explaining the research project as a whole and a draft plan for the discussion. Unfortunately, most of them had some other commitments at the weekend in which the group discussion was planned, and declined to participate in the discussion. I also contacted the latter group in case that no one from the former group accepted the participation. As a result, two from the latter group indicated a great interest in joining the group discussion, but it turned out that they would also have other commitments around the date and would not be able to participate.[64] From the former group, three people agreed to participate in the discussion, and it is confirmed that they would be the discussants for the focus group discussion. Thus, these three participants are members of an academic society whose focus is cultural studies with different disciplinary orientations such as linguistics, foreign language education, intercultural communication study, and psychology. They are one male and two

---

[64] Since one of them was a knowledgeable person on the Japanese academe and the social sciences in Japan, and was very much interested in participating in it and kindly offered me to have an individual meeting on another date, there was another meeting which summarize and roughly analyse what had been discussed on the focus group discussion.

females who work for Japanese universities. Two of them are teaching at private universities, and one works for a national university. Unlike the interview, the balance of age, gender, affiliation, and academic background of the participants is not the central concern of this focus group, and the balance of individual academic background and characteristics are rather incidental.

As far as the number of the focus group discussion participants is concerned, it is often mentioned that around ten people would be ideal (e.g., Lunt & Livingstone, 1996; Morgan, 1997; McLafferty, 2004: 190). However, there is no strict rule about how many people should be involved in a group. As McLafferty (ibid.) notes in this respect, it can be less than five participants in a group, while the participation of around twenty people in a focus group discussion is also possible. It seems that the number of participants is justified mainly because over ten participants would be too big to manage discussion, and less than five would be too small to create views / statements as a group rather than an individual view. Although there might be different effects with different group sizes, Morgan (1997: 34) summarises that such "rules of thumb" are not requirements for conducting focus groups but "a descriptive summary of how they often are done." Thus, in this study, since it was not only a data collection activity but also a collective analysis activity, the number of participants had to be very small in order to acquire intensive and in-depth discussion. It would have been better if one or two more people could have participated; however, it was sufficient and good to have these people who were so much interested in the topic(s) of this study and attempted to provide insightful views on the issues that are asked as well as analytical comments on the interview outcomes.

In relation to the number of participants in focus group discussions, another frequently discussed issue is whether participants should be strangers to each other or acquaintances. On one hand, some advocate that focus groups would be better operated if they consist of strangers than friends (Cohen, Manion, & Morrison, 2007: 377), while others claim that friends and acquaintances could be focus group participants. Morgan (1997: 38) precisely discusses this issue. According to Morgan, it is a valid discussion that strangers should consist of focus groups; however, in reality "social scientists routinely conduct focus groups in organizations and other naturally occurring groups in which acquaintanceship is unavoidable" (ibid.). He argues that focus groups with strangers and ones with acquaintances have different group dynamics, and where group dynamics are not such a concern, a decisive factor is what kind of setting is more practical for a researcher to achieve his / her research goal (ibid.). Regarding this study, I purposefully selected those who had known each other, since it was assumed that the fact that they knew each other would make the atmosphere of the meeting more relaxed than having a group that did not know each other. Especially, this point was not unimportant, considering that the meeting was carried out in a very limited timeframe. Knowing each other's academic backgrounds was certainly helpful to encourage more fundamental discussions among them than having to get to know each other from scratch.

5.2.3.3 Focus Group Practice

Prior to the group discussion, some documents were provided to the participants, [65] including the same documents which were distributed to them when asking for their participation. The discussion language was Japanese, since all are Japanese native speakers.[66] As the environment for the discussion, a meeting room of a small hotel in Tokyo was rented for five hours. Different from the individual interviews, the discussion was planned to be much longer, and it seemed necessary to provide a quiet room throughout the activity with decent facilities for a meeting. The meeting was audio-recorded with a MP3 device for transcription in order to analyse the contents of the meeting. The following is some issues in practicing focus groups:

It is firstly an issue of role of the moderator in the focus group discussions. As McLafferty (2004) indicates, there is also no definite consensus among focus group researchers about who should be a moderator of a meeting. Some studies value the

---

[65] They are documents on interview question topics, backgrounds for the study (including the previous study I carried out for my Master's degree, since this research is closely connected to it), and the group discussion preparation, i.e., introducing the discussants foci of the discussion and informing them about preliminary interview outcomes).

[66] The reason why Japanese language was chosen as the discussion language is the same argument of using Japanese as the interview language. For the details, see the interview section.

participants' own natural flaw of discussion, and others prefer more structured focus groups guided by a researcher him / herself (Bryman, 2008). Again, it greatly depends on what the research project aims at and how it would like to approach the research aim. In the case of this study, a general agenda for the discussion was provided to the participants beforehand, and I moderated the discussion along with the agenda, though I did not attempt to either intervene or to join the discussion unnecessarily. Consequently, the discussion was more a form of group talk than one in which the participants only responded to what had been posed by the moderator. Since the participants are all academics, to a certain extent, they could moderate the discussion by themselves. This point might differ from other research settings, as research participants in other studies are normally considered to be less capable to understand research contents. This negative consideration about research participants in general could rarely be seen in my study not only in the focus group discussion but other empirical part of this study.

Group dynamics could be mentioned as an advantage of focus group discussions. Since it is an interaction among a group, ideas which would not come up in individual interviews could emerge out of the discussion itself (Cohen, Manion, & Morrison, 2007; Payne & Payne, 2008). Kitzinger (1995: 299) also claims that "group processes can help people to explore and clarify their views in ways that would be less easily accessible in a one to one interview." In addition, unlike individual interviews, group interaction dynamics enables participants to ask and explain to each other when they have misunderstandings or uncertainty about what they discuss (Morgan, 1996). Indeed, in the practice of focus group discussion for this study, such attitudes between the participants could be observed, and it is affirmative that the focus group discussion could indicate its positive aspects of group dynamics as a data collection activity, which probably would not have resulted from individual interviews. Although some point out that the focus group is a good means to also observe participants' interaction (e.g., Duggleby, 2005) through a discussion process, this study hardly had such an intention, for its interest is not in people's behaviour and attitude in their interaction.

5.2.3.4 Difficulties in Focus Groups

From a methodological perspective, there are some rules of thumb to carry out focus groups and to analyse data derived from focus groups, and consequently, it cannot be denied that there is some ambiguity in its practice and difficulties how to analyse data (Bryman, 2008). Therefore, focus groups tend not to be a sole research method but can be used with other method(s). Morgan (1996) suggests that surveys and in-depth individual interviews are often combined with focus groups in sociological studies. Although focus groups can be used as the only research tool, it is more useful to employ this method as a part of triangulation (Cohen, Manion, & Morrison, 2007).

In practice, it is frequently pointed out that there might be dominant participants in discussions, who ignore less eloquent participants. Indeed, managing such a collective activity is not straightforward, especially when there are too many participants are present. Even though it is better if the moderator remains reserved during the discussion, it is also necessary that he / she should harness the discussion so that all participants' voices can be heard. Otherwise, the discussion might be pulled towards the dominant participants' voice(s), and the results would be a collection of individual opinions (Cohen, Manion, & Morrison, 2007). This could also relate to issues of roles of the moderator in focus group discussions, that is, how much the moderator should be involved in discussions, how to moderate discussions without being too dominant, and whether the moderator has capability to keep discussions under control (See Stewart, Shamdasani, & Rook, 2007 for detailed discussion on how to moderate focus groups).

There are other challenges in carrying out focus groups, and most of them seem challenging to researchers due to the fact that this method particularly deals with a group of people in an unnatural setting that is provided by researcher. Unlike the participant observation method, in focus groups researchers gather participants in a neutral spot, away from where they live, work, and conduct other daily activities. Participants are not people who naturally gather there but instead are selected by researcher, no matter which sampling strategy is used. Besides, participants are expected to interact as a group, even though they do not know each other in many cases. This unnaturalness seems to contradict what qualitative research normally aims at, which is deriving people's accounts in settings / environment where they feel comfortable. Researchers collect data under such familiar circumstances to research participants by interviews and observations, and then they interpret the data, taking into consideration the context from which the data were obtained. In this light, difficulties raised by focus groups methodologists are inevitable in qualitative research. Supposedly, that is why this method needs supports with other methods for triangulation rather than being the sole research tool.

5.3 Ethical Consideration for the Empirical Research

When a research project of empirical study involves human beings, some ethical considerations should be made, and researchers must proceed with their empirical research according to the ethical considerations which are either set up by academic / disciplinary associations or devised by researchers themselves, in line with contents of those ethical considerations set up by such academic associations. In this section, some fundamental and relevant points to any types of empirical research will be presented. There could be many different implications by the term of 'ethical considerations'; however; this section is confined to ethical issues which exist in the relationship between the researcher and the research participants.

Firstly, the informed consent should be obtained from those who would express their willingness to participate in the research as respondents, interviewees, and people in the observed setting. In the context of this study, informed consent is understood as participants' rights to decide whether they participate in the research, to withdraw from the participation at any stage of their participation in the research, and to be informed about the research, that is, what kind of research project it is, why they are asked to participate in it, and other fundamental information about the research project. Some types of research such as covert observation and other types of research require intentional deception because researchers cannot reveal everything about the research project because such revelations might influence or bias data. Nevertheless, normally obtaining informed consent from research participants is "an important principle" (Cohen, Manion, & Morrison, 2007: 53).

Secondly, privacy of participants as a part of personal data protection practices should be secured. In this study, any ethically sensitive personal information is not required and not involved in the process of data collection.[67] According to Cohen, Manion, and Morrison (ibid.: 64), privacy refers to "more than simple confidentiality," and it is related to what researchers promise to research participants in the informed consent such as rights to participate in or withdraw from research activities, which is explained above. Privacy, thus, could be understood as researchers' obligation to guarantee that a research participants' life will remain the same as when they do not participate in research activities possible.

Similar to privacy, anonymity is an aspect which should be promised to participants. Not only in a research report or a thesis (Payne & Payne, 2008: 69) but also in processed and unprocessed data, participants' identities such as names, ages, place of work, and any other information which might reveal their identity should be hidden by putting pseudonym and masking and / or deleting information where necessary (Brown & Dowling, 1998: 65). Therefore, before they actually participate in the interview or the focus group discussion of this study, promising to keep the participants' identity anonymous was clearly informed to the participants in writing.

Finally, regarding confidentiality, how to handle collected data should be mentioned. This does not directly influence participants' lives, but any researcher should be careful when they obtain and handle a considerable amount of personal information. Even though researchers try to protect participants' privacy and anonymity with their upmost care, there still could be unforeseen accidents that might make personal data / information public without the researchers' consent. In order to avoid such accidents, it is often suggested that researchers should pay a great deal of attention to where and how to store data collected through empirical research. In the case of this study, the interviews and the

---

[67] Such information refers to religious preferences, income, racial prejudices and any other personal information (American Psychological Association, 1973 quoted in Cohen, Manion, & Morrison, 2007: 63)

focus group discussion were all electronically recorded by a MP3 device. The recorded data were stored in my computer, which requires a password to start it, and adding to this, the recorded data file was encrypted with another password which no other people would know. Interview transcriptions were also stored in another encrypted folder with a different password from the recorded file. The questionnaire responses were kept in the same manner as the audio file and the transcription folder.

There are, of course, many other considerations on research ethics, which depend on what kind of research topic is dealt with, what research method for the project is used, who is going to participate in the research (e.g., socially vulnerable people), and how researchers report their research outcomes. Although this study does not involve any particularly sensitive topics, a vulnerable group of people, or unusual social settings which should be closely scrutinized in terms of research ethics, any piece of research involving human beings must respect research participants' private life and should not do any harm, physically and mentally, to their lives (Bryman, 2008: 118) by getting them involved in any research activities.

5.4 Data Analysis Method: Grounded Theory (GT)

So far, the research methods and ethical issues in the research activity with such methods have been explained and discussed. It is crucial that a researcher well recognizes advantages and disadvantages in the use of them to conduct a research project which will meet his / her original research questions / interests to explore the subject matter(s). By doing so, research methods could form a certain framework for responding to the research question(s), and as a result of practicing empirical research based on the framework, the researcher would acquire a large amount of data from the empirical research. Data itself do not interpret what was told by the research participants, but only reveal what was said and how the research participants acted. Therefore, as well as the research methods, a framework for data analysis should also be scrutinized and its validity discussed in a research project. This section, therefore, attempts to explore the basic concept of

Grounded Theory (GT), its origin, fundamental elements of GT, and criticism / drawbacks on GT, and some issues in application of GT in this research such as suitability of GT in this study on one hand and discordant aspects of GT on the other would follow.

GT is chosen among qualitative data analysis methods for this research project as the data analysis method, although it is common in any qualitative data analysis methods including GT that a thematic analysis approach to identify concepts emerging out of the data by coding is fundamentally used. Therefore, the thematic analysis approach is not considered as "a distinctive cluster of techniques" (Bryman 2008: 554), since other qualitative data analysis approaches, such as discourse analysis, content analysis, and narrative analysis, also share, in part, the same activity that is to seek for themes in data. Hence, it is more precise to say that the data would be analysed by GT approach. The details of GT would be described in the next part.

5.4.1 What is Grounded Theory?

GT was generated out of collaborative work of the U.S sociologists, Barney Glaser and Anselm Strauss on patients with fatal illnesses. An intensive empirical research was implemented in a U.S hospital to investigate levels of patients' awareness of their likeliness of dying and ways hospital staff and families of patients handle the patients' awareness. This work was published as a book *Awareness of Dying* (1965), which led Glaser and Strauss to the birth of GT as a form of *The Discovery of Grounded Theory* in 1967. The strong claim they made in the generation of GT is the rejection of hypothetico-deductive model of social research, which starts from a hypothesis based on an existing theory and verifies the hypothesis by empirical research, because, for Glaser and Strauss, this model of research has a limit in social science research. As a background of this claim, at that time, sociologists prioritized verifying theories over generating them.[68] Glaser and Strauss did

---

[68] Glaser and Strauss frequently refer to sociologists in *The Discovery of Grounded Theory*. It is certainly because of their own disciplinary background being sociologists, and it could be assumed that it was social research that meant by the term of sociological research. Today's use of GT is not at all limited in the field of sociology, therefore, it can be concluded that

not deny the importance of verification of social theories; were unsatisfied with the situation, since verification of theory had been overemphasized (Glaser & Strauss, 1967). Simultaneously their uneasiness that the ways that theories normally used to verify do not really fit for studying empirical data was also apparent. They state:

> Theory . . . must fit the situation being researched, and work when put into use. By "fit" we mean that the categories must be readily (not forcibly) applicable to and indicated by the data under study; by "work" we mean that they must be meaningfully relevant to and be able to explain the behavior under study. (ibid.: 3)

Thus, they question whether theories used in empirical research in sociology are really workable and fit in order to investigate what researchers really aim to investigate, and if they are not, there would be a call for "*discovery of theory from data- systematically obtained and analyzed in social research*" (ibid.: 1 emphasis in original).

In short, Glaser and Strauss believed that the hypothetico-deductive model does not fully work in studying empirical reality in social research. Researchers simply used this model because they had never been trained to generate a theory based on empirical data, nor to generate one's explanations by empirical data but by a theory. It seemed to them that these situations originated from the overemphasis on theory verification in sociological research. Therefore, they doubted the relevance of the hypothetico-deductive model of research, and claimed the novel model, grounded theory, to generate theories according to empirical data so that a theory and empirical data fit and work together.

5.4.2 Essential Elements Consist of GT

As we can witness that GT is later further elaborated by Strauss and Corbin,[69] there are diverse understanding of GT, and therefore

---

what Glaser and Strauss meant as sociologists / sociology can be synonymous to social science academics / social sciences in general.

[69] Strauss and Corbin published a book, *Basics of Qualitative Research: Grounded Theory Procedures and Techniques* in 1990, which followed Strauss's own publication *Qualitative Analysis for Social Scientists* (1987).

different procedures in GT approach. Nevertheless, basic GT research remains the same no matter which approach a researcher chooses. The following is the enumeration of essential components of GT.

- Theoretical Sampling

    Despite of the conventional meaning of 'sampling', theoretical sampling is defined quite differently. While the conventional meaning of sampling is that selection of informants and / or research participants in order to obtain possible appropriate data from a certain population that is appropriate for an aim / aims of study, theoretical sampling in GT means "the process of data collection for generating theory whereby the analyst jointly collects, codes, analyzes his [sic.] data and decides what data to collect next and where to find them" (Glaser & Strauss, 1967: 45). Thus, it not only refers to research informants / participants, but to more the phase of activity which is necessary for GT. A possible reason why theoretical sampling differs from other conventional sampling is that it was not favoured to identify and fix even research informants / participants before empirical research starts. Certainly, it is natural to consider that a researcher has some ideas about who should be his / her research participants in the empirical research, therefore, it does not mean that the researcher does not know whom to study at all (c.f. Corbin & Strauss, 1990: 420). However, as a basis of GT, even research participants can be fluctuated dependent on emerged data in the later stage. [70]

After the Strauss and Corbin book was published, Glaser, as one of the founders of GT, rebuked Strauss for having made fundamental changes in GT, which is documented in *Emergence vs forcing: Basics of Grounded Theory Analysis* (Glaser, 1992).

[70] As well as that GT method disagrees with any presupposition at an early stage of a research (e.g., by other theories, literature that is relevant to a current study, etc.), it is considered that data out of empirical research would suggest relevant research participants for the undertaken study. In this sense, it is not the researcher that decides who relevant research participants should be as samples.

Consequently, the research participants cannot be fixed at the beginning of research project in GT method, but can also emerge in the process of empirical research. In other words, the conventional meaning of 'sampling' in GT would be selected by the research process itself, which is theoretical sampling of GT. In the theoretical sampling, iterative activities of data collection and analysis take place, and coding plays an important role during this process.

- Coding

    Coding is the main process in GT, and unlike other analysis methods, it is repeated several times (or many times) until concepts and categories are defined to generate a theory. The activity of coding is identical to the conventional way of coding in other qualitative data analysis methods, in which data are broken down into small component parts (Bryman, 2008: 542) and are labelled on each component. Nonetheless, coding in GT is rather more provisional due to its iterative nature of method. That is to say, same as the research participants in GT, codes can be changed, replaced, or even sometimes abandoned in the process of continuous analyses with added data. This iterative process necessarily made advocates of GT distinguish different three levels of coding [71]: Open, axial, [72] and selective coding (Cohen, Manion, & Morrison, 2007: 493).[73] Open coding is seen as a starting phase of coding in which a researcher carefully reads through data and starts identifying units of analysis (ibid.), comparing, conceptualizing and categorizing data

---

[71] It does not imply that all researchers employing GT should operate with the three coding phases. For instance, Charmaz (2006), who is a well-known advocate of GT, prefers to two phases: initial and selective / focused coding.

[72] Instead of 'axial', it is expressed as 'pivotal' coding. It is a matter of choice of expression, and they have the identical meaning. Axial coding is indicated in the work of Strauss and Corbin (1990).

[73] These three phases of coding are, according to LaRossa, "the most widely accepted" (2005: 840), although there are other diverse understanding and procedures of coding in GT.

(Strauss & Corbin, 1990: 61).[74] It generates some concepts and categories to construct the basic element of an emerging new theory. Axial coding is a practice that interconnection is sought between categories generated in open coding, and it is done by comparing and grouping the data (Payne & Payne, 2008: 108). Then, in selective coding, a core category that is "the central issue or focus around which all other categories are integrated" (Bryman, 2008: 543) is identified and refined. Identifying a core category by selective coding allows a researcher to approach to the central part of what has been studied, which means generating a theory.

- Constant Comparison

The above respective coding occurs in the process of constant comparison. Constant comparison is also an iterative practice in which researchers compare data and categories / concepts with new ones that have emerged from the most recent empirical research, so that categories would fit well with obtained data, and they could finally achieve a core category. It, then, seems that constant comparison aims at saturation in data. Indeed, it is one of the most prominent aspects of GT, emphasized by Glaser and Strauss (1967). Since GT totally relies on data that are collected not only once but several times until a researcher achieves theoretical saturation, this practice of scrutinizing between data and concepts / categories certainly plays a significant role in the entire process of GT. Due to its importance, Glaser (1998) suggests an idea of creating 'memos', which would help researchers to remind what is meant by terms in their analyses as well as to keep their thought on the right track. Memos can be also used to visualize construction of and interrelationship between concepts and categories.

---

[74] According to Payne & Payne (2008: 107), however, researchers should not compare and summarize / categorize data at the phase of open coding.

- Theoretical Saturation

  Theoretical saturation is a status that no more new concepts / categories would emerge even though further data collections and analyses are carried out. It also means that the concepts / categories which have been acquired by the continuous data analyses fit well in the setting that has been studied. At this point, the researcher could stop data collection and analysis, and could start writing up the emerged theory. The theory, in this context, tends to be substantive rather than abstractive, because one of the most significant foci of GT is, as seen before, being workable and fit (Glaser & Strauss, 1967) in actual social situations / phenomena. This inevitably implies that a theory generated by GT method could not stand wider application of the theory to other situations like so-called grand theories claim to do. Therefore, theoretical saturation does not mean that generated concepts / categories by GT are saturated for universal use, but it is theoretically saturated as far as the studied setting is concerned.[75]

Through the aforementioned process the ultimate accomplishment of GT, which is generation of theory that would suit and be able to work in the studied setting(s), would be made. There are some ambiguous terms in the process with which even the founders of GT and those who developed the original GT method further do not agree each other. Below I have attempted to summarize and explain the terms that make up of core parts of the GT method procedure. They are also considered as significant outcomes out of the process in GT at different phases of research.

---

[75] Payne & Payne (2008: 109) suggest that the core category is so refined in the process of GT that it could be used in other studies. However, they also refer to its limitation concerning generalization that theoretical saturation does not mean neither that possible situations / conditions are all covered nor that it could be generalized in other settings / situations.

5.4.3 Core Outcomes of GT

Concepts

Concepts are the smallest analytical unit in the process of GT method, which would appear at the open coding level. Corbin and Strauss state that they "are the basic unit of analysis" and "incidents, events, and happenings are taken as, analyzed as, potential indicators of phenomena, which are given conceptual labels" (1990: 420). Thus, if a researcher finds relevant words / phrases / sentences to generate this minimal unit of analysis to his / her study, they are labelled as 'sports', 'hobby', 'music', and so on. Concepts would increase in the iterative data collections and analyses, while some of them might be dropped off when researchers later find them less relevant than they first seemed. However, at this stage, there would not be seen so much elaboration to label parts of data and it could therefore be more general, leading to the next stage of categorization of concepts.

Categories[76]

While concepts are defined as the outcome of the basic unit of analytical process, categories are created by a researcher based on what they obtain as concepts. Categories can be, therefore, defined as one level higher in hierarchy and more abstract than concepts. They make groups out of respective concepts, and thus take some concepts in one group. Needless to say, categories are also subject to continuous refinement, and not all concepts are categorized in one time analysis. According to Corbin and Strauss, categories play a significant role in theory development and "provide the means by which a theory is integrated" (ibid.). Consequently, having seen in the process of GT, researcher could identify a core category, which is closely related to the phase of theory generation, at the selective coding phase.

---

[76] In relation to categories, there is another term, *properties*. Although it is important to distinguish between properties and categories from methodologists' perspectives, it is very complicated (LaRossa, 2005: 843) and seems controversial among GT methodologists. For instance, categories should involve properties and dimensions for Corbin and Strauss (1990). Since distinguishing them seems of little importance in this study, I will not refer to properties in detail. Properties are understood as "attributes or aspects of a category" (Bryman, 2008: 544).

Hypotheses

Before it achieves the final phase of theory generation by GT, there is a crucial point to be mentioned. Because of the emphasis of its inductive approach in GT, it might be easily overlooked, but GT method does involve a deductive process during the axial coding phase (Payne & Payne, 2008: 108). Despite that GT was generated by Glaser and Strauss as an alternative approach in social research that is against mainstream hypothetico-deductive type of research, it does not mean that GT does not take any deductive approach in itself. Certainly verifying is required in order to achieve theory generation, while hypotheses emerge out of data. Such hypotheses emerged through GT process are an object of verification and re-verification until a hypothesis is confirmed by the activity of verification. Naturally, some hypotheses which failed to verify their validity in the context of research would be rejected or modified by researcher, and by doing so, hypotheses would be also refined and saturated. The important thing here is that hypotheses in GT are not something given by any other existing theories, but are also an outcome of GT process.

Theory

It is the achievement of GT method when a theory is generated by the above procedures. Theories generated by GT can be classified at two different levels: Substantive theory can be the primary one, and formal theory may be the secondary one. GT seeks interconnectedness between data, which can mean empirical reality, and theory, and this interconnectedness inevitably makes a theory more substantive. As a result, it might not be able to be applicable to other situations / settings. Nonetheless, one can generate a theory by the GT method which can be applicable to other settings. That is: Data collection and analysis can be carried out in the same manner as the process to achieve the substantive theory but in other settings, probably with a wider population. If the logic of the GT method as a whole is valid, this iterative procedure of data collection and analysis would lead researchers to a theory that could be fit and workable in other settings. The theory as the outcome of this extended procedure is called formal theory. Though the nature of both types of theory would be, by and large, identical, the latter could provide broader application of the theory in social world / phenomena.

Elements which form GT method and outcomes at different phases in GT have been clarified. In short, GT could be defined as a data analysis method constructed by iterative data collection and analyses that finally lead researchers to a theory which is perfectly fit in studied settings, and, therefore, in which there is little discrepancy between the generated theory and the experiences and phenomena in the empirical study. Thus GT method seems a way of emancipation from the conventional hypothetico-deductive type of social research. Due to the interconnectedness between empirical data and theory, theory does not contradict empirical 'reality', and vice versa. It looks as if problems that often lie between theories and empirical data were solved by the advent of GT; however, GT has also limitation and criticism. In the next part, the criticism and drawbacks of GT are examined.

5.4.4 Criticism of GT

Existing literature, knowledge, and presupposition

Theoretically and methodologically it is quite confusing that GT rejects exploitation of literature and studies which were previously written and implemented.[77][78] Locating his / her own study in an existing knowledge / academic field is a normal and conventional academic practice, and a research project which is going to adopt GT as the data analysis method might have been inspired by precedent studies / knowledge. Similarly, presupposition, assumption, and any other activities that involve anticipation are not favourable in GT, since they could misguide GT researcher to a biased view / views, and consequently to incorrect analyses. The reason why such above activities are forbidden in GT is a belief that data should be the only resource for generation of theory. Therefore, what a researcher knows or thinks prior to his / her research project should not be counted as an appropriate activity for GT method in a strict sense.

---

[77] Glaser and Strauss (1967) are strictly against literature review, while Strauss and Corbin (1990) allow researchers to carry out literature review. According to Dunne (2011), it is not a matter of whether or not literature review should be done in GT, but a matter of when it should be done.
[78] However, there is also an interpretation that Glaser and Strauss (1967) accept literature search before data collection (Allan, 2003).

Although it might be logically understandable, it seems quite impossible for any academic researchers to follow this instruction and practice it. Even though it is not meant that researcher should not bring his / her knowledge at all into data analysis activity (c.f. Dunne, 2011), as Bryman (2008) points out, what we see and understand is likely to be interpreted by ourselves, who have acquired academic knowledge through academic and / or non-academic experiences and activities, and as a result, the analyses through our understanding are less likely to be totally objective or neutral. It can also be pointed out that any academic work has its basis in the existing academic disciplines, and it is naturally oriented from the beginning of a research project towards academic contribution to certain disciplinary fields. Then, the possibility that researcher has no academic or personal presupposition on what is going to be studied would be highly unlikely.[79] Even if literature review is claimed as relevant in the GT method at the later stage of research (Charmaz, 1990; Charmaz, 2006), there still is a big question whether the delay of literature review would make a substantial difference with literature review at the earlier stage. Thus this is a controversial point whether and when literature review is carried out in GT method, and no consensus has yet been achieved among GT practitioners on this point.

Its positivistic orientation

Another major criticism is about the positivistic orientation of GT, which is referred to the origin of GT, *The Discovery of Grounded Theory* (Glaser & Strauss, 1967). The criticism comes from especially sociologists with social constructionist orientation. Charmaz is one of the most well-known advocates of the alternative (social constructionist) GT. From such a viewpoint, the original GT method has too much emphasis on 'discovering reality' out of data, and this implies that data consist of objective reality out there in the field. Although Charmaz and other advocates agree that GT is

---

[79] Dunne enumerates the diverse debates on when literature review should be carried out and why by citing GT practitioners / methodologists. Those who are against the original idea of GT by Glaser and Strauss insist on the impossibility that researchers could abandon literature review in a process of research, and suggest usefulness and necessity of literature review in the GT method (2006: 117).

an efficient data analysis method that is "close to . . . studied world and to develop an integrated set of theoretical concepts from their empirical materials that not only synthesize and interpret them but also show processual relationships" (Charmaz, 2005: 508), GT method is, at the same time, a method "stamped with positivist approval," due to the "assumption of an external but discernible world, unbiased observer, and discovered theory" (ibid.: 509). That is, if empirical data are deemed as reality out there which has no influence of researcher, and, therefore, a theory is discovered as if it was waiting for being eventually discovered by the researcher, as the original GT claims. Then, roles of researcher that are more interpretive and sense making through data analysis would be totally ignored. Charmaz, for instance, somehow solves this problematic matter in GT by suggesting the constructionist GT approach (ibid.), the implication in the original GT method claimed by Glaser and Strauss seems to a number of social researchers quite positivistic, which, in many cases, qualitative researchers are against. Certainly, as shown above in Charmaz's attempt, there would be ways to escape from the positivist orientation that GT might originally involve, and it is probably how GT has been exploited by a great number of social science academics by slightly modifying its method or adjusting its possible epistemological implication to more suitable direction despite of the criticism. Adding to the criticism, are some drawbacks of GT that I will now look at.

5.4.5 Drawbacks of GT

First of all, despite of its popularity among qualitative researchers, GT is not very strictly defined, and, therefore, it can mean different things to different people. As seen so far in this section, it is apparent how GT is constructed and operated as well as its aim though there have been some diverse understanding and conceptualization among GT advocates. However, the term *grounded theory* is defined, and therefore used, loosely. Some might consider GT simply as a synonym to qualitative research, and others might understand it as the founders of GT really meant it to be. Because of such different definitions and understandings of GT, the original procedures might sometimes be neglected by its practitioners (Bryman, 2008). As a result, its meaning and definition has become looser, since it seems dependent on the practitioners to claim what they do is GT.

The second drawback of GT, then, is that there is a certain difficulty carrying out the ideal procedure of GT, which might have a connection to the first point above. Theoretically, GT seems, indeed, to be an alternative to deductive approach to academic knowledge generation, nonetheless, it might be practically less feasible to carry out the entire suggested procedure, which is iterative activities of data collection and analysis. Particularly when researcher has limited financial resource and a short timeframe for a research project, iterative activities to achieve an emergent of theory might not be affordable. Moreover, the GT method does not allow researchers to plan their research activities beforehand if we do not know when we can stop data collection and analysis, and it would certainly make any research project planning impossible, considering that the current research environment is not that generous for a theory emerging without fixed schedule (Allan, 2003). This unforeseeability in terms of research planning might render GT rather undefined and modified so that GT could be practical and usable in respect of actual research planning and activities.

Thirdly and finally, it is questioned whether GT could really generate a theory as it originally claims. Judging from the statement of Glaser and Strauss (1967) in this respect, GT does not aims at generating so-called grand theory but is keen on generating middle-range theory that suits to understand actual settings around us, and, therefore, is applicable to the real life world. Because of the substantive nature of 'theory' that GT aims at, it has a narrow theoretical applicability and some say that GT cannot even achieve the point of theory generation but only that concepts are generated (Bryman, 2008: 549).

To summarize, despite of its popularity in qualitative research, GT has been understood and exploited in a variety of ways. Such diverse usage and understandings result in drawbacks that undermine the ideals of GT which the founders of GT advocated. Further, there are some methodological and ontological concerns among GT practitioners about the original GT method established by Glaser and Strauss. One is impossibility and / or timing of literature review in a course of research project, and another is the positivistic orientation which can be seen in the procedure of GT.

Quite different from the other data analysis methods, GT has been very controversial and therefore has been in a state of flux. Such an aspect of GT may be understood as a limitation, but simultaneously because of its flexibility in usage, GT is sometimes an attractive option.

5.4.6 Application of Grounded Theory to This Study

After having understood what GT is and its unique characteristics as well as the limitations, a clarification should be made why this study exploits GT and how GT is operated in the context of this study. First, and the most important reason for application of GT to the study, is that this field of study is novel, and, therefore, there seems little relevant study on the topic that this study is exploring. Bearing this in mind, first a theoretical framework must be established in which relevant concepts, elements, and categories will work for a study of academic culture. Since academic culture in the context of the studied topic has hardly been well-established, the field in which this study is located requires a sound theoretical framework and a possible theorization of the subject matter. Studies like this should start from scratch to generate theoretical, conceptual, and methodological frameworks without their precedence in the fields. GT, in this sense, is the most suitable approach in order to establish the framework of the field of study, based on the empirical data. In other words, because of the absence of the field of study / topic, the study should exploit what GT could offer through its method as much as possible to generate its theoretical field. In addition, the basic idea of GT that empirical data act as the main role to establish a theory / concepts seems the best workable data analysis method for this study.

Second, this study attempts to exploit a widely thematic analysis approach that aims at extracting themes / concepts through data processing of empirical research, and thematic analysis is a core analytic part of GT. Unfortunately, the ideal style of GT suggested by Glaser and Strauss (1967) cannot be pursued in this study, due to the time and financial constraints; however, the study could share the major methodological approach and the goal with what GT aims at. As mentioned earlier, a drawback of GT is that a number of GT researchers do not follow the ideal procedure of GT and drop a part / parts of it because of restricted resource for research projects. This study also falls into the category of this 'shortened' version of GT. Nonetheless, this does not mean that the aim would not be achieved. For instance, this study employs some different types of data collection method, and the triangulation of the various research methods such as the face-to-face interviews, the open-ended qualitative questionnaire, and the focus group discussion would surely work as the iterative data collection and analysis procedure as GT suggests. Therefore, it is believed that similar effect could be expected by collecting data with different methods, though such process would not occur iteratively.

Finally, since the study is interpretivist, it naturally rejects any implication and orientation of positivism that are said to be involved in GT. Therefore, data are not considered as objective, external reality but as resource onto which a researcher can put his / her own interpretation (as generated through research participants' viewpoints). Moreover, a theory and / or concepts / categories are not waiting to be 'discovered' by the researcher but to be generated through the analysis based on researcher's understanding and interpretation of what is informed by the research participants. Thus, this study takes a position which is closer to what Charmaz suggests as an alternative GT method with social constructionist orientation.[80]

The procedure of data analysis is carried out as follows: After each data collection was implemented, audio data of individual interviews and a focus group discussion was transcribed in Japanese. Written data of questionnaire was filed and summarized in one document file so that responses for each question could be seen and compared together. The authentic GT method does not allow any presupposed ideas before data analysis, however; the framework of academic culture, which was devised for this study based on the concept of Holliday's small cultures (1999), was exploited to underlie the conceptual framework of this study. The reason for introducing the framework before data analysis is to carry out the analysis in a more focused way with the limited timeframe. Had the study been allowed more or unrestricted time, waiting for all concepts and categories by solely a series of data

---

[80] This does not mean that the author of the study is the social constructionist. In respect of the distinction among diverse GT methods, Charmaz's version of GT seems closer to what the study aims at throughout this research project.

collection and analysis would have been affordable. However, this was obviously not the case, and moreover, since the topic of the study is too broad to be unfocused for the investigation of the topic that is also very complex and involves a variety of sub-topics as components of the entire topic, identifying and clarifying the sub-topics was a necessary practice under the given research condition and environment. The collected data, therefore, were processed based on the above-mentioned framework to roughly group the contents of data.[81]

As for coding, it is believed among qualitative researchers that computer-assisted qualitative data analysis software (CAQDAS) such as NVivo would be useful to reduce clerical work related to coding and retrieving of data (Bryman, 2008; Cohen, Manion, & Morrison, 2007). Nevertheless, there are, some concerns among the researchers that CAQDAS would render the data fragmented regardless the context of research. After all, unlike SPSS for quantitative research, CAQDAS would not bring a complete set of data analysis for qualitative research, and data analysis should still be done by researchers to a great extent. Thus, coding, grouping codes, and all the other analysis work were done by manually.

Since there are several different types of data collection methods, some of which were implemented as a part of analysis activity for the primary data such as individual interviews and questionnaire, data were not only interpreted more than one time but also analysed by the researcher and some research participants who were at the same time informants of this study. This modified GT for this study could be supplemented by this horizontal and cyclical analysis which could replace iterative data collection and analysis to a certain extent. Particularly the research participants in this study are all academics, and they can be deemed as people who have sufficient ability to contribute to a part of data analysis. By doing so, although the quantity of data is limited, it could be analysed by not only the researcher but also some other people who are capable of it, then, it would lead to further scrutinization of data than only one researcher's data interpretation and analysis.

As suggested, the coded data were located to the categories that were already identified through the framework of academic culture,

---

[81] The detail of the framework of academic culture is introduced and explained in the section on academic culture.

analysed, and interpreted to find connections between categories as well as between what analysed data revealed and international academic collaboration in terms of knowledge generation. Though it might not achieve a status of being a theory as the outcome of this study, it will certainly be able to generate a framework for similar studies in future by identifying influential factors to better understand the interrelationship between academic work and international academic collaboration.

6. Findings of the Case Study

The empirical research and the data analysis were planned and implemented to achieve the aim of the study, as they were introduced in the earlier sections. This section will reveal what is found through the process, how they are interpreted, and what implications the empirical data can provide us to discuss further about issues around international academic activities beyond the existing discussions. The findings and discussions are structured, based on the framework of academic culture, so that respective factors and elements would be clearly distinguished. The respective factors are at the end to be integrated into one big picture to exhibit the interrelationship each other, in order to explain how they could be influential in discussion of international academic collaboration. Therefore, the findings of the empirical research will be introduced, and then emerged topics will be discussed in the following part of this section.[82]

6.1 Academic Environment

6.1.1 National Science Policy: Prioritized Research Topics and Fundings

The science policy of a nation is very broad and various, and compared with the natural science and technology (hereafter NST), SSH is a much less emphasized and a less focused field in the national science policy. That national science policy tends to neglect the fields of SSH stems from the fact that NST is considered as the scientific fields that would directly contribute to future growth of a nation state as well as that it would be able to solve current problems and concerns to which the nation state faces. Yet, this does not mean that national science policy has little impact on academic work in the SSH field. Funding and prioritized research

---

[82] Referred comments / statements of the research participants in this study are all originally in Japanese. Therefore, they are translated by me where necessary, although each comment / statement does not indicate that it is the translation from Japanese to English by myself.

topics set by the national government seem to influence research activities of social science academics. Therefore, those two aspects are explored in the empirical study, regarding to the factor of national science policy.

- Prioritized Research Topics

National science policy as a whole focuses on NST, and there don't seem to be any topics related and confined to the fields of SSH that are nationally prioritized research topics. Besides, due to globalization, topics which are encouraged to be studied seem to be shared around the world. For instance, interviewee A states that prioritized research topics can be "important issues of contemporaries ... such as globalization, information, life science." In the sense of an important contemporary issue in Japan, it is quite apparent that today's nationally prioritized topic is recovery from the Great East Japan Earthquake (hereafter, the Earthquake), including the accident caused by the failed nuclear power plants in Fukushima. According to the five-year basic plan for science and technology policy released in 2011, "the role of policy for science and technology is understood not only to further promote science and technology, but also to correspond to various challenges with which society of human beings is confronted" (MEXT, 2011: 1, translation of my own), and this document starts with catastrophic damages caused by the Earthquake and by the accidents of the nuclear power plants, and describes the whole situation as "an unprecedented crisis in Japan" (ibid.: 2, translation of my own). There is an interview comment which exemplifies an actual situation where research is closely related to this science policy.

> Currently, a great number of various academic associations / societies go to the regions that were affected by the Earthquake in Tohoku.[83] They carry out research about the situation of the region from various academic / disciplinary perspectives ... in order to reflect the research outcomes on the governmental policy. (Interviewee D)

In the same light, interviewee A also points out that the Science Council of Japan attempts to organize the above-mentioned research activities from different disciplinary fields in order to

---

[83] Tohoku is a geographical region in Japan, where the recovery from the Earthquake is still in progress.

make a contribution to the process of recovery from the catastrophe, and he summarizes:

> Once a challenging topic appears [in society], everyone in academic communities tends to investigate the topic. Therefore, it is possible that politically prioritized research topics can be a reflection of it [the challenging topic]. (Interviewee A)

Although the research topic relating to the Earthquake looks like a particular topic in Japan, the interpretation of the prioritized research topic can be stretched to the world scale. Interviewee A continues the above comment as follows:

> I don't see any particular research topics which exist only in Japan. . . . Disaster can be related to climate change and environmental issues that are discussed around the world. In various forms, issues such as disaster and risk are very important ones. Besides, such issues are also closely connected to globalization and informatization. (Interviewee A)

In other words, it can be understood that prioritized research topics are, generally speaking, shared on a worldwide scale. Interviewee B refers to a term "sustainability" as an example of possible prioritized research topic and explains that it would be more likely to receive research fund "if one keeps up his / her research topic with the times" (Interviewee B). The notion of "keeping up with the times" implies that there are always trends in research topics. Although Interviewee B does not explicitly state that such trends / buzz words in research are shared in the world, and rather talks about research topics in Japan, a term like *sustainability* is seen not only in Japan, but also in any other countries. Indeed, when the aforementioned basic plan for science and technology policy of Japan and an outline of the current research funding programme of European Commission, "Horizon 2020" are compared, the mentioned topics are quite similar. For instance, topics such as "an aging population, food security, energy efficiency" are set as "main societal challenges" (European Commission website, n.d.) to a certain extent coincide with topics raised in the basic plan in Japan.[84] This observation of two

---

[84] Except for topics directly related to the recovery from the Earthquake, stable energy supply, fulfilment of low carbon society including other issues of climate change, and issues of an aging population are mentioned as crucial issues to reach solutions. (MEXT, 2011: 8) This plan also put emphasis on

different documents on research policy or political orientation towards research could confirm the view of interviewee A that research topics are shared in the world scale.

While interviewees stated their views about what the prioritized research topics in Japan are, some touched on relationship between research topics and the science policy. An interesting comment that the prioritized research topics which could attract the national research fund is a matter of "whether or not the research topics can be national interests" (Interviewee B). This comment seems to be corroborated by the documents seen above in the cases of Japan and of Europe regarding the focused research topics. That is, Japan as a nation state put the science policy in practice in order for it to make a growth by innovation, to enforce its power by contribution from science and technology, and to play more prominent role in the world by solving challenging issues which the world faces on. Therefore, some academics like interviewee B may tend to connect the research topics with the national interests. On the contrary, others may not find such obvious relation between science and policy, and / or influence that science policy of a country might put on academic research. Interviewee E contests that he cannot recall that he has ever had to adjust his research to the then science policy. However, interestingly enough, when Interviewee E was asked about globalization of Japanese academe, which is a part of Japan's science policy today, he responded, "It is like that I look into the government's face." This means that interviewee E, as an individual scholar, did not react to the science policy when he planned his own research project, but policies on academic activity in general, which more could broadly impact academic activities as a whole, rather than on activities of individual academics. Thus, in a broader sense, interviewee E also admits that the national science policy could influence ways in which academics plan and carry out their research activity.

---

tackling challenges not only to Japan but also those that the whole world are facing. For instance, it reads, "it is assumed that issues Japan faces . . . can be shared issues in the world" (ibid.: 21, translation of my own).

- Japanese National Research Fund: *Kakenhi*

Like any other countries in the world, there are various national or private funding programmes available to SSH academics in Japan. However, the most important funding source for Japanese academics is Grants-in-Aid for Scientific Research (so-called *kakenhi* in Japanese),[85] which is provided once a year by the Japan Society for the Promotion of Science (hereafter JSPS).[86] This research grant called *kakenhi* seems a possible biggest financial resource for research activities in all scientific fields among academics working in Japan.[87]

Naturally, with regard to the relationship between the science policy and academic work in Japan, *kakenhi* became the main topic during the interviews and the discussion implemented in this study. As a commonly shared understanding of *kakenhi* among the research participants, it could be stated that it is important to be awarded *kakenhi*, and universities they work for encourage them to apply for it. Despite of the shared understanding, grounds for trying to receive it seems to vary. First, seemingly the most

---

[85] As the outline of Grants-in-Aid for Scientific Research (Kakenhi), JSPS describes that "Grants-in-Aid for Scientific Research are competitive funds that are intended to significantly develop all scientific research (research based on the free ideas of the researcher), from basic to applied research in all fields, ranging from the humanities and the social sciences to the natural sciences. The grants provide financial support for creative and pioneering research projects that will become the foundation of social development. The research projects are selected using a peer-review screening process (screening by multiple researchers whose field of specialization is close to that of the applicant)." (JSPS, n.d. retrieved from the JSPS English website at: http://www.jsps.go.jp/english/e-grants/index.html on 1 February 2015)

[86] JSPS is an organization equivalent to Deutsche Forschungsgemeinschaft (DFG) in Germany. JSPS is the funding organization which provides research fund to scholars and scientists who are Japanese nationals and foreign scholars but working for Japanese universities or other research institutes in Japan. Although it is the independent administrative institution, it is closely related to the Japanese government, especially to the Ministry of Education, Culture, Sports, Science and Technology (MEXT). Therefore, JSPS acts as an organization to develop science in Japan, which accords with the science policy, as well as promotes international scientific collaborations with foreign countries' academic circles.

[87] It refers to as grant applied for individual / collaborative research projects. There are other bigger-scale research programmes that provide a greater amount of fund by JSPS, but they are occasional and rather targeted on research universities to apply to.

fundamental and reasonable ground for applying for *kakenhi* is receiving financial support to carry out research. This simply means that any research activities cost some amount of money, and any additional financial support for research is favourable. Academics working for a university in Japan on a full-time basis normally get some amount for research expense from the university; however, the amount also varies from one university to another, depending on what type of university they work for, and in many cases the amount provided by the university is likely to be insufficient for an ideal research project. Interviewee B, for instance, strongly emphasizes:

> It [research fund such as *kakenhi*] must be acquired. Funding should be obtained.... Funding is necessary.

Interviewee B expressed the strong necessity of additional research fund as the supplement for research expenses which she receives from the university she works for, and it is a simple demand from academics to receive more research expense in order to fulfil his / her academic interests by carrying out a possible ideal research project.

Similarly, there seems another demand for acquiring *kakenhi* for a research project. In this case, it is not only to fulfil a personal academic interests, but also to educate and train postgraduate students and young researchers.

> Especially, if one works for a national university[88] and supervises a number of postgraduates, he / she should play an important role to organize a research group in order to educate undergraduates and young researchers. In such a case, a big-scale research project should be planned with the financial support of *kakenhi*, and it is indispensable for this to be continuous for some years to acquire *kakenhi* for this purpose. (Interviewee A)

That is to say, carrying out a research project has another implication that it is something an established academic person should do in order to train young researchers and students as mature and proper academic researchers. Certainly, research ideas and interests come from the established academic person who would organize the entire research project funded by *kakenhi*;

---

[88] What interviewee A meant by "a national university" can be understood as a research university, considering the academic background of the interviewee.

however, the purpose of acquiring *kakenhi* in this context seems more educational than the previous ground expressed by interviewee B, which is to genuinely pursue personal academic interests. Interviewee A also points out that there are mainly two patterns of motivation for applying for *kakenhi*: One is implementing a small-scale research project in which individual academic interests would be pursued with relatively small amount of *kakenhi*. The other is the aforementioned case to organize a research team of "around twenty people" (interviewee A), which consists of colleagues of the research project organizer, postgraduates, and / or postdoctoral research fellows, with a large amount of fund. Although the each motivation might look different, it can be understood that they are still substantially the same ground for applying for *kakenhi* that the main motivation is carrying out research activities regardless of the scale of research project.

On the other hand, there is another ground for trying to apply for *kakenhi*. If the aforementioned patterns are to be defined as the research oriented motivation, this pattern would be defined as the evaluation oriented motivation. That is to say, *kakenhi* is one of the evaluation factors for research activity of a university, of which result would be open to public, and this would directly influence the domestic university ranking in Japan. It is quite apparent in the interviewees' comments:

> For instance, as a kind of publicity for the university, it is very important to mention that our university acquired *kakenhi*. (Interviewee C)

> The university put a kind of pressure on faculty members that we should apply for and acquire the fund [*kakenhi*]. [The interviewer asked why it was so] It is for prestige of the university. (Interviewee B)

> The university administration insists that faculty members should apply for *kakenhi*, because it would be pointed out if the number of applications and adoption rate were too low when university evaluation takes place. . . .It would be all open to public such as total amount of fund that a university received, which university received the most among all Japanese universities, and so on. (Interviewee A)

> From a certain time, total amount of *kakenhi* a university received, number of foreign faculty members a university employs, and other factors which had not existed before [as evaluation items] were introduced in the evaluation system. . . . Then, our university realized that we would also have to be committed to research that involves *kakenhi*. . . . As a whole, *kakenhi* is one of

the most important evaluation factors in terms of research activity. (Interviewee F)

As seen above, the motivation for applying for *kakenhi* in this case does not seem to voluntarily come from academics who are the practitioners of research activity, but rather from the university administration. In other words, the first two patterns are spontaneous motivations which are closely and strongly related to research activity itself, while the last one is rather forced or passive with few motivations connected to research. That is, applying and acquiring *kakenhi* from the perspective of university administration has little to do with research activity itself, but is considered as an indicator of willingness and activeness towards research activity for universities in Japan. Similarly, there seems another strong reason for the university administration to encourage academics to acquire *kakenhi*.

> It [kakenhi] is greatly appreciated, because such competitive research fund would bring the university some additional financial resources. (Interviewee C)

In this context, the university administration refers to overhead costs [89] that would be provided to universities when *kakenhi* applications are approved. Although the overhead cost for *kakenhi* should be spent in relation to the research project that has been successfully granted (MEXT website, n.d.), in reality, it sometimes seems to be spent for other purposes. Interviewee A notes that some parts of the overhead costs are stored in the university and used for young researchers in the university to promote their research, which is out of the context of *kakenhi* projects. Indeed, no matter how the overhead costs is spent in each university, *kekenhi* seems to play a significant role in respect of university administration. Other interviewees also confirms that

> The university could also get some amount of money if the external fund is granted. That is why [the university urges us to apply for such fund]. (Interviewee B)

---

[89] Thirty percent of the total grant amount would be provided as overhead costs. (MEXT, n.d., retrieved from MEXT website published in Japanese: http://www.mext.go.jp/a_menu/shinkou/hojyo/07071108/007.pdf on 6 February 2015)

Thus, research funds, especially the national competitive research fund (*kakenhi*) seems to play a significant role for academics as well as for university administration. It can be concluded that demand and motivation for acquiring *kakenhi* are twofold: One comes from the academics' willingness for research activity, which matches the aim of the funding organization to support scientific research that develops scientific knowledge. The other is based on an accreditation system that was gradually introduced in the Japanese HEIs from the beginning of twenty-first century. According to Amano (2006), the accreditation was originally required only for the national universities, because they had been managed and run by the national tax. Therefore, private universities that are run by student fees, donations, and other private financial resources were exempt from this accreditation system because private universities had accountability only towards their students, parents of students, and other private stakeholders. Nonetheless, when the government decided to deregulate the standards for the establishment of new universities, the idea of accreditation was emphasized instead of a rigid examination of application for a new university establishment (ibid. 162). This means that founding a new university became less difficult, while survival via competition among other universities by results of the university accreditation system became keen. Until then, it was not as it is now in private universities with regard to *kakenhi*. Private universities in Japan, except some private universities which are considered as research universities, did not seem to have to be eagerly committed to research for a long time. Rather, many of them were founded to educate certain groups of people with certain aims. Some private universities were founded to educate sons and daughters of wealthy families, and others were founded by Christian missionaries to ingrain Christianity in the Japanese society through education. Thus a number of Japanese private universities originally had other interests than research. A comment of interviewee C underlies this change in Japanese private universities in regard to research as below:

> We are now all told to carry out research at the university, but it is a very recent current [to be urged by the university to acquire *kakenhi*]. . . . I was employed here in a teaching position, and there are so many people working here in this university who have started their jobs with agreement with the university that the given positions were not in research. (Interviewee C)

Interviewee F comments of the past experience related to *kakenhi*.

> When I was successfully granted *kakenhi* ten years ago, I was told by the university administrators that it was only a nuisance for them, because the work concerning my *kakenhi* research project would be extra work for them, adding to the ordinary routine work. They had no idea of *kakenhi* in this university, because they thought that research funded by *kakenhi* should be carried out by people in national and municipal universities, not by us from private universities. (Interviewee F)

Thus the big change of universities' attitude regarding *kakenhi* can be seen, especially in private universities, due to the aforementioned introduction of accreditation system to all Japanese universities. It is now a shared view among not only academics but also HEIs in Japan that *kakenhi* is one of the crucial items when discussing and evaluating the extent of research in which academics in Japan are engaged. In other words, *kakenhi* can be considered as a benchmark of research activity in the Japanese HEIs.

When the importance of the national fund for both academics and universities is discussed, the place of employment of successful applicants is often raised. As seen in the comment of Interviewee F above, it is believed among academics and universities that applications from certain (research) universities for *kakenhi* and other funding programmes implemented by JSPS are more likely to be approved, compared with applicants from other universities. For instance,

> Whether 'big name'[90] is joining your *kakenhi* project, and whether applicants of *kakenhi* obtain PhD degree[91] though I am not sure if it [the latter notion about PhD degree] is really true.... I have heard that national universities tend to be granted more than other universities. (Interviewee B)

---

[90] Interviewee B meant by the notion of 'big name' as research universities and / or other universities that have a strong research orientation.

[91] Currently, it is hard to get a position in Japanese universities without a PhD degree, nevertheless, there are a number of people working for Japanese universities as academics without PhD degree. It is because Japanese universities did not award doctoral students in the social science PhD degree for a long time until recently. This situation has been changed in recent years, but there are also a number of people who obtained their PhD degrees abroad, due to the limitations of the old regime.

Although Interviewee B cautiously states that there may be a relationship between the likeliness of being granted *kakenhi* and obtaining a PhD degree, it seems to be well-known and believed among academics in Japan that national universities and other research oriented universities have an advantage in obtaining *kakenhi*. In the similar light, Interviewee F states that "COE, Global COE,[92] and other similar national funding programmes target the former imperial universities [93] and big private universities." (Interviewee F)

What they would like to express is that there are certain criteria such as type of universities and applicants that allow academics to successfully acquire national research funds. Indeed, if we observe the most recent data released by MEXT, which reveals the adoption rate and granted total amount of *kakenhi* for universities and national research institutes in Japan, we can see in the table below that the top ten organizations are all national universities, of which the majority is the former imperial universities.

---

[92] COE is officially "21st century COE programme," and Global COE is the follow-up programme of 21st century COE. COE (Centres of Excellence) was introduced and implemented to "cultivate a competitive academic environment among Japanese universities by giving targeted support to the creation of world-standard research and education bases (centers of excellence)." (Retrieved on 10 February 2015 from JSPS website: http://www.jsps.go.jp/english/e-21coe/index.html)

[93] They are today's University of Tokyo, Kyoto University, Tohoku University, Kyushu University, Hokkaido University, Osaka University, and Nagoya University, which are considered as research universities in Japan.

Findings of the Case Study

	Name of Organization	Number of adopted project	Granted amount	Overhead costs	Total grant amount
1	University of Tokyo	3690	16831488000	5049446000	21880934000
2	Kyoto University	2961	11016351000	3304905000	14321256000
3	Osaka University	2644	8814198000	2644260000	11458458000
4	Tohoku University	2534	8060990000	2418297000	10479287000
5	Kyushu University	1962	5714260000	1714278000	7428538000
6	Hokkaido University	1724	4650120000	1395036000	6045156000
7	Nagoya University	1720	5662760000	1698828000	7361588000
8	University of Tsukuba	1214	2890140000	867042000	3757182000
9	Hiroshima University	1134	2259200000	677760000	2936960000
10	Kobe University	1081	2286721000	686016000	2972738000

The amount is Japanese Yen

The ranking is decided by the number of adopted project, not the grant amount.

Table 2:   Adoption Rate and Granted Total Amount of *kakenhi* for 2014
(Source: MEXT, 2014, data 2-2 on overview of number of adoption and grant amount by respective organizations for year 2014 in pdf document from the MEXT website,[94] modified and devised by the author)

Thus the data published by MEXT seems to support the interviewees' comments on the relationship between the type of universities and the likeliness of being granted *kakenhi*. However, this view is contested:

---

[94]   Retrieved on 11 February 2015 from: http://www.mext.go.jp/a_menu/shinkou/hojyo/__icsFiles/afieldfile/2014/10/20/1352401_2.pdf
The document (data 2-2) was originally published only in Japanese, therefore, it is translated and modified by the author where relevant.

> Fundamentally, whether or not one works for a well-known university has little to do with the result of adoption for *kakenhi*. . . . I would say, it is less likely that they were selected [to receive national grants] because of the name of university. Rather, it can be a matter of training system [for young researchers / post graduate students] in a university, or a matter of recruitment of faculty members [that could be decisive factors that such research universities are always selected for national grant programmes]. (Interviewee E)

What Interviewee E points out is that the name of university is not a reason for being awarded the national research grant, but a consequence of the training and recruitment system that those universities established and maintained in order to obtain better trained / qualified researchers in the universities. That is why, interviewee E continues, "the rich would become richer." Interviewee E has an experience of programme officer who evaluates application documents of the national research funds, and therefore has a profound insight into the evaluation system for the national research funds. The reason why Interviewee E insists that the name of university does not matter to be successful grant applicant is the fact that evaluators cannot know the name of institutional affiliation of applicant when evaluating all applications. Therefore, it is impossible for any evaluators to judge the quality of research only by the name of universities. Interviewee E concludes that it happens to be applicants from well-known research universities who are successfully granted the national funds, simply due to the good quality of research project applications.

Kakenhi and other national research funding programmes are funding programmes which anyone working for universities or other research institutes in Japan could apply for, regardless of the character of his / her organization and whether or not it is a well-known research oriented university. Nevertheless, there seems to be a segregation among Japanese universities between research oriented university and less research oriented / more education oriented ones. This segregation results in difference in adoption rate of *kakenhi* among all universities in Japan.

Relating to the segregation between national universities and the others, observing the number of doctoral students in national and private universities may be useful to better understand the connection between the type of university and likeliness for getting national research funds. The table below is one of the data published by MEXT, which shows the number of doctoral students in national and private universities respectively.

Private universities

Year			
	Total	Male	Female
FY 2013	18,174	11,578	6,596
FY 2014	18,229	11,595	6,634

National universities

Year			
	Total	Male	Female
FY 2013	51,061	35,033	16,028
FY 2014	50,686	34,782	15,904

Table 3: The Number of Doctoral Students in the Japanese Universities
(Source: e-Stat, 2014:[95] data 12(8-4) and 12(8-6), modified and devised by the author)

The total number of doctoral students in national universities is almost three times as much as the one in private universities. What one can interpret from this data is that national universities are more committed to not only research activity of faculty members, but also education and training for future academics. Earlier, the comment of interviewee A that *kakenhi* is necessary when one works for a national university and has many postgraduates is introduced, and the background of this comment can be that there are more doctoral students in national universities to be trained as future academic researchers. Further, the previous comment of Interviewee E can also related to the aspect of difference in the number of doctoral students in national and private universities. That is to say, research project applications for *kakenhi* from national university organizations often turns out good quality to be approved in comparison with ones from other universities, and the grounds for Interviewee E's comment is that there are well-trained / experienced researchers due to the recruitment and training system that national universities tend to maintain. In other words, national universities, particularly the former imperial universities, attract more and seemingly better human resources as well as obtaining relevant training systems which are necessary for research. As the consequence of such research environment,

---

[95] The data is retrieved from Gakkou kihon chousa Heisei 26nenndo (Basic research on educational organizations in Japan for the fiscal year 2014) released by e-Stat, which publishes governmental statistic data in Japan. Due to the data written in Japanese, the table above is translated and modified by the author. The entire data can be retrieved on e-Stat website: http://www.e-stat.go.jp/SG1/estat/NewList.do?tid=000001011528

adoption rate of *kakenhi* for national universities are higher than the other universities.

Thus, this good circulation of financial and human resources seems to lead certain (mainly national) universities to a position of research university in Japan. Simultaneously, it should be mentioned that the former imperial universities and some private universities are deemed as flagship universities in Japan (Yonezawa, 2007: 483),[96] and the notion of research university and of flagship university can be used and understood almost interchangeably in the Japanese context. No matter what they are called, it is clear that the position of research university defines their role among more than seven hundred universities, strengthens their position further as research university, and renders concentration of funds, human resources, and prestige. This is what the comment of Interviewee E "the rich would become richer" means.[97]

---

[96] Yonezawa defines the Japanese flagship universities as follows: "the seven former imperial universities (Tokyo, Kyoto, Hokkaido, Tohoku, Nagoya, Osaka, and Kyushu); the Tokyo Institute of Technology (the top national university in engineering); and three leading private universities (Keio, Waseda, and Ritsumeikan)" (ibid.). However, there may be slightly different perceptions and definitions of the Japanese flagship universities, especially on private universities, to which some people would like to add a few more.

[97] In fact, there is a national commitment to strengthen Japanese research universities in order for them to match their capability as research university to international standards. It aims not only to promote their research activity in general, but also to maintain better research environment by allocating research administrators whom Japanese universities widely lack, inviting eminent scholars and scientists from foreign countries, and supporting the establishment any other research infrastructure which would promote the research standard to match the international standard. This commitment commenced in 2013 for ten years. 22 organizations are selected and the annual budget for this national commitment in 2013 and 2014 was 6.4 billion Japanese Yen (ca. 4.7 million Euro) for each year. (MEXT, 2014) Retrieved on 6 January 2014 from the MEXT website: http://www.mext.go.jp/a_menu/ka gaku/sokushinhi/__icsFiles/afieldfile/2014/04/21/1333815_03_2.pdf

160   Findings of the Case Study

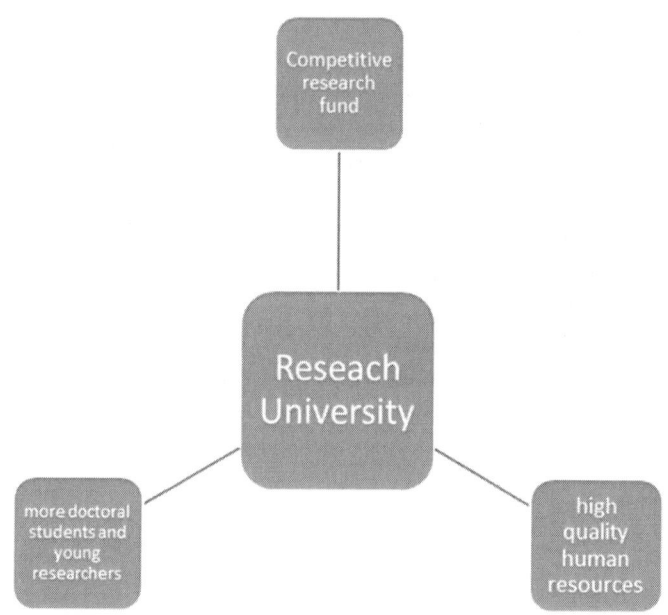

Model X: Concentration of Human and Financial Resources on Research University

The model indicates the summary of the analysis above. The research university is the place where those three resources are concentrated on, and competitive research funds including *kakenhi* and other national research funds tends to be funnelled more to particular universities which are classified as research / flagship universities. Although it does not mean that those who are working for the other universities do not get national research funds,[98] the tendency of resource concentration is significant as seen in the table 2 given earlier. In such conditions that there seems segregation among universities in Japan in terms of research

---

[98] There is a research funding support programme for private universities to support the establishment of research base of those universities. However, the programme does not fund the full amount that universities applied for, but mostly a half of the proposed total amount. The information (MEXT, n.d.) was retrieved on 13 February 2015 from the MEXT website: http://www.mext.go.jp/a_menu/koutou/shinkou/07021403/002/002/1218299.htm

activities relating to the national funding programmes, what difference in distribution of *kakenhi* and other national funds informs us is that although people working for Japanese universities may be all considered as people who are committed to research, education, and social contribution / contribution to local communities, they are not necessarily evenly provided a similar level of research environment. That is, the type of university they work for can be a decisive factor in what kind of academic work they carry out, the extent to which their work is related to research activity, and what type / scale of research they tend to carry out. As seen, if one works for a research university, it is more likely that he / she will receive the national research funds and work with abundant human resources of good quality. If not, the situation for one's research environment can be rather contrary to the one in a research university.

To summarize this part on science policy, firstly observing the prioritized research topics informs us that these seem to be widely shared in the world, because a number of concerns on various aspects of our lives is witnessed not only in one particular country but also many other countries in different global regions. Scientific / academic knowledge is expected by government to find solutions that people can use to solve them. The concerns to be researched are not necessarily restricted to ones that a particular country is suffering for, but can be challenges that other countries / regions undergo, since it seems also crucial from political perspectives to contribute to help solve such challenges for the international society.[99] As interviewee A commented, research topics nowadays are closely connected and shared among countries around the world. Even though there is a view as of interviewee B that prioritized research topic might have something to do with national interests, this does not mean that research topics are

---

[99] The basic plan for science and technology policy of Japan refers to the contribution to solve world scale problems. It reads, "Japan is required not only to aim at development of its own science and technology, but also to contribute to actively solve various problems which occur in world scale with cooperation of other countries and collaboration with them" (translation by the author, MEXT, 2011: 24). Research on issues relating to the climate change, energy security including finding alternative energy resource, and infectious diseases are mentioned as examples for world scale scientific contribution.

confined to situations and status of one country, but rather mean fundamental connectedness between policy on science and research, which national policy could influence how academics plan and carry out research activity.[100]

Second, regarding national research funding, the type of research topic and the type of universities which the nation state is more likely to fund can also influence research work. Earlier in this section, I reviewed various notions whether the adoption rate of Japanese national research fund, *kakenhi*, is connected with applicants who work for a national university. The analysis reveals the necessity for a bigger scale of research fund in national universities, and possible reasons why applications from national universities seem to be funded more than the other types of universities. It is, then, concluded that the type of university one works for, to some extent, defines the way he / she is engaged in research.[101] That is to say, national universities, particularly which are considered as research / flagship universities in Japan, attract a great portion of national research fund as well as human resources of good quality. Due to this positive circulation of financial and human resources that are necessary for research activity, as interviewee E expressed, the privileged ones become more privileged in terms of their condition for research activity and of status as research / flagship universities. Although influence of science policy on research activity in respect of *kakenhi* seems rather indirect and subtle, there are certainly other national funding programmes that clearly target research universities, as Interviewee F pointed out. Then, it can be said that research funding programmes other than *kakenhi* more clearly indicates the influence and connectedness between science policy and research activity. However, it was apparent from the comments of interviewees as well as from the data on adoption rate of *kakenhi* that the research universities have quantitatively benefited from the national funds, even though it does not seem that their applications are intentionally selected.

---

[100] Murakami refers to the basic plan for science and technology policy of Japan and comments that "scientific research is political issues" (translation by the author, 2010: 52) as long as research is a part of the governmental plan.
[101] Here this is mentioned from a perspective of funding opportunity.

6.1.2 Roles of Higher Education and Institutional Research Policy

Already seen in the previous part on the science policy, it is noticeable that there are different types of HEIs in Japan. For those who are not familiar with the system of Japanese education in general, it will be hardly possible to understand this part in particular, without some background knowledge of the education system in Japan. Therefore, in this section I will devote careful attention to information about Japanese HE system and universities. What is implied here is that there might be diverse understandings and roles of HE in different countries. That is, what we all call as 'university' might not be a totally identical entity in different geographical settings. The relevance, therefore, of exploring roles of HE and respective HEIs' research orientation in this part is to not only understand what interviewees informed us but also to realize a possibility of different understanding of roles of HE from those of readers' own country.

Before starting to explore roles of HE in Japan, types of Japanese university should be referred to, because different types of universities may have different expectation, aims, and consequently roles in the country. Generally, it is understood that there are three different types of universities in Japan,

> the so-called former imperial universities, other national and municipal universities, and private universities like Waseda, Keio, and Ritsumeikan. . . . These can be called research universities in Japan. Next is the liberal arts university . . . and the last one is a university which is adhere to local community where the university is located. This type is very close to a concept of community college in the U.S. Respective universities in Japan belong to one of those types. (Interviewee F)

The classification above is widely shared in Japan. The first one is also classified as flagship universities as seen in the previous part,[102] and the other two types in the above classification of interviewee F consist of private universities. A line is drawn between the first one (research universities) and the rest, because,

---

[102] Although not all of the national and municipal universities are normally considered as flagship university. It should also be pointed out that some other private universities than those appear in the comment of interviewee F could be classified as flagship university.

as seen already, research universities maintain superiority in financial, human, and other resources over the other universities. As of 2014, there are 781 universities in Japan (e-Stat, 2014), which is more than twice as many as the total number of universities in Germany,[103] and more than 600 universities out of the total number are private universities. That is, the liberal arts type and the community college type are mostly private universities. Unlike national and municipal universities, the aims and missions of private universities are various and do not necessarily reflect the aims of national / regional administration. As a result, most of them, except a few, have remained as rather less research oriented universities.[104] Therefore, interviewee F continues, "we [as employees] are also restricted by it [the type of university we work for, in relation to way of working]."

Some relate the role of Japanese HE to the current status of academic work.

> University education [in Japan] used to be education for elite. It then entered mass status of education, and the massification has accelerated further. Naturally, academic ability of university students has also become vulgarized. (Interviewee D)

> Universities nowadays are like high schools. (Interviewee G)

> Universities in Japan have become popularized and vulgarized entirely. Therefore, the [academic] level of students is getting lower, and university education is closer to high school education. (Interviewee B)

The above comments may only refer to middle-level of private universities; nevertheless, considering that this type of universities make up the majority of universities in Japan, the expressed

---

[103] According to the website of Embassy and Consulates of Germany in Japan, there are 376 universities in Germany. The number includes universities, universities for applied science, universities for arts, music, and film, and private universities (Embassy of Germany in Japan, n.d.). The information was written in Japanese on: http://www.japan.diplo.de/Vertretung/japan/ja/08-kultur-und-bildung/studieren-in-deutschland/Hoschschulsystem.html

[104] Amano widely discusses the Japanese HE system from its incunabula to today. According to him, "most of the private universities (before the World War Two) had low standard of research, and . . . had a similar characteristic of American private universities that had been called 'college'." (translation of the author, Amano, 2006: 37)

phenomenon that Japanese universities are vulgarized due to the massification and universalization of HE in Japan can partly provide a certain image of today's Japanese universities. What those interviewees hoped to express is not the low-level academic ability of Japanese university students but what kind of organization today's Japanese universities are. Before the Japanese HE entered the mass status and universal level of accessibility, originally it was considered as a place for elite education, which German universities were the model. In other words, the comments imply that Japanese universities are used to be, or are meant to be educational organizations for selected people. However, what the interviewees wanted to emphasize is that it is not the case today, and most of universities in Japan are not given a role as educational organization for elites. Therefore, when the interviewees were asked about the role of HE and universities, a common view that university is seen as "a place one must graduate from" (Interviewee A) emerged:

> Students want a qualification that they graduated from a university so that they could successfully get their first job. (Interviewee D)

> Japanese companies employ new graduates all at once, and one cannot go onto such a job market in Japan unless he / she graduates from a university. (Interviewee A)

This may be a peculiar aspect of social system in Japan that the job market for new graduates is regulated by an agreement between universities / colleges and companies about when recruitment activity can commence, when companies officially inform job applicants that they would employ them, and many other timings which relate to annual recruitment for newly graduated people. This is because all companies receive new employees in April every year, while universities / colleges hold a graduation ceremony in March.[105] Before students graduate in March, in order to keep this yearly employment activity in order, most of companies, especially listed companies on the stock market in Japan, decide whom they would employ before job applicants complete their study in university / college. It may be changing that new graduates are accepted only once a year, since, for instance, this schedule that

---

[105] In Japan, academic/business calendar starts in April and ends at the end of March the following year.

new graduates start working at the same time in April every year does not match schedule of those who studied abroad or those who are not Japanese nationals.[106] However, generally speaking, this is still how the job market for new graduates operates in Japan. In this situation, applicants are required to obtain, at least, a bachelor degree.[107] That is, obtaining a bachelor is considered as one of the necessary conditions to apply for Japanese companies. Moreover, as touched on in the interview comments, it is said that Japanese HE reached a phase of *zen'nyu* （全入）which means that all of today's eighteen-year-olds can enter universities unless they stick to only privileged universities to enter, due to the universities being mass education status in Japan together with declining population of the youth. Although such a phenomenon of *zen'nyu* does not happen in a practical sense, it can be said that the rate of advancing to the HE has been increasing, compared to some decades ago. With such societal and educational changes, the consequence of popularization of advancing to the HE seems to change the essence and role of universities.

> [The aim of undergraduate education is that] we try to help all students getting a full-time job [after graduation]. [Interviewer: What ability would a university try to provide students?] Basic ability [which would be required at work] such as reflecting things . . . reading books, writing, and discussing. (Interviewee B)
>
> University education is education of human beings . . . to develop ability as human and ability to work [in companies]. (Interviewee D)

---

[106] Changes as a strategy for internationalization of university in some universities have been seen. For instance, the University of Tokyo decided to partly start its academic year in autumn as the Western universities. The university expects more incoming foreign students as well as outgoing domestic students studying abroad by matching the starting of the academic year (Yomiuri shinbun newspaper, 8 October 2011). Some other universities also considered and started to introduce so-called 'autumn entrance', however; it does not seem to impact the entire HE system in Japan, because the beginning of business calendar (fiscal year) still remains as the beginning of April. Consequently, the recruitment schedule for the new graduates tends to remain the same as before.

[107] This does not mean that Japanese companies do not employ anyone that graduated from only high school. They do employ people with a high school certificate, but the salary would be lower than the one who have higher educational degrees.

The above two comments indicate a connection between HE and development of students' ability for the labour market, and their understanding of the role of universities is more inclined towards and focused on enhancing 'employability' of students. A participant of focus group discussion also confirms this role of universities, and states:

> It seems to be our mission to graduate students after four years and to help them get a full-time job. The pressure for us to fulfil this mission is very high, therefore, we have to spend a lot of time and effort to do it. (GD participant A)

It can be explained that it is a taken-for-granted view of and an important role of universities in Japan from society in general that the university is a place where various ability which is required for being employed successfully, and as a result, it goes back to the aforementioned point about how the university is understood. While this strong connection between HE and the labour market is observed, there is another view on the role of HE.

> The aim of university education is that we help students develop and train themselves in whatever forms. There is no other aim of university education. (Interviewee A)

> I really hope that students would be people who could demonstrate their ability wherever they go. (Interviewee C)

They also refer to development of ability of students, but do not directly imply the ability as labour force. Rather, the ability in their comments meant in a more abstract sense that is not necessarily confined to work situations, and the interviewees seem to consider that university is a place to train students themselves as humans in a broader sense than the previous comments relating the role of universities to employability. Even though all interviewees work for Japanese universities in the same social condition, it is interesting that those two rather different views are expressed. The views might be influenced by some factors such as their experience as academics and type of university they work and / or they have worked for, and it seems not wise to define and fix the role of HE in one definite form.

Bearing in mind that there are those different views on the role of HE among academics in Japan, we should briefly observe how they teach undergraduates and postgraduates. Although their comments obviously relate to the teaching part of their work, questions were not asked to understand their teaching work, but to discover their views on the role of HE from their teaching approach. For instance;

> For undergraduates, I try to provide views that there are diverse ways of seeing things, which could turn usual ways of seeing things upside down. . . . [As an academic person] it should be postgraduates who train as researchers, therefore, I try hard to do this. (Interviewee E)

> I do not emphasize pragmatic ability [that may be useful to get a job] in teaching, because my field of discipline is not pragmatic. I think the best thing in social and human science is probably that we could analyse and understand what we feel strange or resent by using words. . . . Basically, my teaching approach is the same whether they are undergraduates or postgraduates. (Interviewee F)

It may depend on the academic subject they teach, but those comments are related to the substance of their own academic disciplines. In other words, they have little consciousness in their educational practices, whether intentionally or not, that the role of HE is often considered in the connection with generation of new (and more skilled) labour force.

On the contrary, a different type of education and an approach to education can be seen in the below.

> Our graduate school aims at training of professionals with a high-level of specialization. Therefore, it may be different from other graduate schools. . . . The majority of the students is those have full-time jobs in local administration, NPO. . . . They are not academics . . . and our graduate school is not an organization fostering academic researchers. (Interviewee B)

This is a type of graduate school education that has a professional school orientation,[108] and it implies that the contents of the education in such a graduate school are pragmatic. Although the professional school is considered as a kind of postgraduate school, its education has little in common with graduate schools that aim at fostering academic researchers, as interviewee B admits. The above comment refers only to graduate school education, but it can often be seen that business people, who do not have relevant

---

[108] The U.S model of professional school was introduced to the Japanese HE system by the university reform in Japan at the beginning of twenty-first century.

academic qualification such as masters and doctoral degree, teach undergraduates in Japan.

> Business people can play great role in today's Japanese universities. (Interviewee B)

> There are a number of business people teaching at Japanese universities ... those who are used to work for media, travel industry, and so on. (GD participant D)

Given that non-academics can also teach in Japanese universities, it is no wonder that educational contents in Japanese universities, in part, tend to be very pragmatic and work-related. The explanation for this would go back to the comments earlier that students want to enter a university to be qualified for job hunting.

Thus the role of HE and universities in Japan seems to be mixed. One can be explained as the relationship between universities and labour market. That is, university qualification is necessary for students to enter the labour market, and some parts of university education are, therefore, closely connected to job-oriented contents. In such a situation, people from diverse industries are appreciated as lecturers to feed students more pragmatic information which may be useful in actual work situations.[109] Some academics also feel that they are given a mission to train students as skilled, employable people so that those students would be welcomed in the labour market. In this sense, the role of universities in Japan seems to have a strong orientation to adjusting the contents of education to demand from the labour market for favourable human resources from companies' and / or industries' viewpoints.

The other role of universities is expressed in a more abstract manner as the role of HE. Although it does not mean that the interviewees who much less emphasized the relationship between HE and the labour market do not have a concern about the future of students in respect of job hunting, they seem to consider the role of HE from academics' viewpoints. They do not try to provide students something that takes effect at once for job hunting or in working practices, but offer something through academic knowledge and / or academic approaches so that students could live their own lives with their own ability. In other words, they look

---

[109] Sometimes they are given a status of specially appointed professor.

at the role of HE in a long-term perspective, rather than just equipping students with employability.

Those two different understanding of the role of HE in Japan may also be related to the aspect of different types of university and the societal situation, regarding the universal stage of HE in Japan, as seen earlier in this part. Since there is a relatively clear division of labour among Japanese universities,[110] the role of HE / HEIs may be affected by the type of university which the interviewees come from. It is not difficult to imagine that research universities are unlikely to employ ex-business people without academic background as lecturer, because that would undermine their prestige as research universities. Contrarily, less research oriented universities may attempt to attract new students by pragmatic, job-oriented education and / or by the rate of students who successfully get a job, because such aspects could be a big appeal for university applicants (and their parents) to choose a particular university. Depending on the position of a university, the role of HE / universities can be, thus, very diverse.

To summarize, it is pointed out that the declining birth rate and massification of HE in Japan has lowered the academic level of students as the popularization of HE is intensified. Some interviewees characterized this as 'high-schoolization of the university'. The expression implies that university education has to look after students' academic performance that is still rather at the high school level. Despite of the situation that the academic level of university students is declining, it is a necessary condition in Japan to obtain, at least, bachelor degree in order to join the competition for job hunting, especially to enter stable, big listed companies in any industries. Due to this direct connection between university education and the labour market, Japanese universities are considered as the place for students to get qualified for being employed with better conditions (i.e., salary, holiday, social security, etc.). Such societal and educational conditions tend to lead many of the Japanese universities towards the pragmatic, job-oriented type of education in order to satisfy the demand from both the labour market and the students as future employee of

---

[110] In the previous section of science policy, it is observed that there is a political inclination to fund certain (research) universities. Therefore, those universities become more and more research oriented, together with their own efforts to recruit and train high-quality human resources.

companies. Thus there is a view among the interviewees that HE in Japan should enable students to be employable human resources that various industries would appreciate. On the other hand, some interviewees insist that HE should equip students with the ability with which they could manage their lives in a long-term life perspective. Since there are diverse views of the role of HE, it seems to be less meaningful to determine one definite role of HE / HEIs in Japan, especially considering that there are three different types of universities and each of them has distinct aim and *raison d'etre*. As one of the interviewees pointed out, academics are restricted in their way of working within what his / her employer aims at as a university. This is an important point in observing and analysing academic working life in Japan, since views and perception of academic work can be influenced by such a personal environmental factor.

6.1.3 Mission of Academics in Society: Roles and Expectations in Society

In the previous section, the university as the place where academic work is located was examined, and the role of HE / universities explored. Similar to the science policy part, the type of university one works for seems to have a relationship with the perception of the role of HE in Japan.[111] In this section I will focus on the mission of academics in society. Having understood the conditions and the role of their work place, the main focus is shifted to the academics themselves. As certain societal conditions seem to influence lay people's perception of the role of HE, what those people and / or society expect academics to do and how academics are perceived could impact academic work. Thus, in this part, the interviewees were asked about the image of academics which is likely to be drawn by non-academic people in society, as well as about expectation from society towards them as academics. In doing so, I attempt to clarify the relationship between academics and society as a part of working environment where academic work is located. As a starting point, the ways they are perceived will be described.

---

[111] Adding to the type of their employer (university), their own academic background might influence the view of the role of HE. However, it is premature to discuss it at this phase of the study.

There are mainly three types of image of academics. First, they think that they are understood as 'teacher'.

> I think I am considered as a teacher . . . especially because I teach English language in university. . . . People do not think I am a scholar. I am teaching in university but not a scholar, I wonder. (Interviewee B)

> When I say "I am teaching English," I feel people's impression about me is downgraded. [Interviewer: Why is it so?] Because it is a language subject, and I feel they do not recognize me as an expert so much. It is also the case in the university I work for. (Interviewee C)

It seems coincident that the above interviewees both teach English language (not literature) in university. They both find the reasons for the impression which people tend to have is because of the fact that they teach language. Interviewee C makes an interesting comparison as follows:

> People think it is enough to learn English at language school. Then the image of me suddenly becomes the image of language school teacher. Before I tell them I teach English in university, they may have an image of expert in Shakespeare [when I say, "I work for university"]. (Interviewee C)

What she intends to express is that language is not classified as a part of academic world by the public, while English literature can be a field of academic expert. Interviewee C also refers to her position in the university as a lecturer of English.

> Such prejudice about language subjects exists also among academics. They might think that it is enough to appoint a person who has only one-year contract as a language lecturer. (Interviewee C)

Thus not only the public but academics consider those who teach language as a kind of 'teacher', despite of their expertise in language.

Interviewee B seems to share the view described by interviewee C; however, she not only refers to the aspect of teaching English but also mentions that the image of 'teacher' could apply to academics in general.

> This is my own impression, but . . . until some time ago if one says "I am professor," then people's reaction was like "Wow, he / she is a professor." Nowadays, almost everyone goes to university, and that makes people's perception of academics as teachers. (Interviewee B)

Her understanding is that generally academics are not so much considered as someone academically so special, due to the massification of university education in Japan. In her own case, although she is in a position of professor, she considers that teaching English seems to give people the impression that she is a teacher, adding to the general impression above.

The aforementioned comments may give readers an impression that academics in Japan are not respected, since the comments sounds rather negative. However, it is a very common impression from the public in society that people are respectful towards people working for university.

> When I say, "I work for a university," then the first reaction is like "Wow, it's great." (Interviewee C)

> It is an impression with a kind of respect. If one does not know so much about university, they would react with respect. . . . In Japan, respect towards people who are engaged in any teaching job would be paid. . . . My neighbours also call me 'sensei'. [112] (Interviewee E)

Thus it can be understood that academics are paid a certain respect by the public in society, as people recognize them as someone doing special work. However, considering that some academics are understood as 'teacher' rather than scholar or researcher, it is difficult to suppose that members of society perceive any particular characteristics of academics. Rather, academics are seen as someone different from ordinary people, therefore, they can be respected. On the other hand, they are not precisely perceived as someone related to academic work and / or academic knowledge.

Such an ambiguous perception by the public towards academics may lead to the following impression:

> Generally speaking, we are probably seen as someone argumentative, naïve, or someone that follows fundamentalism [to think about things]. (Interviewee A)

> A reaction [to be informed that one works for university] is that *sensei* in university is useless. The public consider us as people who do not know reality in their daily life and live in the world of books. (Interviewee E)

---

[112] *Sensei* in Japanese means teacher, master, professor, lecturer, and some other occupations. Medical doctors are also addressed as 'sensei' in hospital. Thus, the word *sensei* is for addressing someone who is in a position above people. As an anecdote, Japanese politicians are often addressed as 'sensei', as well.

Again, the comments indicate quite negative impressions about academics. Simultaneously, judging from the expression above such as "naïve" and "live in the world of books," it can be said that academics are perceived as people who live in a detached place from the people's daily life. This impression can be understood as a similar impression of academics that people in society often describe as "living in the ivory tower." This detachedness from the public could explain the above-mentioned ambiguous image of academics. Although academics are understood as someone exceptional (as *sensei*), contents of their work remain widely unknown. Consequently, they are assumed that they live in another different world from the ordinary public.

Then, with such impressions of them, how do academics understand expectations from the public? For those who think that they are understood in a negative way, they could not go beyond this negative image. Therefore, they did not refer to any expectations from the public. Similarly, those who commented that they were seen as teacher seemed to think that they were only expected to teach students. However, there were a couple of comments about this aspect.

> There is nothing but that the public would like us to solve problems they are faced with. (Interviewee A)

This interviewee does not mean that they are expected to solve people's problems through their academic expertise. No matter what his / her own academic expertise is, academics are "relatively far away from interests in society" (Interviewee A). Therefore, academics seem to be suitable people to deal with and solve people's problems. That is, academics are considered as the third party in various social relations and situations, due to the detachedness from society. In this sense, interviewee A understands that academics are seen as a kind of mediator to deal with people's problem from a position of neutrality in society. This is why he considers that people would like academics to solve various problems in society. While this perception indicates general expectations from society towards academics, there is another perception of social expectations regarding academic knowledge.

> I was told that academics should provide people with knowledge that people cannot know at all through their ordinary life, even though the knowledge is impractical. (Interviewee F)

This expectation expressed above is more focused on academics in relation to academic knowledge. If the first case is named as expectation for problem-solving, the second one can be called as expectation as provision of academic knowledge to the public. Although these are quite different types of expectations, a sense of detachedness can be seen in the second case, and the detachedness is referred not to academics but to academic knowledge which is impractical. Since the role of academic knowledge will be discussed in the next part, I will not analyse it further here. However, it can be summarized that academics are considered as people who are detached from the public, therefore those things that academics do or produce such as academic knowledge are also considered as something detached and impractical for the public in society.

So far, impressions of and expectations towards academics by the public through academics' own eyes have been observed and analysed. In the following part, I will explore how academics themselves contribute to and / or would like to contribute to society. Previously, a certain detachedness of academics and academic knowledge from society was observed. This detachedness can be deemed as passive perception by the public, but it is assumed that there should be active perception drawn by academics about themselves. In other words, they place themselves in society as academics, and what they perceive they are doing or are expected as academics will be described.

> I would like to contribute to construct sustainable society. . . . [It is] a contribution from academism towards society. (Interviewee B)

> I think I carry the very foundations of fostering human resources [as an academic person]. (Interviewee C)

> I would like to establish scholarship that could appreciate diversity of people's lives and efforts made by them. . . . The best thing would be that I suggest institutional designing that could reflect diversity or plurality of people in various contexts. (Interviewee F)

> Ultimately, I should only provide people with the ability to train and educate themselves. (Interviewee A)

The aspects of what they described as their missions as academics are various, and it is not feasible to narrow them down to one definite aspect. While interviewee A and C refer to fostering humans / human resources, Interviewee B and F are more interested in constructing new models of society from academic standpoints. However, there is a common point they all raised, which is that they all mentioned how they can contribute to society, and what they can do as academics in close relation with society. This is interesting in comparison with the impressions of academics from the public, which seem to consider academics as someone detached from society. Although they realize that they are not perceived as people who are closely connected to non-academic society, these comments reveal their attitude to face up to society / reality in front of them with diverse approaches.

To sum up, this part focused on roles of and expectations towards academics in society. These aspects were described from the academics' own viewpoint as well as academics' perception how the public see them. The impressions which the public seems to have about academics are both negative and positive. To some extent, academics are respected as people who have expertise which the public do not usually have. Nevertheless, the public do not quite know what academics do, and therefore, tend to think academics work in a separate place from ordinary people's life. From these impressions, it can be stated that academics live a detached existence from society. This nature of detachedness seems to influence the expectations that the public is assumed to have. That is, on one hand, there seems to be an expectation that academics should solve problems which people confront. The interviewee who suggested this view of the public explained that academics are, more or less, free from public's daily life interests, and that such people may be suitable to mediate any conflictual social situations. In this view, the detachedness of academics from the public is considered as a good condition to be a mediator in society to solve problems. On the other hand, another interviewee stated that academics are expected to provide the public with academic knowledge. In other words, trivial knowledge which anyone could know by any information channels in their daily life is not what the public expect of academics, but knowledge which ordinary people cannot easily reach should be provided by them. The detachedness is applied to the academic knowledge in this context, and academics are seen as a conveyer of such knowledge to the public. However, unlike the impressions and expectations from the public which indicate detachedness from society, academics are inclined to place themselves in society and would like to contribute to society for various aspects in society. It can be, then, concluded that the public does not really understood what academics attempt to do in society. However, under such a social circumstance, academics would like to contribute to society with their expertise and by their unique existence that is not seen as involved in society.

6.1.4 Academic Knowledge in Society: Roles and Perception of Knowledge

Having observed what academics are in society in respect of their roles and missions, it is academic knowledge that will be investigated in this part. To be more precise, while academics as practitioners of academic knowledge generation are analysed in the previous part, how academic knowledge is understood and where it is placed in society will be clarified in this part. Since it seemed confusing for some interviewees to distinguish between roles and perception of academics and those of academic knowledge, some failed to respond to questions in this part properly. Further, a concept of academic knowledge did not seem to be rooted in some interviewees' thoughts. Therefore, they seemed to experience difficulties relating their academic work to academic knowledge. This part consists of three points. First, roles of academic knowledge in society or relationship between academic knowledge and society will be explored. Second, perceptions of academic knowledge in society will be discussed. Third, how academics themselves perceive academic knowledge will be analysed.

6.1.4.1 Roles of Academic Knowledge in Society / Relationship between Academic Knowledge and Society

> The most important thing is that we academics should be responsible for society. . . . I think it is crucial that we collaborate with society. In a sense, [each discipline] works to bring academic knowledge to society. . . . It is also important that academic knowledge is open to the public, and we generate knowledge which could operate well in society. That is the most important. . . . In Japan, academic knowledge seems more appreciated as a means to enlighten citizens than to establish solid academism. (Interviewee A)

> I think what I can do [with academic knowledge] is to send people who could continue to learn off to society. At least, I hope that I could do something for educators of English language with academic knowledge. (Interviewee C)

> I think it is meaningful that academically specialized topics are explained to the public audience, rather than to specialists and / or students studying the same or similar fields. [Interviewer: In terms of social contribution or...?] Yes, I think so, in terms of that. (Interviewee G)

Although individual comments seem rather unfocused, each interviewee attempted to depict what they were asked. The respective comments turn out to relate to each other. For instance, the notion which interviewee A made that academic knowledge is more used to enlighten the public can closely relate to the comment of interviewee G about the importance of informing lay persons about academic knowledge as a kind of social contribution. Both also refer to the openness of academic knowledge to society / the public, that is, academic knowledge should prevail in society, although the form of knowledge should be simplified so that the public could understand fundamental contents of it. Moreover, it could be stated that a view seems to be shared between Interviewee A and C in respect of their attitude that they would like to contribute to society with academic knowledge they generated, even though which parts of society to be contributed are indefinite.

As stated at the beginning of this section, the relationship between academic knowledge and society seems similar to the relationship between academics and society. If it is supposed that academics exist in society via academic knowledge which they generated, it seems valid to say that the role of academic knowledge in society equates with the role of academics in society.

Academic Culture: An Analytical Framework 179

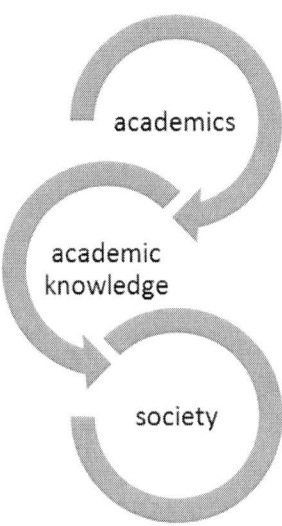

Model Y: Relationships between Academics, Academic Knowledge, and Society

That is, as the above model shows, academics are considered to exist with distance from society. They generate academic knowledge through their work, and outcomes of their work contribute to society in diverse forms. The relationship between academics, academic knowledge, and (non-academic) society is, thus, clarified. Compared with the role of academic knowledge based on the academics' own perception of it, how academic knowledge is perceived in society will be observed in the next section.

6.1.4.2   How Is Academic Knowledge Understood, Valued, and Interpreted?

Academic knowledge, from the above discussion, seems to be intermediary between academics and society. Despite of detachedness of academics from society, academic knowledge which is a product of academics, on the contrary, seems to be open and accessible to society. In order to clarify how academic knowledge can be intermediary between academics and society, looking at perceptions of academic knowledge is not unimportant.

Therefore, comments on this aspect will be enumerated below, followed by analytical discussion.

> [Academic knowledge offers] a means for living for everyone. I think that people [in society] understand academic knowledge as something that may relate to problems they have. . . . In general, people choose what is sympathetic to their problems in a broad sense as knowledge. (Interviewee A)

> It [academic knowledge] is not recognized as something significant. . . . It is more knowledge in paperbacks rather than academic knowledge. . . . It is not far away from society [people's daily lives]. (Interviewee B)

> I wonder if academic knowledge is something that people relate to their own interests very much. However, what I generate as the outcome of my work is not scientific knowledge, but skills. Language skills. Therefore, I and my colleagues do not consider the work we carry out every day as scholarship. (Interviewee C)

> It is specific knowledge which is not useful in society. . . . Therefore, academic knowledge is considered as special knowledge that is useless for the public. (Interviewee E)

> [Confined to the knowledge in cultural anthropology] Exoticism is the perception of knowledge of my field. (Interviewee F)

> [Referring to academics in Japan who often publish paperbacks as non-academic writings by exploiting their disciplinary knowledge] It is a normal reaction that one would leap onto something that digestibly explains what one is interested in, I think. (Interviewee G)

Two different views are seen among the above comments. One is that academic knowledge is connected to people's interests, benefit, and problems (Interviewee A, C, and G). In a broader sense, the comment of Interviewee B that academic knowledge is not far away from society can also be included in this view. In other words, even though people pick up academic knowledge quite selectively for their own interests, academic knowledge, which is outcomes of academic work, is adopted in people's life, and seems to thrive in society. The other view implies a rather negative impression of academic knowledge, which is considered as too special / academic and alien to the public. Consequently, there does not seem to exist a close connection between academic knowledge and society in this perception.

Similar relationship was seen in the earlier section, relating the role of academics in society and expectations towards them from society. That is, while academics feel that what they do at work is not necessarily understood by society, some of them suggest that they are expected to solve people's problems and to provide people in society with academic knowledge. Further, a similarity can be observed in the previous section of the role of academic knowledge and the relationship between academic knowledge and society. In respect of the current topic, different perceptions described by the interviewees may stem from different natures of the disciplines they are engaged in. Hypothetically, however; interviewee B, C, and G teach foreign languages, while interviewee E and F teach subjects in the social science such as sociology and anthropology. As expressed earlier by interviewee B and C about the role / perception of academics in society, teaching a language subject implies that the subject is not academic but more practical. As a result, they feel that they are not considered as academics but as teachers. On the contrary, academic disciplines such as sociology and anthropology may distance themselves from the public, because they do not seem to acquire familiarity and / or popularity among the public, or, at least, in general life of the public, unless one is particularly interested in those disciplinary knowledges. Thus their views seem to be influenced by individual working circumstances and disciplinary orientation. In this respect, the most prominent comment is the one from interviewee C that it is not academic / scientific knowledge but language skills that she deals with in her work.

As a summary of this part, two distinct perceptions of academic knowledge are revealed. One expresses the perception that academic knowledge has a certain closeness and connectedness to society, and therefore, it is considered that it has something to do with the interests, benefit, and problems of the people in society. The other holds a rather opposite view, that academic knowledge and society are distant from each other, because there does not seem to be common ground between academic knowledge and the public in society. Especially, knowledge in academic disciplines may be considered by the public as too specialized to relate to the life of ordinary people. As seen in other sections of this dissertation, such contrastive views could coexist in discussing one certain topic. Although they look as if they opposed to each other, the opposing views do not mean that one is correct and the other is not. Rather, as the distinct views in this part shows, each of them may have different backgrounds and conditions for work that could influence their views and understandings of academic knowledge, of themselves as academics, and of relations between the academic world and society. It seems more important that each of these aspects is interconnected with other components of the factors. That is, there are interrelations between components within a factor (e.g., the role of academics in society, the role of academic knowledge in society, the role of HE, etc.) as well as between the factors, as seen, such as the relationship between the science policy and the role of HE / universities in Japan. Bearing this in mind, the next section will move to the perception of academic knowledge.

6.1.4.3 Perceptions of Academic Knowledge: the Academics' Perspectives

The public's perceptions of academic knowledge was depicted through academics' eyes in the previous part. Now, how academic knowledge is perceived and / or defined by academics will be introduced and analysed here. First of all, the perceptions of academic knowledge expressed by three interviewees are given below:

> For me, academic knowledge is systematized exercises of mind at the highest level. . . . It is the exercises of mind that dynamically and flexibly move. (Interviewee A)

> To nicely put, it is creativity and originality. . . . The disciplinary knowledge is not directly applied and used in practical situations, but I can say it is interesting. One may surprise other people [by academic knowledge], or may use it when confronting difficulties in non-academic situations. It is when we can show real ability of academic knowledge. (Interviewee F)

> It may sound a bit too ordinary, but [it can be said as follows] "what I do not know is knowledge. Therefore, I would like to acquire it." (Interviewee G)

These expressions are very different and seem to have little in common among them. However, the comments of interviewee A and G can be understood that there is a point that they can share. What interviewee A refers to as "exercises of mind" is an attitude of academics that attempts to inspect problems in society from various angles and to solve them. According to interviewee A, the exercises of mind are required to the fullest possible extent for the above-mentioned purpose. Although one might think that he / she achieved the aim that a solution for the problem he / she has been working on is found, it would not be the end. Since situations around the problem could change, the solution may not be valid any more. Then, it is necessary to destroy what one found as academic knowledge, and to restructure or find a new solution, That is, academic knowledge should be flux rather than something fixed. Therefore, academics are required to continuously work in order to pursue their mission as academics. This comment is more related to ways of knowledge generation than a perception or definition of academic knowledge. On the other hand, interviewee G refers to academic knowledge acquisition with a very brief expression. At a glance, they seem to talk about different aspects, nonetheless, a commonality between them can be seen when the focus is narrowed down to a question what academic knowledge is for them. As interviewee G states, if we consider that academic knowledge is what we do not know, then the "exercises of mind" are carried out endlessly towards what we do not know, i.e., academic knowledge. That is, the comments of interviewee A and G respectively reveal the grounds for generation and acquisition of academic knowledge. Although they refer to academic knowledge from quite different aspects, it can be concluded that the both interviewees seem to perceive academic knowledge as a means to understand something unknown to us.

There is another view expressed by interviewee F, which also looks different from the ones of Interviewee A and G. It is different because the comment seems confined to his own disciplinary field, and it does not refer to knowledge in the social science in general. The focus of this comment is ways in which academic knowledge is used, judging from his utterance that one may find a solution for difficulties he / she confronts with in daily life through such disciplinary knowledge despite of its impracticality. Interviewee F commented for other questions that he thinks the best thing in social and human science is that we could analyse and understand what we feel strange or resent by using words. This implies that he presupposes that (disciplinary) knowledge is a means for understanding what one does not know. Thus, although the ways of expressions and the points of emphasis are diverse among the above comments, it can be concluded that academic knowledge for academics is a means for knowing and understanding what they do not know.

Findings of the Case Study

In this part, academic knowledge is observed from different angles. Firstly, the role of academic knowledge and the relationship between academic knowledge and society were explored. It is clarified that it is considered that academics exist in society via knowledge they generated. Simultaneously, the role of academic knowledge in society seems to synthesize the role of academics in society. Second, the perception of academic knowledge in society was discussed. The perception of academic knowledge in society described by the academics is that academic knowledge is something closely related to people's life, dependent on their interests, benefits, and problems. However, there is another perception of academic knowledge, which is more distant from the public, and therefore, it is less appreciated in society. This contesting view may have something to do with what academic knowledge the interviewees refer to. If the view is restricted to discuss certain disciplinary knowledge, one is less likely to find a connection between such knowledge and society, due to the nature of specificity of disciplinary knowledge. On the contrary, if what one deals with at work has more popularity and practicality in society, such as language subjects, it is not so difficult to find a connection between academic knowledge and society. Third, I asked academics what academic knowledge is for themselves. Despite diverse views, one commonality is that academic knowledge is a means for understanding what they do not know.

As pointed out earlier, all these individual points tend to have connections with, and to form coherence between other factors and / or components of a factor. Therefore, it is premature to draw a complete picture of working life of SSH academics in Japan. In this sense, summaries and conclusions of each parts are partial; however, what is expressed in the academic environment could provide us with certain impressions which were not apparent at the beginning of the study. In order to better understand what practically academics do at work, we will move to the academic practices. Together with what is depicted at the sections of academic environment, it will bring us more details as well as a clearer view of academic work in relation to academic knowledge generation practices.

6.2 Academic Practices

Backgrounds and surroundings of academic work have been observed and analysed as academic environment. As a result, it has become apparent that societal, educational, and political frameworks can be decisive factors in defining how and what academics are, and what academic knowledge is in society. Moreover, those perceptions and understandings about academics and academic knowledge by the public as well as by the academics themselves have close connections to each other and help in understanding the substance of academic knowledge and academic people. Thus an outline of academic knowledge and people engaged in generation of academic knowledge has emerged.

This section attempts to describe details inside of academic work and to analyse them in order to acquire further understanding of academic work. Academic work here means not all aspects of it but work aspects related to activity of knowledge generation. I keep to this focus because the aim of this study focuses on investigating academic work in the context of international collaboration. Knowledge generation is considered as one of the core activities in international academic collaboration; therefore, the following six aspects are identified as relevant academic practices in relation to knowledge generation, and are investigated mainly by the questionnaire research.

- Academic discourse practice
- Publication practice
- Managing academic activities
- Knowledge acquisition practice
- Disciplinary practice
- Social relations

Outcomes of this section will provide us with not only a closer look at details of academic work but also the interrelationship between the above academic practices as well as the interrelationship between them and with the aspects of the academic environment.

6.2.1 Academic Discourse Practice

First, aspects of academic discourse practice will be observed in this part. Academic discourse practice means discourses with colleagues at work and in disciplinary association / society to which they belong. In order to understand the influence of interaction with colleagues, I ask whether or not there are discourses with colleagues, the frequency of such discourses, places of discourses, methods of discourse communication, and whether such discourses with colleagues influence their research activity and / or educational (teaching) activity.

First, the respondents are asked: "Are there discourses with colleagues in university and / or members of disciplinary associations which you belong to? (Topics of discourse are limited to topics which relate to research and educational activities)." All of the respondents answer that there are discourses. Second, they are asked the frequency, forms, and contents of discourse. Interestingly, only respondent C answers that the discourse takes place every day in the form of face-to-face meeting, and email. The response of the others is that it is irregular (respondents B and D) or once a month when participating in a workshop by interested people and alike. If annual conferences held by a disciplinary association / society is counted, it takes place once or twice a year (respondents B and E). As a form of communication, therefore, it is more face-to-face meetings, as far as workshops and conferences are concerned. Respondent B and D state that email is the main means of communication. The telephone seems to be a rare form of communication; however, respondent D confesses that he sometimes uses the telephone as well. As for contents of discourse, most of them mention that it is about organizing events / conferences for the disciplinary association and about topics concerning their research activities. That is to say, the core of discourse topic seems to be something connected to research activities rather than educational activities. None of them indicates contents of discourse with colleagues at work as a response to this question, even though the first question does not exclude possibility of discourse with colleagues at work. There could be various interpretations about the point that discourse with colleagues in university was referred to by none of them. However, responses to the next question may reveal a bit more details about it. Therefore, the third question: Do you think such discourses could influence your research and / or educational activities? If so, what are the grounds for that? All valid responses indicate that the discourses they suggest in the previous question influence their academic work both in research and in education. Respondent B and E show similar aspects. For instance respondent B states that discourses with colleagues influence her work "because we can exchange information about the same research topic / theme," and respondent E agrees with the view of respondent B by explaining that there is an influence with respect to the examination of research trends and his point of view on research topics / themes. It can be said that respondent A also has a similar orientation towards this point. He refers to a workshop that is regularly held by his own initiative and explains that it requires considerable preparation and capability to maintain discourses with the participants. In other words, in order to organize and maintain discourse with colleagues from the same discipline requires ceaseless efforts, not only to catch up with topics the colleagues may refer, but also to lead such disciplinary discourses. Again, they only refer to discourses in the research context. Judging from this, they lay more emphasis on discourses related to research work, and educational aspects are not in their focus when considering discourse as a part of academic working life. By contrast, respondent C mentions that both aspects of research and education influence her discourses. Her comment is as follows:

> We have to design a course that diverse lecturers are satisfied with, because our department is run under the concerted curriculum. Therefore, we often exchange our opinions closely. I suppose that communication between educators is the centre of educational activities. Regarding research, I participate in collaborative research projects, and frequent discussions of research contents, direction, and methods take place. Additionally, I participate in a regular workshop with my colleagues, which enables us to understand what we did not know, to find literature, and to read it together. (Respondent C)

Although she mentions research activities in relation to the influence of discourse, she is the only one who refers to the educational aspect. Besides, the aspect of research which she raises seems primarily an activity of research, compared with what others mention about the same scope. It may be because her academic and institutional background is teaching / education centred. Indeed, she informs us in the interview:

> The stance of my university is obviously on education. Therefore, there are few people who would like to carry out research work, and even if there is, they would not stay in this university. . . . In fact, such people moved to national universities, because they could not be engaged in research work while working in this university. (Interviewee C)

Thus it is not only her own personal tendency to be more committed to teaching, but the characteristic of university where she works obtains strong tendency to concentrate on education over research.[113] This implies that how individual academics define themselves, in this case, as either educator or researcher, seems to define the central nature of academic work for them. Further, characteristics of respective universities seem to influence the ways academic people work, as also seen in the analysis in the academic environment. That is, if one considers his / herself as a researcher, the main focus of their academic work is likely to be research, and if one thinks he / she is an educator, educational aspects are prioritized in the academic work. Respondents may have unconsciously written their comments; nonetheless, their identities seem to appear out of the perception of their own, as well as the characteristics of university where they work.

To summarize, regarding discourse practices with colleagues at work and / or in disciplinary organizations, it is clear that there are various kinds of discourses. The major forms of discourse seem to be face-to-face meetings and emails, and the frequency of discourse varies from being irregular, once or twice per year, to every day. As for the contents of discourse, planning to organize disciplinary events / conferences, discussing disciplinary research topics / themes, and other matters relating to research activity are mentioned. Thus research related topics seem to be mainly discussed through such discourses. On the other hand, there is another aspect of discourse contents—that which is related to education, though this aspect is suggested by only one respondent. Judging from this respondent's reply, which includes both aspects of education and research as the contents of discourse, she is

---

[113] However, this does not mean that this university has little interest in research. Interviewee C states in the section of science policy that the university encourages the employee to apply for national research fund.

engaged in research activity as well as education. However, it is an interesting point why other respondents do not include educational aspects as a part of discourse contents, given that they are all engaged in education as well. A supposition that this difference may originate from how they see themselves and what kind of institution they work for emerges. As seen in the science policy section, the nature of university which they work and / or used to work for can be a decisive factor of what kind of academic work respective academics are engaged in. If the explanation is valid, the above supposition could also make sense.

Regardless of whether they are more engaged in education or in research, all respondents agree that discourses with colleagues influence their own academic work. For some, discourse is useful to update research trend in the discipline and to examine their own views on topics / themes which their discipline is concerned. Discourse is also significant to develop his / her own academic knowledge. In terms of educational aspect, discourse is an important means to reach consensus about planning for educational activities. Although research and educational aspects have totally different standpoints and significance in relation to discourse practice as a part of academic work, discourse practice seems important in both aspects in order to share information and knowledge, to examine his / her own understanding of certain issues, and to develop own capability for teaching / research. In this respect, this competence development through discourse practice can be suggested as a significant factor in academic work.

6.2.2 Publication Practices

Publication is certainly one of the significant aspects of research activity. When academic collaboration is discussed, publication by co-authoring has almost the exact meaning of collaboration, because it is assumed that publication is an ultimate outcome of collaboration. Needless to say, as seen and discussed earlier, the use of citation databases to benchmark quality of academic work places great value on publication for today's SSH academics. Judging from this trend, for academics publication is an important signifier of their academic work to others. Therefore, in this section, the respondents are asked about their experience of and / or future plans for publication, types of publication, and the importance of and reasons for publishing their work.

They are firstly asked about their experiences with publications, and they all answer that they have experiences in having their work published in the past. The next question is what kind of publication their work was published in, and the responses vary from academic books, journals, and bulletins to non-academic books that aim at enlightening non-academic people. Although most of the responses relates to academic publication, questionnaire respondent B, C, and E mention that they published books for non-academic people. This is what was expressed in the role of academic knowledge in the academic environment aspect. That is, publication for non-academic people (the public in society) means reification of the role and perception of academic knowledge discussed in the previous section. As some admit in the interviews, academic knowledge to the public could appear as something "useless," but, at the same time, if it is written in a way that non-academic people could also understand, academic knowledge could play a role in society. This is what interviewee G means in his statement that it is normal that one would jump at publication that digestibly explains what one is interested in. Thus while publication of non-academic book is one possibility, it seems that the majority of publication activities are located in and confined to academic fields. The respondents are asked in the next question: "How important do you think publishing academic work is in fields of SSH in Japan? What is the reason for that? If you do not think it is important, please also provide the reason." The following are the responses to these question:

> Important. It is because one would be recognized as a scholar / researcher in the field [by publishing one's work]. (Respondent A)

> Important. Because publication can be counted as one's achievement of academic work. Also, it gives a record of research outcomes for future [academics or work]. (Respondent B)

> When trying to get a job position, publication [number and contents] is considered as an indicator of "contribution to the disciplinary field." In this sense, publication is an indispensable activity for those who would like to work for a university. In a broader perspective [apart from getting a job], it is important to disclose one's research outcomes in a sense of "contribution to the field" and contribution to society. I suppose that publication exists as a form of such contribution. (Respondent C)

> Very important. First, for development of research and mutual critique. Second, for enlightening the public audience. Third, (generally speaking), useful for evaluation, promotion, and job hunting. (Respondent E)

All agree that publication is important; however, the grounds for that are various. The classification which respondent E makes is very straightforward and comprehensive. Firstly, it can be mentioned that publication is important as an activity of knowledge generation, which is related to "contribution to the field" (respondent C). Respondent E expresses it in a more detailed manner, but the first point raised by him certainly means that publication is important as a contribution to the field. In the same light, part of the statement by respondent B that publication can be a record for the future also suggests that publication as a written form remains over times for future work in the field. The second point that publication is for enlightening the public audience is the point above, which refers to publishing non-academic books. Although respondent B, who responds that she published / will publish non-academic books, does not include this point as the reason for importance of publication, respondent C and E, in fact, published and / or planned to publish non-academic books, and a coherent activity between publishing and a reason for publication can be observed. That is to say, for them, publication for non-academic people is a kind of contribution to society with an aim of enlightening people by academic knowledge. Finally, the third point agreed by respondent B, C, and E very frankly admits that publication is an important evaluation factor for them. It is not only for getting a job at a university but also necessary in today's academic work as a part of evaluation system. The following comment from the Focus Group discussion confirms this aspect of publication as a means of evaluation[114]:

> We are given credits by publishing our work when the university carries out the evaluation of its faculty members, so it directly impacts merit rating which takes place once a year. Naturally, if one does not do anything, the rating [of the person] goes down. However, some people require some years to write a book, therefore, it is not simply judged by a unit of one year only. (GD participant A)

---

[114] Although this section is intended to exploit outcomes of the questionnaire research in order to observe academic practices in details, some comments from the Focus Group discussion are inserted. It is because of the relevance of such comments from the Focus Group to the topic(s) discussed in this section.

This seems to be the recent system introduced in the fields of social sciences. GD participant D recalls:

> Long time ago, when I was young, it would be fine if one wrote one article / book that is really what he / she wants to write during his / her entire academic career. Nevertheless, considering getting a job nowadays, young academics enumerate publications as their achievements. It is inevitable under the current academic circumstance. Everything becomes credits nowadays. (GD participant D)

Probably this is one of the strongest reasons (and motivations) for publishing their work under the current circumstances of academic work. The emphasis that publication is important for promotion, job-hunting, and internal evaluation for merit rating is put by relatively young academics who are around their forties, while established academics like GD participant D understand the current situation around the evaluation and publication, but do not concern themselves with it so much as a personal interest. Respondent E raised this aspect of evaluation as a ground for publishing work, but he put it in brackets as "generally speaking," and this indicates that he personally does not concern himself with this point either.

To summarize, it is apparent that publication has a great importance in academic work for those who obtain a tenure position in a university as well as for those who try to get into the academic work or to move to another university. Although this is the common view of academics on publication activity, the grounds for it can differ from one person to another. When publication is considered as a part of knowledge generation activity, academics understand the activity as the contribution to the field. In terms of contribution, publication of non-academic writing can be deemed as the contribution to society, which aims at enlightening the public audience by academic knowledge. On the other hand, publication seems a vital activity in today's academic work. Which aspect one puts more emphasis on seems to relate to one's individual position as an academic person. That is, if one is close to retirement age or is already retired, the motivation for publishing work tends to relate to development of academic knowledge and / or of the disciplinary field one belongs to. On the contrary, young academics are more involved in the aspect of evaluation related to publication. Thus the driving forces for publication in academic work are mixed depending on the position and needs of the individual academics.

6.2.3 Managing Academic Activities

This part differs from the other sections, for it asks about more general aspects of academics' daily working life. The relation to knowledge generation may seem rather indirect. However, because academics' working life consists of things other than research, I believe that observing the ways in which academics work out of the context of research activity is relevant to my research. In other words, it is not unimportant to understand under what kind of working conditions they carry out research activity. Therefore, they are asked: What is the proportion of their respective work (education, research, and others), how they learnt to carry out daily work (and by whom they were trained), and work contents that can be classified as daily work.

    First, respondents are asked about how much time they spent on which activities in their everyday working life. Since most of the university employees in Japan are employed to teach, unsurprisingly commitments to teaching seem to occupy their daily working life. However, the proportion of teaching and work related to teaching varies from one person to another. Respondent C stated that teaching took more than 80 percent and research is less than 20 percent of her daily work. Similarly, respondent A indicated that teaching and research occupied about 60 percent of his work; the other 40 percent goes to administrative work for university. The administrative work includes faculty meetings, committee meetings, administration of examinations, and any other work related to neither teaching nor research. It seemed that relatively a great portion is spent for work which is not so much related to academic work. Respondent B also stated that teaching, research, and other activities such as university administration and contribution to local society required one-third of her entire work respectively. On the contrary, respondent E informs us that 70 percent of working time is spent for research, and teaching takes up only 30 percent. Thus the majority of them spend more time for teaching and administration in university, and only respondent E stated that work relating to research is more prioritized in his daily working life. This does not mean that the majority of them do not value research work in their daily working life.

> Most of the researchers in Japan belong to universities, therefore, on one hand, they are teaching staff, and are researchers, on the other hand.[115] Which part is attached more importance for them depends on individuals. It is also pointed out whether he / she considers research work as a "job." In my case, I consider the teaching part of my work as a job, because I get salary for that. When I ask myself if the research part is my job, I am not sure if I have such a perception that research is my job. (GD participant A)

This is an interesting point that some academics in Japan may not consider research work as a part of their job. It may sound too exaggerated, but respondent B also mentions that research activity can only be carried out during weekends and holidays. In other words, although they carry out research activity, it cannot be a part of their daily working life, due to the other commitments such as teaching and administrative work. Although the basic principle of missions of universities in Japan rest on the three pillars of education, research, and social contributions, it seems that most of these academics experience difficulties in including research activity in their daily working life.

Having observed the proportion of their work, the contents of daily work in respect of both teaching and research will be studied. What is enumerated is not so diverse among the respondents. As an educator, lecturing, seminars for postgraduates, supervising students, preparatory work for lectures, planning a course curriculum, together with administrative work in university are mentioned. As research work, writing articles / books, research activity such as data collection and searching literature, giving speeches at conferences / meetings, organizing workshops / conferences, and commitments to disciplinary associations / societies including administrative work in such organizations are

---

[115] Weber states, "The youth who consider that scholarship is their vocation should know that his [sic.] mission as a scholar has a kind of duality. This is to say, He [sic.] should have not only quality as a scholar, but also as a teacher. These two qualities do not necessarily accord with each other." (translation of my own, 1980: 18) This statement of Weber suggests that it is common for academics to perceive their job with this duality. Nevertheless, the above comment rather expresses that academics in Japan may not take this duality for granted as components (qualities) of their job. Rather, they tend to think that they live from teaching, not from research.

seen. Judging from the comments and descriptions of proportion of each component of their daily work, education can be the centre of their daily work, and research is carried out rather outside of the routine work in university. The comment from respondent D may give a supplementary explanation about why in Japanese universities research activity is pushed away from the daily work.

> Generally, I wonder if an image of academic life that prioritizes research work is no longer a reality in the fields of SSH. Due to declining birth rate, universities in Japan have entered the era of survival. As a result, an image of today's universities is rather a place to provide educational services, which is most prioritized. The traditional image of academics was that they were firstly committed to research, then to education, and university administrations were the last thing they should commit to. . . . Today's Japanese academics strive to commit to both education and research in the above-mentioned situation. (Respondent D)

This aspect has been observed and analysed in the section of role of universities in Japan as a part of academic environment. Particularly, if one works for a less research oriented university, this tendency of providing educational service to students seems quite strong. Without considering this background of their working life, it would be hard to understand why academics in Japan spend so much time on teaching and administrative work, and less time on research. Simultaneously, the proportion of daily work and the contents of it support what is described in the role of HE and role of academics in society that they are more teaching oriented, and therefore, academics are considered as "teacher" (or *sensei*) by the public.

The contents and the proportion of respective work of academics are clarified, but how they acquired and / or established their own ways of working remains unanswered. Generally speaking, most of them express that they were not given any particular training but that they established the ways of teaching and research by "learning by doing." In respect of research, training was given during their postgraduate period, since such training is one of the purposes of education at graduate school. However, there seems no training system for teaching. For instance, respondent A mentions that he learnt teaching by looking at the way his supervisor taught, and respondent E similarly enumerates colleagues, supervisors, and himself as people from whom he learnt. Respondent C says that she learnt from her senior colleagues as well as by collecting information from various people, while respondent B recalls that she devised her own way of teaching while carrying out teaching. Unlike other educational levels such as primary and secondary education, those who give lectures at HE level in Japan are not required to obtain any official qualification.[116] In other words, even though they are considered as teachers / *sensei*, what defines them as *sensei* is very subtle. The background that teaching at university does not seem to require particular training and qualification like primary and secondary school teachers can be an explanation for the aspect seen in the role of HE in Japan. That is, business people could also play a role in Japanese universities as lecturers or specially appointed professors. As a reflection of the above situation, GD participant D points out:

> Academism or world of scholarship in Japan has never been established as a solid form. It is all mixed and confused, but it is fine in this country. . . . In this sense, the academic world in Japan is considerably different from ones in Europe and the U.S. (GD participant D)

This comment suggests that there is not a clear separation between the world of academism and the practical daily life world in the Japanese HE system. Therefore, *sensei* in Japanese universities seems to be quite an elusive substance, which does not require a qualification for teaching while most of them are nowadays required to obtain a doctoral degree when applying for a job position at university.[117] That is to say, people obtain the highest academic degree which allows them to enter the job market for HEIs, and once they successfully get a position in university, they are rather expected to spend most of their working time as a

---

[116] Qualification for teaching at primary and secondary education can be obtained through a course for teacher training at most of universities in Japan. The licence is issued by the prefectural board of education. However, it can be considered as a quasi-national qualification, because the course for teacher training offered at Japanese universities is certified by the minister of Education. People who obtain this licence could take an examination for employment in publicly established schools of each prefectures. Thus, in terms of qualification, the primary and secondary teachers in Japan go through various trainings and examinations.

[117] Though it is the current situation, it was not a precondition to apply a job at university until some time ago. Therefore, it was possible to become even a professor in Japan only with a master degree.

teacher, which they were not trained for. Academic competence is required to enter the academic working life, but afterwards, this required competence does not seem to be used on a daily basis. In such a situation, it is not surprising that academics, more or less, train themselves as *sensei* to adapt to the demand in the working environment

It has become apparent by observing how academics manage their working life that most of their working time is spent teaching and working for university administration. This coincides with the perception of academics by the public that they are teachers / *sensei*, rather than scholars or academic researchers, under the circumstance that holiday period and weekends are the only time when they can concentrate on research activity. On one hand they are *sensei*, being busied in teaching and dealing with meetings and paperwork in university; on the other hand, they remain as academics by carrying out research, writing articles / books, and committed to activities in academic societies / associations. Yet the balance between teaching and research is not even, and there seems to be discrepancy being teachers without systematized training or qualification and being thoroughly trained academics with specialized postgraduate educations. As a result, they train themselves as teachers by learning by doing in response to the demand.[118] Thus, the way academics manage their working life can be seen as the response to the expectation from universities where they work as well as to the role of respective universities towards society.

6.2.4 Knowledge Acquisition Practices

Acquiring the existing knowledge is essential if one wants to generate knowledge in a certain disciplinary field. Simultaneously, acquiring knowledge can be the first step of research work to understand what has been studied in the disciplinary field, as well as inspiring him / her towards the work which is going to be formed and planned. Considering such significant roles of knowledge acquisition, in this section I will ask: What are methods and places of acquiring knowledge, the motivation for knowledge acquisition, and how is acquired knowledge used?

---

[118] The details are discussed in the role of HE in the academic environment.

As a starting point, I raise the question of where academics acquire disciplinary knowledge. For this question the following alternatives are given for the respondents to choose: Academic journals published in Japan, academic journals published in foreign countries, academic books in Japanese, academic books in foreign languages, [119] non-academic writings (Japanese), non-academic writings (foreign languages), speeches and presentations at conferences in Japan, speeches and presentations at conferences abroad, workshops held by interested persons, websites including web-journals, blogs by academics, and others. [120] The most frequented responses are academic journals published both in Japan and foreign countries, academic books in Japanese and foreign languages, speeches and presentations at conferences in Japan and abroad, and workshops held by interested persons, and websites. These are directly related to academic work carried out by other academics, regardless of place of origin of such academic knowledge. This could imply that they are conscious of acquiring knowledge generated not only in Japan but also in foreign countries. Moreover, acquiring academic knowledge is not confined to written sources, but includes attendance of conferences and workshops where human interactions occur.

Then, what motivates them to acquire knowledge by the above-mentioned means? A slight distinction can be observed between those who are rather young academics and those who are in more established phase as academics. Young academics like respondent B and C direct their responses towards practical situations of their own. That is, they are motivated to acquire academic knowledge in order to use it for individual achievement. Respondent B mentions that the motivation for acquiring academic knowledge is improving her career prospects as a researcher. The comment from respondent C is rather indirect, compared with the one from respondent B, and tells us that it is due to intellectual curiosity. Simultaneously, respondent B refers to improving the quality of teaching. Although this is more directed towards the aspect of teaching work, it can still remain as an individual purpose / achievement. On the other hand, those who are older and well

---

[119] In the Japanese context, a foreign language can be normally English. Nevertheless, the author had no intention of excluding other foreign languages as the alternative.

[120] If one selects 'others', he / she is asked to describe what it is / they are.

established as academics more often refer to broader views that are not confined to their own achievements. For instance, the comment from respondent A sounds even philosophical. It reads: "I could not select by myself to be born as a human, nevertheless, I think I try to respond to that [the fact of being as a human] as much as I can [by acquiring academic knowledge]." Respondent D states that he longs for fundamental understandings of social changes in Japan and abroad by acquiring academic knowledge, while respondent E's comment is more research oriented. For respondent E, the motivation for acquiring academic knowledge is development of research in the disciplinary field, and to make good use of academic knowledge for social practice. The commonality of those three comments is that they do not refer to academic knowledge as a means of individual benefit / achievement in their practical working life. Rather, they place more importance of academic knowledge in relation to society.

As the response to the foregoing two questions, they are asked how the acquired academic knowledge is exploited. Consequently, the similar tendency to the previous responses on the motivation for acquiring knowledge is seen. That is to say, because the motivation for young academics is directed to more practical working conditions, the use of acquired knowledge is also practical. Respondent B simply puts it that the acquired academic knowledge is used for "writing academic papers." Respondent C who would like to acquire academic knowledge for educational purposes as well as for her own intellectual curiosity also connected the motivation with the use of academic knowledge. Her comment states that the main purpose of use of academic knowledge is that the acquired knowledge is reflected on her teaching activities and curriculum in the course. Adding to it, she mentions that it is used for her own research.

Similarly, the aforementioned senior academics also connect the use of knowledge to the motivation for acquiring it. Respondent E repeats the same words for the response to the last question as the response to the previous one. That is, it is used "for development of research in the field and for social practice." Respondent D also links this question to the previous one, and states that he uses the acquired knowledge to check how much he could understand matters which he is interested in. Respondent A states that he tries to ingrain knowledge in the nation by acquiring the knowledge. Although this response from respondent A less refers to the comment to the previous question, his standpoint is apparent from his comments during the interview that academic knowledge should be useful for and available to society. Thus academics who are already established and do not need to work to compete with others more often relate academic knowledge to society and / or development of knowledge, compared with the younger academics.

On the whole, the knowledge acquisition practice is similar to the publication practice. As seen, purposes of publishing their work for younger academics have quite practical aspects, which closely related with and influence their academic life. Knowledge acquisition is a process towards publication when one is concerned with the aspect of research in his / her academic life. Simultaneously, if one is more committed to the teaching aspect in his / her academic life, knowledge acquisition is considered as sources of teaching materials. Although this does not mean that younger academics do not concern themselves with development of knowledge and / or contribution to the disciplinary field, individual motivations and interests prevail over the other roles and purposes of academic work. Contrarily, senior academics do not relate knowledge acquisition with their own perspectives of academic work as much as their younger colleagues do. I assume that they have this attitude because they are mature and well-established as academics. Therefore, as the attitude towards publication as outcomes of their work also indicates, individual achievements and interests are less obvious in relation to knowledge acquisition practice. Instead, their emphasis of knowledge acquisition practice is put on the aspect of academic knowledge *per se,* i.e., academic knowledge as public good. From this viewpoint, knowledge acquisition practice is emancipated from the view that knowledge acquisition is a means to accomplish individual aims. Rather, knowledge acquisition for those senior academics is intended to contribute towards much broader settings than individual interests. Describing this duality of knowledge acquisition practice does not attempt to judge which is correct, but to draw attention to manifold nature of academic work. Nonetheless, it can be assumed that academic working life of different generations may suggest different perceptions of work, diverse orientations towards work, and different natures of work, even though they all carry out similar, if not the same, academic activities in their working life.

6.2.5 Disciplinary Practices

Disciplinary fields can be an important place for knowledge acquisition, generation, and dissemination for academics. In respect of collaboration, there are increasing possibilities nowadays to collaborate with people from other disciplines. Similarly, when international collaboration is considered, contents of disciplinary activity may differ between domestic and international settings. Therefore, this section will focus on whether there is / are unique aspect(s) in methodology, conceptualization and theorization of knowledge, compared with other disciplines, and if so, what kind of aspects these are, whether there is any different activity between domestic and international disciplinary associations, and if there is, what it is.

 First, are there unique and / or different aspects in their own discipline, compared with other disciplines in the fields of SSH? Except for one respondent, they all answer that there are unique aspects in their disciplines. Second, they are asked about what they think the unique aspects in the disciplines are. Respondent A and E come from the same discipline, but their responses take different directions. Respondent A states that the discipline he belongs to encroaches on other disciplines by taking theories and concepts that exist in other disciplines into the discipline. Respondent E does not refer to the point that respondent A mentions, but rather relates the unique aspect to activities of the discipline being transnational as a consequence of practice of transnationalism. That is, the discipline respondent E belongs to practices the academic concept of transnationalism by forming transnational academic networks among scholars in the discipline. Both respondent A and E relate the uniqueness of the discipline to conceptual and / or theoretical aspects in the discipline. Respondent C points out that the discipline she belongs to is unique in respect of that achievement / result of education in the discipline can be measured by external examination systems. Further, she mentions that people who do not have expertise in the discipline frankly express their opinions about how the education in her discipline should be. From her point of view, these aspects do not exist in other disciplines. In comparison with the discipline of respondent A and E, respondent C refers to more practical situations than conceptual and theoretical aspects of the discipline. The difference between those two disciplines may arise from the different nature of respective disciplines, which is also seen in the section on the role of academic knowledge in the academic environment analysis. Respondent C teaches English, and respondent A and E come from sociology. Also as discussed as the academic environment aspect, the distance of the disciplines to the public / society can be applicable to explain the difference. That is to say, English language, as an academic discipline, is not considered as a traditional academic discipline even among those who are engaged in teaching this subject, as respondent C stated in the interview. This is apparent from her statement that what she does as academic work is not academic knowledge but skills. This may bring the differences which respondent C describes above, while sociology has a different academic standpoint that is more theoretical / conceptual from languages. Given that disciplinary practice is directly concerned with academic knowledge, that the aspect of the role of academic knowledge in the academic environment is again found here is not a coincidence. Rather, it can be stated that the ways respective disciplines exist influence activities in the disciplines, and therefore, diverse uniqueness of each discipline emerges when comparing each with other disciplines.

Third, the focus shifts from the contents of domestic disciplinary practice to the contents of the activity in the same discipline in different geographical settings, which are in domestic disciplinary associations and in international ones. Therefore, the following question is given to respondents: Is there any difference in activity between the domestic association and international one? As a fourth question, they are asked to exemplify the difference(s) between the domestic and the international disciplinary associations, if they think there is any. If comments from the respondents of the same discipline are juxtaposed, both respondent A and E agree that differences between activities in the domestic and international associations exist. Nevertheless, when they are asked what the difference is, the comments from them look quite different, even though they belong to the same associations both domestically and internationally. Respondent A states that it is still rare to send one's own article which is in progress to colleagues in the domestic association in order to get feedbacks, while such an activity can be seen in the international setting. On the other hand, respondent E mentions that the only difference is whether they use the English language or not, i.e., he does not seem to find any considerable difference in working practice between the domestic and the international associations. Respondent C comments that there is little difference in working practice between the domestic and the international associations. However, she adds that English education and learning in Japan seems to influence both on research and teaching. Those three comments have little commonality and / or interrelationship between them, but at least, respondent A and C refer to some particular characteristics of the domestic circle / circumstance, and none of them comments on characteristics or particularity in practice of international disciplinary associations. As far as respondent C is concerned, her main viewpoint is placed that there is little difference between the domestic and the international associations. In this sense, her standpoint is rather closer to the one of respondent E, who states that the difference is only the language which is used for communication. Although a concrete statement cannot be made at this very moment, it can be assumed that there might be little difference when we compare one domestic disciplinary association and the other international and / or foreign association. Because, if one shares the same discipline, the contents of academic work within the discipline such as the methods for research activity, employed concepts / theories for research, and current research topics / themes are less likely to be different to a great extent. This point seems to have an interrelationship with the discourse practice in respect of domestic work, and also with the publication practice in the both respects of domestic and international academic work. Those practices are carried out, in part, to share the information / knowledge among colleagues, and to update and check their knowledge. In other words, the above-mentioned practices are possible as long as the disciplinary background is shared, regardless of the associations being domestic or international / foreign. Of course, the degree of shared understandings, information, and practices within the same discipline could be diverse; however, it might not be the difference of 'all or nothing'.

Thus, to summarize, there seem some unique aspects in respective disciplines, compared with others. This uniqueness is understood in diverse ways, and appears to have some relationship with the role of academic knowledge which is observed in the academic environment. That is to say, if the discipline is a traditional academic discipline such as sociology, anthropology, and other SSH disciplines, the orientation of its practitioners is likely to be influenced by the nature / characteristics of discipline. As seen as a part of academic environment aspects, such characteristics have connections with how academic knowledge in the discipline is perceived by society as well as by academics themselves. For instance, in the case of those traditional academic disciplines, knowledge generated in those disciplines is deemed distant from the public society, and therefore, it can be understood by the public that such knowledge has little to do with people's daily life. It might be because knowledge in the disciplines has strong ties with concepts and theories that non-academic people / ordinary citizens are not familiar with. Reversely speaking, then, the academics who are committed to such disciplines tend to judge things such as the uniqueness of the discipline based on theoretical / conceptual ways of thinking. On the other hand, if the discipline has a more pragmatic dimension than the aforementioned disciplines, viewpoints of those who are committed to the discipline which is of more pragmatic use could also be influenced by this characteristic, and be rather pragmatic.

Regarding differences in disciplinary practice between the domestic associations and the international / foreign ones, there seems little difference between them. Although some respondents stated that there was a difference, it seems rather a difference of degree than that one party has a certain characteristic which the other party does not. The grounds for this are based on the understanding that most of the practices carried out within the same discipline could be widely shared across the national borders. In a broader perspective, it seems that research topics / theme are shared in all global regions (see the section of science policy in the academic environment section).

As far as the academic practice is concerned, the discourse practice and the knowledge acquisition practice indicate that academics exploit those practices in order to obtain and share information related to research work and knowledge. If activities in the domestic and the international / foreign disciplinary settings were so heterogeneous to a great extent, such above-mentioned practices would make little sense. At least, the basis of academic work within a discipline is likely to be shared around the world, and therefore, little tension seems to be observed in comparison of activities in the domestic disciplinary associations to the international / foreign ones.

6.2.6 Social Relations in Academic Work

This section will be focused on social relations which might influence academic work. Social relations in this context mean general communication and interactions between humans at work. In other words, I am interested in whether styles of communication and interactions with colleagues, aspects of so-called national culture,[121] and other traits which exist in Japanese society influence academic work. Although this study is not interested in defining people by their nationality and / or national cultural traits, it does not totally eliminate the possibility of influence of them on academic work by human relations, communication styles, and any cultural traits.[122] Any work which involves human relations cannot escape from influences that are caused by interactions between humans, then, academic work is also not an exception. Thus in this section I do not focus on national cultural traits which might cause any influence on work, but explore whether there is any such factor that could influence

---

[121] Although the main emphasis in this part is not an analysis related to national culture and / or peculiarity of Japanese people's behaviour and utterance, it is not excluded as a focus of investigation in this part. Because of the presupposition of the author that national cultural traits do not necessarily influence academic work, using the notion of national culture can be inapplicable to this study as the other study about disagreement discourse of Japanese SSH scholars in international collaborations (Okamoto, 2010a) suggests that national cultural traits do not seem play an important role in analyses of academic work. However, since the interviewees may find influential aspects of national culture relevant, the notion of national culture is included.

[122] In this context, "cultural traits" refer not only national culture but also other cultural aspects, for academic culture might also have certain traits. Regarding traits of academic culture, it is not yet certain what they are at this moment, but exploring this aspect of social relation related to academic culture is relevant.

academic work, and if there is, to clarify what it is. May it be either positive or negative, influential aspects related to social relations are enumerated by interviewees.[123]

> I think there is little influence which is advantageous or disadvantageous for work itself. Generally, there is not. . . . However, in the case of Japan or Asia, age could influence, to a certain extent [when we elect a new president of an association or alike]. In this sense, age may influence. . . . Being female may be disadvantageous, judging from the fact that the rate that females become a head of organization, department, etc. Reasons for that can vary, but this is not only in Japan, but in other countries as well. The higher hierarchy is, the less females we can find. (Interviewee A)

> It may depend on respective universities and disciplines. Females are in the majority in my discipline, and there were many advantageous occasions because of being female. [Interviewer: For example?] Being female is appreciated because we are the minority in number as a whole. . . . I do not see any hierarchical relation in this university, especially in my department. . . . I am not talking about my department here, but, regarding promotion, I have heard that there are many cases in which one could not be promoted because he / she was out of favour with a certain person. It seems quite common. (Interviewee B)

> Japanese is exploited as handy people to American faculties in my university, and we are not respected by them so much. . . . It is like America in the 1930's. I wonder why they are so haughty. . . . Every day is intercultural exchange. . . . In terms of status, tenure, non-Japanese, male faculties tend to behave arrogantly in my university. (Interviewee C)

> I heard that one would get a job position if he / she was well recognized and appreciated by certain people in a big research university in the western part of Japan.[124] . . . Whichever university one works for, it all depends on one's effort, unless he / she works in really bad conditions. (Interviewee F)

---

[123] Some interviewees were asked orally by the interviewer, but the same question was given to answer in the questionnaire as well. The respondents of the questionnaire and the interviewees are the same except two participants, who did not send the questionnaire back to the author.

[124] In reality, the name of university was mentioned by Interviewee F. However, it seems too specific and does not mean so much to disclose the name of university in the context of this study. Therefore, I have given a broader description of the university.

Fundamentally, I think everywhere is the same. In Japanese universities, foreign researchers are not so favourably accepted. They are welcomed as guests, but are not really welcomed in terms of working and carrying out research together, I think. In a sense, regarding hierarchy, I feel it is stricter in Germany.[125] . . . However, it is allowed in Germany to say something very important even though one is in the lower hierarchy at work. (Interviewee G)

Judging from the above comments, it is suggested that particular Japanese culture and / or communication styles do not impact academic work. Interviewee B and F refer to the relation between job promotion and human relation that it would be easier to get promoted if one is favoured by someone higher in the hierarchy. Even though there is such a tendency, it is not easy to define this as a characteristic of Japanese social relations that could influence academic working life. An interesting point raised by interviewee B regarding gender does not certainly match the cultural stereotype of Japanese people / society, which is rather defined as and related to masculinity and patriarchy (e.g., Hofstede, 1984). However, on the other hand, the following view of the relationship between gender and promotion is expressed:

> Female employees in Japanese universities have to make a lot of effort in order to work within a scheme which is male-centred. We have to play according to the rules that males established. . . . Being female is disadvantageous when [one runs in] the election of head of department [in my university]. (GD participant A)

Although the emphasis of the above comment is put on the working conditions of "Japanese universities," it might not be confined to the Japanese universities.[126] As interviewee A points out, the relationship between gender and job promotion is likely to be seen in other countries, and the points raised above generally seem to not be bounded by national peculiarity.

As for the comments of interviewee A, B, F, and G, they do not emphasize that so-called Japanese culture influences academic

---

[125] Interviewee G used to work for a couple of German universities.
[126] The data released by OECD in 2014 states that the employment rate of women who received higher education in Japan is at the lowest level among 34 OECD countries (Source: Asahi Shinbun, 10 September 2014, retrieved from http://www.asahi.com/articles/ASG996X2YG99UTIL05T.html on 28 February 2015). This may corroborate the comment of GD participant A. However, the OECD data does not match what interviewee B mentioned, as opposed to the disadvantageous condition of female academics.

work. Rather, like interviewee A and G, some clearly state that aspects of social relations including cultural aspects have little influence on academic work. Moreover, they assume that it is not so different from one country to another.

The comment of interviewee C is very unique among the other. English and Japanese languages are used as official languages in the university she refers to, and some faculty members come from the United States, due to the fact that the university was founded by Christian missionary from that country. Therefore, the working climate in the university may differ from other ordinary Japanese universities. The interesting thing is that certain types of foreign colleagues in the university have quite great influence over others, despite the fact that it is a Japanese university. It is assumed that it is unlikely that peculiar Japanese cultural and / or communication styles will be seen in such situations. Rather, it sounds as if what was being described could have been any foreign university. Interviewee C also admits that it is impossible to make consensus-building in a Japanese way, thus, we can see that the location of the university does not necessarily reflect the national culture of the location. That is to say, there might be something else that could influence academic work other than national culture or peculiar communication styles of a certain national. Judging by the comment of interviewee G, foreign employees at Japanese universities seem to be treated as guests. However, in the case of interviewee C's university, certain foreign faculties seem to have more authority over Japanese counterparts. This contrast between the comments of interviewee C and G could suggest us that it is not national culture *per se* but working climate and conditions of respective universities that could influence the academic work of people who are employed there. Then, it is understandable that most of the interviewees state that peculiarity of Japanese culture and communication style has little influence on academic work. Further, some interviewees advocate that they do not see absolute influences on academic work caused by social relations, which could not be overcome.

As a whole, the influence of social relations on academic work is little seen, and this could support the view that exploiting theories of intercultural study, particularly of essentialist approach, for analyses of academic work is less pertinent (Okamoto, 2010a). Some interviewees understand that an aspect they exemplified is born of the Japanese national culture, nonetheless, it is difficult to judge whether or not it is originated from the Japanese culture, unless the same aspects are observed in foreign settings.

Apart from the influence of national culture and particular communication style, the questionnaire asks about other aspects such as how one's position in institutional affiliation and in disciplinary association, nationality, university from which one graduated, and obtaining a PhD degree influence academic work. All who completed the questionnaire state that their position in their university and / or disciplinary associations influences their work, but the reasons / explanations for it vary. Interviewee B briefly but clearly states that her position is taken into consideration when a new research project or other academic event is planned, because the organizer of the project / event may decide to invite participants by looking at their academic background.[127] Others refer to the amount of workload and contents of work as results of influence caused by the position. For instance, interviewee E states that the quantity of work would increase when one sits in important positions in various academic associations / societies. Similarly, interviewee A mentions that there would be more and broader opportunities given to receive research funds, to publish articles / books, and to give speeches at conferences / meetings. Interviewee A provides more details of what interviewee E refers to as the quantity of work. Thus one's position in university as well as in academic associations is assumed to be an influential aspect which could decide the amount and the contents of their work.

Another common understanding of influential aspect is nationality / native language. It is obvious that those who point out such an aspect presuppose work situations which involve interactions with foreign counterparts. As often referred to, it is not very common that Japanese academics especially in SSH are proficient in English or other foreign languages. They may be able to read, but the number of Japanese academics who could communicate in foreign languages is still limited. Therefore, if one is capable in foreign languages, especially in English, there would be more international academic opportunities to participate in

---

[127] Interviewee B also includes the aspect of obtaining a PhD degree as influential aspects over academic work.

(Interviewee A). Reversely, interviewee C refers to Japanese language as a mother tongue. Considering that the university she works for accepts English and Japanese as official languages, interviewee C focuses more on the fact that she is a native Japanese speaker. This aspect also increases the amount of work for her as being bilingual, compared with her foreign counterparts who do not speak Japanese. Although this is an unusual case in Japan, it seems to have the same influence on work as that some Japanese academics are proficient in English. That is, there would be more work opportunities and / or workload if one could command foreign languages.[128]

Interestingly, more advantageous influences such as more opportunities and favourable work conditions are mentioned in the questionnaire research, while some disadvantageous aspects are raised in the interview research. Nevertheless, a commonality between the responses in the questionnaire and those in the interviews is that the respondents emphasized little about any peculiar cultural and communication aspects in Japan. In the interviews, gender / other human relation and job promotion is the most frequent issue as an influential aspect over academic work. Some suggest that it is the Japanese peculiarity; however, it seems to be a matter of extent to which such mentioned phenomena are seen in Japan and in other countries. We will have to wait for future studies in other countries to see whether the above-mentioned aspect is confined to Japanese setting or not. In the questionnaire, on the other hand, issues of positions and native language / nationality are raised. These two are considered as influential aspects which could increase opportunities and quantity of academic work. Again, emphasis on Japanese peculiarity in them is little seen. Therefore, it is anticipated that the aspects explored about social relations in academic work have little to do with peculiarity of Japanese academics in their academic work.

---

[128] In the case of interviewee C, Japanese language can be considered as a foreign language to her foreign colleagues. Therefore, foreign languages in this context do not only imply languages other than Japanese.

7. Discussion of the Case Study

7.1 Japanese Universities and Higher Education Policies in Japan

Roles of universities and expectations towards them are introduced and interpreted through the data analysis. It is found that there are three different types of universities in Japan, and that they have diverse missions, roles, and aims, which are either set up by universities themselves or allocated by HE policies. Since they seem to impact on academic work, it is relevant to look further into details of HE system and of HE policies in Japan. In this section, therefore, the overview and the structure of universities in Japan will be observed together with the situation of HE in Japan, which could be also an influential factor in the nature of Japanese universities. Then, different roles among them, which are allocated to due to the previously introduced structure, will be discussed. Simultaneously, some examples of political initiatives which underlie this structure of universities in Japan will be exhibited.

7.1.1 The Structure of Universities in Japan

Although the word *university* is applied to more than seven hundred Japanese HEIs, it has become clear from the outcome of the empirical study that respective universities play rather different roles which are the responses to missions and aims they set up and / or are provided by HE policies. Broadly speaking, in Japan, there are national, municipal, and private universities, and the total number of them are 781 as of 2014. The number of universities informs us that Japan has entered the status of mass or even universal level of HE,[129] which means almost half of around eighteen-year-old population enters the HE system (Amano, 2006:

---

[129] As of 2013, the rate of population advancing to universities was 49.9 percent (MEXT, 2013: 4). It will lessen, due to the low birth rate of the country. The border line between mass and universal level is said to be fifty percent of the above rate (Amano, 2006: 186). Considering that this rate was only three to four percent before the Second World War (ibid.: 185), the drastic change of the educational situation in Japan can be understood.

186). At a glance, it looks like that Japan generates highly academically qualified people, however; the high rate of advancement to HE does not necessarily secure the high academic quality of those people. It is because there is a large number of universities available, regardless of academic levels. In other words, one can be called as a university student even though one has quite low level of academic achievement before entering the university, while another is also a university student who has a good record of academic achievement, thus studying at a top / research university. As seen in the data analysis section, the Japanese HEIs are structured as the image below:

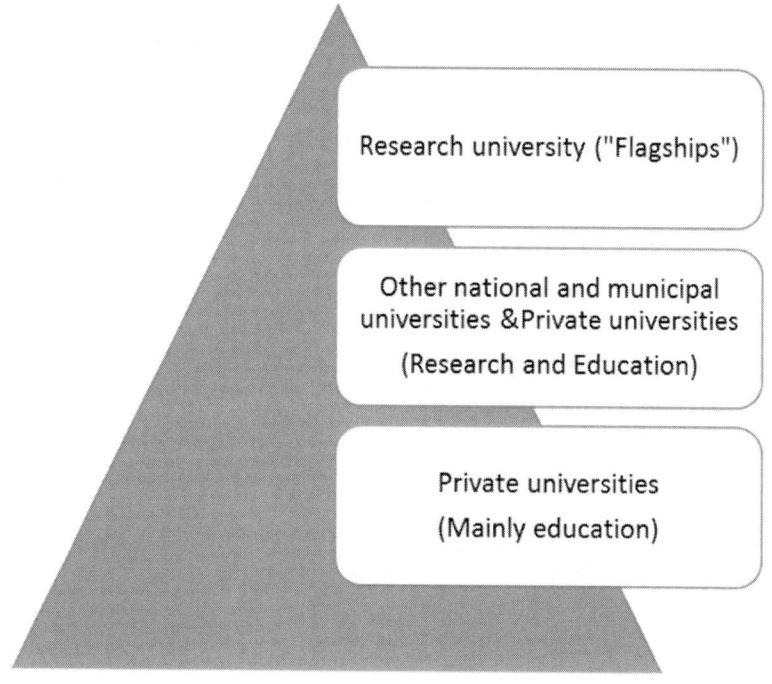

Image X: An Overview of Structure of Universities in Japan

The lower in this pyramid, the lower the academic level of university will be. As expressed as "high-schoolization of university" by some research participants in the interviews, the academic level of students seems to have been deteriorated. Thus, under the same label of 'university student' and / or 'university', the academic level of respective students / universities is quite heterogeneous.

7.1.2 Different Roles and Definitions of Universities

It is, then, natural that there is a certain division of labour among the universities with their different abilities, characteristics, and aims. As the image X above indicates, the peak of the hierarchy is the research oriented university, and as one goes towards the bottom, it would be more likely to be education oriented. Further, contents of research seem to have different characteristics, based on the above structure model of universities in Japan. For instance, GD participant A refers to the quality of research in the fields of social science in Japan, relating to diverse nature / characteristics between national / municipal universities and private universities:

> Although national universities take a form of 'national university corporation',[130] I think it is an environment that we could carry out research without considering making profit by research. On the other hand, private universities are made for 'private customers', and consequently, they tend to create more pragmatic knowledge or even shallow skills [through research they carry out]. (GD participant A)

This comment provides an image that national universities can carry out research that does not necessarily adhere to demands of the working world. On the other hand, research carried out by private universities may tend to be attached to interests of certain groups of people, who could influence management and / or benefit of universities. Therefore, the above research participant uses the notion of "private customers," and implies that such knowledge generated for private customers can end up with being pragmatic, and that it is not even entitled to as knowledge but as

---

[130] At the beginning of the twenty-first century, there was a university reform in Japan. As one of the main parts of the reform, national and municipal universities became 'corporations', which allow individual universities more autonomy in management, salary increase and promotion, and involving non-academic experts in decision making process. For national universities, the reform was enforced in 2004. (MEXT website, n.d. available on http://www.mext.go.jp/a_menu/koutou/houjin/03052704.htm) Before the enforcement of the law, national universities were operated directly by the MEXT with the 'top-down' system in a broad sense of university management in general.

mere skills. The notion of "private customers" indicates that the university reform in Japan has also brought a big change to the general role of HE / HEIs, which can be seen as a consequence of implementation of New Public Management into the HE system. This division of labour in research activity between national and private universities seems quite important, because about 80 percent (about 2.2 million students) of all university students in Japan are enrolled in private universities , and about twenty-two thousand academics are employed by them (MEXT website on roles of private universities, n.d.). Particularly, considering the fact that the proportion of SSH departments in private universities is higher than NST, and the number of SSH academics in private universities is overwhelmingly larger than those in national universities (ibid.), it is important to look into profiles of private universities such as their roles both in education and in research. Generally, such implications which roles of private universities in Japan can suggest with regard to research and educational activities seem to have been overlooked in discussions of academic work, especially those at the national level. Consequently, looking at only academics working at research universities will provide us with the very limited view of academic work in Japan, particularly in SSH fields. For instance, if the category of research universities (so-called flagships) in the above model contains only a couple of private universities, it means that we only look at the limited number of national universities, and that we generalize something about HE in Japan out of barely about 1 percent of the total number of Japanese universities. Although the research universities may be considered as the representative form of universities in one country in discussions regarding research activities, the situation which should not be forgotten is that "there is a great number of academics working at private universities, who have quite high achievement in research; however, their potential is not sufficiently exploited" (translation of my own, ibid.), due to the lack of funds for investing in research facilities, different national funding scheme, and difficulties in making a base / bases for research among private universities (ibid.). Even though academics working at private universities are less visible than those who working at national / research universities, this does not mean that they do not have to be involved as the object of discussions with regard to research activity. Because private universities and academics working for them certainly form the majority group of the Japanese academics, especially in the SSH fields, then, impacts coming from them on any research and educational activities are not to be overlooked.

With this background of HE in Japan, as GD participant A mentions, the contents of knowledge generated in respective universities play significant roles in discussions about which type of universities influence what kind of knowledge that is generated. That is to say, if the structure of the Japanese university and the shift of knowledge contents are considered, it can be stated that the majority of knowledge generated by academics in Japan seems to be more pragmatic than abstract and grand. GD participant A indicates her concern that the contents of knowledge generated by social science academics in Japan would be directed towards and limited to pragmatic aspects of social phenomena in Japan. She states that it might cause a deterioration of academic knowledge in the fields of social sciences in Japan. As a response, GD participant D suggests:

> In the current situation of HE in Japan, there seems a separation that some carry out academic research and others do research in more practical fields. In any occupation, there is a hierarchy that some limited people make a fundamental grand strategy for their business and the employee of the company will put the strategy into practice. It is all this division of labour. Within such a system, knowledge is very important at a certain level, but more practical aspects are more important at the lower level. Knowledge-based society consists of this big hierarchy, therefore, the meaning of 'knowledge' will be different, dependent on which place in this hierarchy one is working.

In other words, it is the inevitable phenomenon that the above-mentioned division of labour is seen in the universities as places of generation of knowledge.

7.1.3 Political Influence on Being of University

In fact, recent movements in HE policy and political initiatives in Japan seem to try to accelerate this division of labour. Enumerating some, there is a programme that aims at shifting some universities from their current position to one that is more attached to and collaborative with local administration.[131] Although the applicants can be any types of university, including national universities, a clear intention of reorganization of a part of universities in Japan by providing them a new role, or rather, by emphasizing one of the roles of universities, which is contribution to society, can be seen. Naturally, being close to a local community can influence the contents of education and of research, because topics they teach and research would be more likely to be confined in the context of the local community. It does not necessarily mean that they cannot play any other roles than being a university for a local community, however; judging from the impact of this type of university on academic and educational activities of the university, it is also more likely that they will be, to some extent, fixed as this new type of university, once they join the programme.

Similarly, though it is not yet put into practice, a suggestion was made by a governmental body called the Education Rebuilding Executive Council in March, 2015 that universities in Japan which have been inclined to curricula with academic subjects require a reform towards fostering human resources that can be an immediate contribution to industries in Japan (Nikkei online on 5 March 2015). Moreover, the council members suggested in an earlier meeting that not all universities in Japan have to be 'mini University of Tokyo', and that differentiation of university functions / roles should be promoted (ibid.). These suggestions and opinions from the above-mentioned council can be interpreted

---

[131] The programme is called "Chi no kyoten (地（知）の拠点)", which can be translated as "Base of knowledge," and commenced in 2014. The programme put great emphasis on collaborating with the local administration and working for local community where a university is located. For the application of this programme, applicants are supposed to suggest a plan / plans to introduce a new curriculum and innovation of organization, which would make applicant universities an educational and research organization that deals with issues concerning the local community as well as fostering students as human resources that is useful for the local community. Equipping with such systems and study programme / curriculum may change the type and the characteristics of a university from, for instance, the traditional academic type of university which focuses on research and education to a new type that is rooted in the local community to deal with local concerns and interests. Details of the programme are available on the MEXT website (MEXT, January 2014): http://www.mext.go.jp/component/a_menu/education/detail/__icsFiles/afieldfile/2014/01/28/1343326_0 1_1.pdf

to mean that more universities would be transformed in near future into educational organizations that teach students practical work knowledge and skills. The notion from the member that not all universities have to be 'mini University of Tokyo' seems to express the similar, if not the same, intention as the aforementioned "Base of knowledge" programme. That is, the majority of universities in Japan should contribute to fostering human resources which will contribute to development and innovation of Japanese industries than trying to teach students traditional academic disciplinary knowledge, which is less useful in practical work situations in the non-academic settings.[132] Under the name of 'diversified roles of universities', differentiation of university functions would be further promoted, and, as a result, a small number of universities would remain as 'university' where academic / disciplinary knowledge is generated and taught.

While middle and lower level of universities are to be asked to play a role of organization that would foster employable and productive people in industries and local communities in Japan, top level universities are provided a way to promote academic knowledge with which they can compete with their foreign counterparts. In 2014, a new funding programme, named "Top Global University Project" was introduced.[133] The aim of the funding programme is stated as follows:

> The Top Global University Project is a funding project that aims to enhance the international compatibility and competitiveness of higher education in Japan. It provides prioritized support for the world-class and innovative universities that lead the internationalization of Japanese universities. Selected universities are expected to press forward with comprehensive internationalization and university reform. (MEXT, September 2014)

---

[132] This attempt by the government to reform universities in Japan started around the 1990s. According to Inoki (2009: 124), the pressure on universities in Japan from industries to foster and provide employable people for immediate contribution to them ruined the education of liberal arts subjects such as philosophy, literature, and history in Japan. This reform regarding the liberal arts education has been discussed and often accused of among Japanese academics (e.g. Hayashi, 2004; Amano, 2006; Murakami, 2010).

[133] In an English document released by MEXT, the name of the programme is stated as "top global university project." However, in other documents in Japanese, the name is "super global university project." I follow the English name of the project in this thesis to avoid any confusion that they are different funding programmes.

There are two different categories for the funding: Type A is named as "Top Type" and Type B is as "Global Traction Type." Type A, as the name suggests, is expected to play the most important role as the representative of Japanese universities, and therefore, they are aimed at being ranked "in the top 100 in world university rankings" (ibid.). Needless to say, Type A universities are not expected to play the roles of the above-mentioned types of universities, which provide local communities and industries in Japan with people who could work in those confined settings. Rather, they are expected to concentrate on competing with universities of foreign countries as research universities. Thus, the aim is very straightforward that the Japanese research universities should be more competitive in the world of science at the global level. Type B, on the other hand, does not seem to be given such a significant role, compared to Type A universities; nonetheless, they are expected to "lead the internationalization of Japanese society" (ibid.), which is one of the prioritized political issues. Although it is not clearly mentioned, internationalization, which is the aim of Type B, can imply enhancement of competitiveness of Japan by collaboration with foreign universities such as building a joint degree system, increasing foreign faculties and students, and providing more lectures in English. Therefore, both types of this funding programme fundamentally aim at intensification of international competitiveness of Japan in and through scientific knowledge. The total annual budget of this programme is 7.7 billion Japanese Yen (ca. 600 million euros) for around thirty projects.[134] The total number of successful applicants for this programme (for the both types) is equivalent in only 3 to 4 percent of total number of Japanese universities. In other words, it is considered by the government and the bureaucracy that a limited number of universities is sufficient to play this type of role as HEIs, and that such universities are worth concentrating on spending the national budget to achieve the national aim of enforcement of international competitiveness of the Japanese academia.

Thus today's universities in Japan are not only classified by the type of university such as national, municipal, and private, but also by the aforementioned governmental initiatives / policies which

---

[134] For the year 2014, 37 universities were successfully granted the fund for this programme.

attempt to lead the universities in different directions by providing project funds and / or by establishing a new standard of university. The implication of recent governmental initiatives is that moulding respective universities into the above types as top global, adhesion to local society, and generation of employable human resources for industries could change the essence of the university. Though the priority in each university is diverse, the essence of the university in Japan has been research, education, and contribution to society, and all those activities have been carried out with different balance, dependent on the type, missions, and aims of respective universities. The division of labour between different types of university, as GD participant D notes, has certainly existed, nevertheless, this division of labour does not mean that each university is moulded into one certain type and should be specialized in particular academic activities such as fostering employable people. Even though some universities have such a tendency to focus on teaching more practical knowledge and skills than academic / disciplinary knowledge, this tendency did not restrict each academic person working for them to pursue academic / disciplinary knowledge. In other words, it has been the different balance between research, education, and contribution to society that respective universities intentionally set up, and it does not imply specialization in one of them. If this balance each university selected influences and results in academic quality / level of its academic employee, and vice versa, a hierarchy between universities as well as academics would inevitably emerge. Regarding this hierarchy among academic researchers, Hayashi proposes an interesting account:

> In any fields of profession, a professional community does not consist of only the first-class people. If you imagine such a community as a form of pyramid, the only limited number of the first-class people occupies the peak of the pyramid. The rest of the community members, who is the majority, occupies the middle and the bottom part of it. Naturally, the same could be said about the academic / scientific community. However, one thing should be remembered that it is this majority of academics who support the whole pyramid and contribute to the formation of the community. (translation of my own, Hayashi, 2004: 155)

Hayashi admits that there is such a hierarchy in academic work, nonetheless, his emphasis is placed on the point that all members of the academic community, regardless of the class, make certain contribution to maintain the community. He continues that it is important to be conscious of one's own position and roles as a member of academic community in order to fulfil his / her responsibility for the entire community (ibid.: 156). That is, it is incorrect to consider that only the first-class academics can make important contributions to the development of academic knowledge, because it is also important to carry out research on topics which the first-class academics may overlook. Then, such research carried out by non-first-class academics would have significance in terms of contribution to development of academic knowledge.

However, the aforementioned recent governmental initiatives seem to have a different emphasis from the division of labour which Hayashi (ibid.) mentions. While the latter indicates the different levels of academic contribution, all of which is vital to form a particular academic / disciplinary community, the former is intended to separate the academic work for different aims which government set up. Especially, the attempt for differentiation of university function towards education of pragmatic knowledge and skills could put at risk the fundamental philosophy of universities, and consequently, some or even many universities might become organizations for vocational education in near future. It is assumed that the differentiation of universities in Japan could also mean differentiation of work of academic people, because, as observed in the empirical part of this study, the nature / characteristics of the university for which one works could be a decisive factor in the way he / she carries out academic work.

In this section, I have focused on depicting heterogeneity of universities in Japan, which is based on the roles of respective universities. Research, education, and contribution to society are the essential missions of universities in Japan. However, which mission is most emphasized in each university depends on the kind of university it is (national, municipal, or private) and the political initiatives the nation state directs at the universities. In both cases, the role and mission of universities are likely to be decided directly or indirectly by HE policies and political initiatives on HE. In this sense, 'autonomy' or 'freedom' in academic work, as a part of discussion of university governance, seems to be an illusion. Even though individual academics could still obtain their freedom and autonomy to carry out academic work, it is a limited autonomy within the context of academic work already decided and allocated to by the interests of nation state. This differentiation of universities could imply differentiation of academic work, and as a result, the academic profession in the future may consist of different occupations such as researcher, teacher, and those who work for a local society with academic approaches. To a certain extent, therefore, the differentiation in academic work among academics in Japan can be observed as a consequence of differentiation of university functions. Thus, in the following section, ways in which academics in Japan perceive themselves under this particular working circumstance will be discussed.

7.2   Self-Perception of Academics in Japan

'Working at a university' tends to be considered as the same anywhere around the world. If you come across a Japanese academic person at an international conference, you may unconsciously imagine that this Japanese academic is more or less similar to academic people in your country, working at university that you know from your own country's setting. However, as seen in the previous part of discussion of Japanese universities, Japanese universities may look different from what you know as universities, and the circumstances under which Japanese universities exist may not also be as identical as ones you have been familiar to. Consequently, people working at Japanese universities, therefore, may be someone that you have never imagine them to be. The academic profession and / or academic people appear to be quite identical throughout the world when reading through literature on them (Boyer, 1994; Altbach, 1996; Marginson, 2000; Shattock, 2001; Lechuga & Altbach, 2006; Teichler & Höhle, 2013). Certainly, they are, to some extent. Especially, if only those who are 'working at a research university' in various countries are the subject of the topic. However, it is not necessarily always academic people working at research university that participate in international conferences, events, and international research projects. There are committed academic researchers who work at less research oriented universities, and they would also participate in international academic work. Given that there are more than seven hundred universities in Japan, describing and discussing only academic people from research universities seems insufficient for discussion of international academic collaboration, though such confined perspectives would be also interesting and undoubtedly important.

Some interesting aspects relating to identities of Japanese academic people emerge in the findings of the empirical study. Therefore, discussions will be deployed in this section about the following points. First, the discussion will focus on the perception of themselves as academics. In the findings section of the academic environment, the perception of academics in society is explored, but it does not ask who they think they are. At the beginning of this study, academics were defined as those who carry out research in connection with knowledge generation activity. This was a taken-for-granted view of people working at universities, and this view will be scrutinized in this part. Second, reasons why they see themselves as they have described themselves above will be studied. There should be grounds for the description of themselves, and it will be meaningful to understand why they consider themselves what they are. After studying the reasons for their self-perception, other background factors which can influence their self-perception will be examined, in order to understand not only the subjective accounts of academics for their self-perception, but also what makes them perceive themselves in the ways they expressed. As a result, the entire picture of their self-perception will emerge, and from this will flow applications to other academic settings for future studies on topics that can share similar perspectives to that of this study.

7.2.1 Who Are You? : Self-Perception of Japanese Academics

First of all, careful attention should be paid how academic people working at university are conventionally understood and defined. According to Arimoto (2008), the academic profession is defined[135] as "professors, associate professors, lecturers, and research associates working at university, who are dedicated to a

---

[135] Though Arimoto defines academic profession as follows, he states that it is not easy to make an intensive definition of it, due to other precedent studies on academic profession. Therefore, the definition does not seem to be exclusive, but other diverse definitions could exist in different research contexts.

disciplinary field, engaged in academic activities, and obtain a peculiar culture" (translation of my own, ibid.: 14).[136] He elaborates more about the definition of the academic profession and enumerates some representative characteristics of academic profession.[137] He firstly asserts that the academic profession is not merely the teaching staff at a university but a profession which relates to a long-term experience of teaching, disciplinary knowledge, social authority, and high level of academic productivity. He claims, as the second point, that work related to the academic profession consists of and is based on knowledge (ibid.: 14–15). From these two characteristics, Arimoto understands the academic profession as a highly specialized occupation in which knowledge is placed at the centre. He even states that it is not a mere teaching job, although he simultaneously admits involvement in teaching experiences as a part of the profession. In other words, the academic profession is defined as a profession which is organized around and related to academic knowledge. This perception almost matches the perception of the academic work in this study. Therefore, as seen in the structure of the investigation, the role and implication of academic knowledge are given significant emphasis, and academic people are considered and dealt as people who work for the generation and dissemination of academic knowledge.

However, it became apparent through implementation of the empirical study that this perception did not necessarily coincide with the perception of research participants working in the "academic profession" as defined above. In the analysis regarding the role of academics in society, some participants mentioned that they were seen as rather "teacher / *sensei*" than academic researchers / scholars. Although this is the perception from the public, this seems to also reflect their own perception of

---

[136] It is not very apparent what Arimoto (2008) means with the expression of "culture." Judging from other parts of the text, he seems to suggest that there are diverse ways of working, norms, and working climate in respective academic disciplines (ibid: 15). Therefore, it can be assumed that he means disciplinary cultures, which Becher and Trowler (2001: 23-24) also define culture in academic work in a similar manner.

[137] The third and the fourth characteristics seem less relevant in the context of the topic here, and are not introduced in detail.

themselves. While some participants have quite a firm perception that they are academic researchers, others disagree with this view:

> I think it is difficult in Japanese universities to consider ourselves as academic researchers. . . . The pressure that we have to render students employable in four years is so strong, and we have to take most of working time towards this aspect. (GD participant A)

This participant further explains that 70 to 80 percent of her routine working time is occupied by teaching and administrative work such as meetings and paper work. This is the aspect analysed in both academic environment and academic practice. The proportion of teaching and administrative work is much bigger than research. Therefore, the above GD participant A points out that it is impossible to carry out research if one prefers not to work on weekends. It does not seem to her personal experience, but another person in the interview mentions the exact thing:

> It is about one month [pausing for thinking], in total, one and a half months per year that I can really concentrate on my own research. It might have something to do with my ability, but research requires a certain block of time, and I cannot say that I do any research work during weekdays. (Interviewee B)

The amount of time for research interviewee B suggests is the time that she is away from the university. That is, she uses her holiday period to carry out and concentrate on research. She also mentions that people working at Japanese universities which are not classified as an "elite university" are working like her in respect of research work. It is yet uncertain whether the proportion of working time really influences the perception of themselves; however, there is an interesting observation about the perception of academic people's identity:

> Words such as *researcher* and *academic profession* do not necessarily seem to be the words which [Japanese] university professors in the fields of SSH are familiar with. It seems to me that there are many of them who understand their occupation as educational or scholarly job; nonetheless, there are relatively few people who recognize that the central part of their job is researcher. (translation of my own, Hayashi, 2004: 60)

Hayashi also notes that the terms of researcher and academic profession in Japan are normally understood as and used for researchers in NST, those who engaged in fieldwork in social research, and employee at think tanks (ibid.). Indeed, GD participant A used to work for a think tank before acquiring a position at university, and notes a similar difference in her self-perception between working at university and working for a think tank. Given that a person who has experienced both occupations notes such a change of self-perception, it may be generally a common perception that SSH academics working at Japanese universities less often consider themselves as academic researchers. This means that working at a Japanese university is not a synonym of being an academic researcher in terms of their self-perception.

Particularly, those who studied abroad seem to have a tendency to refer to different working conditions and circumstances as researcher between Japan and other countries as grounds for their self-perception. This may have some connection with the reference of the proportion of working time which could be spent for research. For instance, interviewee B started the interview with the following comment:

> When thinking of doing research in Japan, the first obstacle is that we have too little time to dedicate to research. . . . Compared to researchers abroad, time and energy spent for research is too little [in the Japanese academic setting]. That is the biggest barrier for me. (Interviewee B)

Reinforcing this view, GD participant A recalls:

> In the country I studied as a postgraduate, they can spend so much time for research that I agree to call them as researcher. In fact, researchers abroad seem to have a proper pride in being researcher. However, if one tries to get a job at a Japanese university with the same attitude and pride as I have just mentioned, as researcher, he / she will fail to do it. Therefore, I think that working at a university that European or American people imagine is different from working at a university in Japan. (GD participant A)

Both of them obtained their PhD degree from universities of English-speaking countries. While they emphasize the observation that academic people working in those countries could spend more time on research than their Japanese counterparts, interviewee B points out the more rigid working conditions of being a researcher abroad:

> The pressure for research work in countries I know is much stronger than in Japan. Although I only know working conditions as a researcher in some other countries, it is like "you must write a certain number of academic articles per year, of which a certain number should be refereed, and then you should publish a book within a certain period. Otherwise, you will be fired!" This is not uncommon [in those countries]. Given that, therefore, they are very much proud of being a researcher. That is so different [from us]. (Interviewee B)

Thus it is not only the amount of time but also the expectation, or even obligation, towards researchers that seems to make for a different identity of academic people in other (English-speaking) countries from Japan. As seen in the section about national research funds (*kakenhi*), Japanese academics are also encouraged by universities to apply for the national funding programme(s). However, it must be remembered that it is nothing more than encouragement, not the condition for obtaining the job position at university. Although there certainly is an annual merit rating for respective academics in all universities, if one has already got a tenure position, it is most unlikely that he / she would lose the position because they were not successful in getting national funds. Needless to say, as far as SSH fields are concerned, publishing in international refereed journals is less common among Japanese academics.[138] Besides, there seems no definite research obligation for them. Interviewee B mentions this point that Japanese academics do not necessarily do research work, due to the condition that not doing research work would not deprive them of the job position. Thus, to review my findings, for those who are willing to carry out research, they feel that they are not given sufficient time for research, because of other commitments at university. Therefore, they find it difficult to call themselves researchers. Consequently, they tend to define themselves as teachers at a university rather than researcher. At the same time, it should be noted that there are people working at universities in Japan who do not commit to research so much. In this case, it is

---

[138] It is not confined to international refereed journals, but it has been an issue that academic work carried out by SSH academics in Japan is less visible from outside of Japan. JSPS released a report on internationalization of SSH in Japan in 2011, and the report also refers to this point. The concluding part of the report points out that there are few incentives for Japanese SSH academics to publish in English (JSPS, 2011: 206).

not surprising that they consider themselves teachers rather than researchers.

Kano (2008) states that Japanese academics used to be research oriented until late 1980s, and seeks causes for the shift from research to teaching / education in the academic profession in Japan. He explains that the Japanese policy of HE / HEIs around the last couple of decades of the twentieth century changed the content of work of academics. That is, a series of governmental reports critiquing the academic profession was released by the university council, which is a part of the MEXT. Especially, a report released in 1998 put an emphasis on roles that academics should play as teachers, because the Japanese academics then were still seen by policy makers / bureaucracy as too research oriented, despite the changes around HE in Japan such as massification of Japanese HE and diversification of demands from university students. Kano points out, as a result of those governmental reports, referring to how Japanese academics were rendered more as teachers than researchers,

> Firstly, it was "target of achievement" [to shift from research oriented to teaching oriented], then it was "obligation to achieve," and finally, by means of laws and systems, it became really obligatory. This process resulted in binding activities of academics strongly. (translation of my own, 2008: 49)

Accordingly, an evaluation system for academics was gradually introduced to respective universities (ibid.: 52), and teaching became one of the core components of the evaluation, which cannot be ignorable for academics. Certainly, the extent of the emphasis on teaching can vary from one university to another; however, Kano expresses his concern that this change in academic work in Japan led by HE policy could blur the border between secondary education teachers and the academics working at university, since the emphasis on research, which is done only by academics, has been reduced by the policy (ibid.: 60). Therefore, one can conclude that academics in Japan tend to see themselves more as teachers than researchers because of the changes in HE policy since the late 1980s. If this policy that rendered Japanese academics more teachers than researchers is a decisive factor in overall academic work, it could not be only a matter of individual academic people's effort to be oriented towards research activity. Even though some academics try very hard to remain as researchers by sacrificing their weekends and holidays, there would be a limit to do it. Thus,

> ostensibly, it looks like that we also carry out research, and there are experts here in university. However, in reality, it is the system which totally relies on individual efforts [to carry out research work]. Therefore, the part of being a researcher is gradually crushed, and it seems to me that our identity is mainly 'what subject we teach in which university'. (GD participant A)

On the other hand, this does not mean that academics in Japan totally give up aspects of researching in their working life. Despite of the above-mentioned working conditions and circumstances, there are academics who claim that they are researchers. Among them, are two types: One is academics who are rather senior and established in terms of their status. They seem to take for granted that people working at university are in any case academic researchers as well as educators. GD participant C and D express that it is incomprehensible that some academics in Japan state that they are not researchers. That is to say, being a researcher is a part of academic working life, therefore, aspects of being researcher are indispensable as academics. Thus, the fundamental understanding is that being a researcher is an unquestionable identity of academics. Nonetheless, they also point out why academics in Japan do not consider themselves researchers. For instance, GD participant C mentions that those who are committed to undergraduate education should prioritize the aspect of teaching more than research. Consequently, he concludes, they are less likely to define themselves as a researcher. This notion implies that types of education they are committed to could influence their self-perception. It is probably because undergraduate education has less of an orientation towards research,[139] while postgraduate education is more based on disciplinary expertise of those who teach, i.e., postgraduate education is more closely related an academic's own expertise and research interests. Another point is

---

[139] It is also evident from the analysis of the role of HE in Japan in the findings section. Undergraduate education in Japan seems to be more interested in generating employable human resources for the labour market. Interviewee E, for instance, states, "It is postgraduate students that I can train in a true sense of academic knowledge. Therefore, I always intended to try my best to foster them."

that identity of academic people in Japan seems to be influenced by their institutional affiliations. GD participant D explains:

> Certainly, the proportion of teaching seems to be more than other countries. . . . Unless one works for a research university, in other words, if one works for a private university, teaching would be the main part of the work. Here what I mean by 'research university' is the seven former imperial universities, the limited number of private universities such as Waseda, Keio, Jochi,[140] and Hitotsubashi and Kobe which are national universities but not former imperial ones. Those who working the above universities and playing a big role in those universities consider themselves as researchers. (GD participant D)

In other words, there is a division of labour between research universities and non-research universities, and that means the majority of Japanese universities is, more or less, a teaching oriented / prioritized type of universities. In such universities, GD participant D points out that it is not so easy to be conscious of oneself as a researcher. This point, raised by GD participant D, finds support in Hasegawa (2008: 209), stating that academics working for private universities spend more time for teaching / education, while employee of national universities spend more time for research.[141]

Also among the younger generation of academics, the willingness to remain as a researcher rather than educator persists, despite of the uneasy working conditions and circumstances as discussed above. It seems to depend on the individual motivation and preference to be researcher, especially if one does not work for a research oriented university. As an example, interviewee B expresses the following:

> When I think with which situation I would be more satisfied, I would say it is when my article appears in a major international academic journal. It may be only my self-satisfaction, but I am conscious of being a researcher. (Interviewee B)

---

[140] Jochi University is widely known as Sophia University. GD participant D uttered it in the Japanese name and the transcription tries to be true to what was said in the Japanese language. It is also to avoid any misunderstanding that it is a foreign university in the expression as "Sophia University."

[141] However, the time spent for teaching at national universities has a tendency to increase in the comparison between the year 1992 and the year 2007. Regarding the time spent for research has the tendency to reduce in both private and national universities in those fifteen years. (Hasegawa, 2008: 210)

Similarly, interviewee G notes that he is unwilling to have a bigger commitment as a member of the directorate in the disciplinary association which he belongs to. Because he considers himself as a scholar, and thinks that work other than research could hold him back from research work. Thus it seems that it is not only the working conditions but strong individual willingness to be, or remain as, researcher that could influence the self-perception of academics. In other words, although the majority of academics in Japan is seen themselves as educators rather than researchers, some struggle with the working condition which is practically and politically geared towards teaching in order to maintain the identity as researcher. Certainly, the amount of time which could be spared for research plays an important role to define what they are; however, this is not the exclusive factor that defines the identity of academics in Japan. As GD participant A points out, whether they remain as a researcher in the above-mentioned working condition, which is very much teaching oriented, depends on efforts and will of individual academics.

Indeed, the same can be true in other countries regarding the relationship and balance between research and teaching. A work by Leisyte, Enders, and de Boer (2009) discusses the exact point, and some similarities can be found in the cases of Dutch and English universities in the context of university governance. According to Leisyte et al., the introduction at universities of new public management that values productivity of organizations has created strong tensions between teaching and research. The notion of productivity is closely connected to evaluation and accountability, because productivity is measured and evaluated to indicate to public society that organizations (in this case, universities) have certain values to give to society. In the case of universities, the values given are the fostering of employable people through university education, carrying out research whose outcomes could be appreciated by not only academic experts but also (non-academic) society members, etc. Universities are confronted with evaluation by a national body such as Research Excellence Framework (REF) in the United Kingdom that is tasked with determining allocation of national research grant monies for respective universities (Research Excellence Framework, 2014).[142] Since this REF evaluation is vital for each university in the United Kingdom in terms of receiving national research grants, university management tends to put pressure on academic staff to meet REF productivity criteria. According to the above-mentioned study, teaching consequently becomes "a punishment for not producing good enough research outputs" (Leisyte, Enders, & de Boer, 2009). That is to say, if one could not prove his / her capability in research by a publication list, he / she would be given a teaching-only position. This means that the person will be excluded from research activity in his / her career at the current employer. Then, it will make sense that the research participants of this study emphasized that researchers in other (English-speaking) countries seemed to be committed to more research work than academics in Japan. Interviewee B noted that academics in those countries have more pressure / obligation in research as university employees, and she seems to have made a proper observation in this respect.

On the other hand, she assumed that they spent more time on research than academics in Japan, and this seems rather incorrect. Even though the research condition and environment looks better than the one in Japan, Leisyte and her colleagues points out that "roughly 60% of their working time goes to preparation for and teaching of classes, correcting exams, student supervision and related paperwork and meetings" (ibid.). This almost matches what the research participants in this study also estimated as the time for teaching and administrative work in their daily working life. Moreover, Leisyte et al. also found out that academics in England have to stretch their working hours even to weekends and holidays (ibid.). This is exactly the same situation that academics in Japan experience. Probably, with the comparison of the aforementioned work about teaching-research nexus in Dutch and English universities, a slight difference seems to be that it is possible and even encouraged by university administration in England to obtain external funding to "'buy-out' teaching" (ibid.) so that academics could reserve time for research. In Japan, this does not seem to be the case, and academics in Japan have no other choice but carrying

---

[142] It is formerly known as Research Assessment Exercise (RAE) in the United Kingdom. Although it was modified as REF, the major role of the organization remains the same. The activity details of REF can be found on: http://www.ref.ac.uk/ (Research Excellence Framework, 2014)

out both teaching and their own research by themselves. Instead, as mentioned earlier by interviewee B, it cannot be seen in Japanese universities that academics in SSH are forced to publish their research outcomes in order for a university to submit a good assessment application document for keeping the university in a good status in terms of getting national research fund.

What we can see from the comparison between this study and the study of Dutch and English universities is the very similar working environment for academics, regardless their locations. Although the other study does not refer to the self-perception of academics in the mentioned countries, it has become quite obvious that today's academics certainly have struggles between teaching and research. The struggles can originate from the evaluation-based system which seems to be a consequence of university reforms around the world following the practices of private corporations in making academic organizations more productive, accountable, and efficient. Thus the struggles seem to influence how academics perceive (and define) themselves.

Going back to the discussion of the case study, the self-perception of academics in Japan has been discussed from two different points of view. One account comes from a rather senior and established generation as academics. The other is from the younger generation in their forties. The former tends to more positively define themselves as researchers, as well as educators. Despite recognizing that the current working condition is unlikely to provide them with an ideal work environment for research, they seem to believe that being researcher should be a part of their academic identity. On the other hand, the latter indicates more hesitation about calling themselves researchers, mainly due to the lack of time for research work, which seems to be the consequence of a series of political decisions to render academic more teaching oriented. Although those two generations coexist in the same working condition, why do they perceive themselves differently?

Given that the form and roles of HE and universities, which are decided and defined by policies on them, could also influence academic work, it can be presupposed that the time the senior generation spent as academics or even as university students could have been in a time / era in which academics in Japan had more spare time for research with less educational and administrative work than now.[143] Therefore, although the working conditions have been gradually changed during the past twenty years or so, their working philosophy as academics is still based on the working life experiences of their prime as academics. Further, once they are established with a certain status as academics, or reached at a certain age level, the workload in teaching at undergraduate level could be less than the amount that the younger generation carries.

Reversely, the younger generation experiences a more evaluation-based style of academic work, which was introduced in the late 1990s. That is, the whole academic work is segmented as teaching, research, administrative work, and contribution to society, and academic people are evaluated for each category (Kano, 2008: 52).[144] This evaluation for academics seems almost the same as the university ranking system. Consequently, the better the evaluation result is, the better the treatment received from the university would be for academics. In such a situation, it is understandable that they have to balance these four work components. Especially if teaching is valued more than research, teaching would be the central part of their academic working life.

---

[143] There is an observation made by a Japanese academic from the field of West Asian history in the report on internationalization of humanities and social sciences (JSPS, 2011: 17). The person states that historians of the senior generation in Japan did research with quite high quality that scholars in other countries also recognize and quote this senior historian's work. It seems to him because his senior colleagues had more time for research. He state, "It was a time that the life in university was not so busy with less teaching slots, and less administrative work. Therefore, our seniors could collect various literatures from other countries and read them. To put it simply, they could devote themselves to research work. That is why they could carry out such high quality work. . . . Time is, after all, a considerably big factor [to carry out research]."(translation of my own, ibid.) Although the main focus of this statement is about the quality of academic work, it is worth noting in the context of this part of the study.

[144] According to Kano (ibid.), this is not only to evaluate respective academics working at university but also to show willingness of a university to related political / governmental bodies that they rightly follow the accreditation system that was introduced when national universities became individual corporate bodies. If the evaluation of academic people is reflected on salary and other incentives for academics, it is appreciated by the political / governmental bodies that this university effectively manages itself as a corporation. This makes the evaluation of the university higher. Therefore, the evaluation of academics as above is directly related to the evaluation of the university as well.

Moreover, contrary to the senior generation, the younger generation seems to have more teaching commitment to undergraduate education. Different from the postgraduate education, as noted in the section of the role of HE, undergraduate education in Japan has assumed great responsibility for creating employable human resources, i.e., academics are also expected to work to fulfil this responsibility by successfully sending all the graduates to available companies on the job market. This can put great pressure on academics, and as a result, they would be pulled more towards the educational work.

By and large, it can be stated that those different generations of academics seem to have different working conditions and backgrounds of academic life. Even though they are in a way contemporaries, due to the aforementioned different working conditions and backgrounds their self-perception is respectively defined in a different manner. Since this senior generation still often plays major roles in research / disciplinary activities both in domestic and international academic circles, the impact of how academics define themselves on research activities is not yet clearly seen. Nonetheless, when the younger generation starts to occupy central positions in research and / or in disciplinary activities, there may be different situations in research, given that the majority of them consider themselves to be educator. Or the segmentation of academic work may be seen among academics,[145] and it may become a reality that research work will be the work only for those who work at research universities.

Apart from the differences of self-perception in being a researcher and an educator, a notion of intellectual profession is seen from comments of the research participants. Mostly, they compare themselves with their foreign counterparts, and conclude, "Self-consciousness of being an intellectual elite that Western academics seem to have exists to much lesser extent among Japanese academics" (GD participants B). This understanding can be the consequence of what has been discussed so far, that is, the emphasis on teaching transcends research in the Japanese setting. GD participant D states that eminent Western academics are

---

[145] Kano is concerned with this point. He states, "There is a possibility that the academic profession [in Japan] would be split into two: One is only a few academics who prioritize research, and another is the majority of academic population who emphasize education." (translation of my own, 2008: 60)

intellectuals, whose existence is very distant from the public. Further, he states, those people can devote themselves to research, and teaching and looking after students are rather out of the scope of their academic activity. As an example, he refers to his own experiences that he made research trips abroad with his students. He recalls:

> It is inconceivable for Western scholars [that an academic makes a research trip with his students]. They would say to me, 'How do you dare to do that? You would not have time for your own research if you do such a thing with students.' Thus, their existence as intellectuals is really different from us, Japanese academics. (GD participant D)

Although he considers himself as academic researcher, he explains that relationships of academics, students, education, and research seem to be relatively close each other in Japan, compared with those in other countries. This closeness of Japanese academics to education and students seems to render Japanese academics someone different from Western intellectuals. However, it is not so easy to conclude and to draw a general picture of academics in Japan from this aspect, because, simultaneously, GD participant D mentions that this difference is prominent only when we compare quite prominent scholars / well-known research universities with working condition of ordinary Japanese academics. According to him, the majority of academics in any country mainly plays the role of educator in their academic life, but they struggle to carry out research while they have teaching commitments at the same time. In this sense, there is little difference in working conditions between Japan and other countries. Conversely speaking, there seems to be Japanese academics who do not take care of their students as much as others do,[146] and therefore, they are not so close to students and educational practices. Judging from this, even though the number may be smaller than that of other

---

[146] Interviewee E gives an example of a professor at the University of Tokyo as this type of academic. Instead of spending much time for teaching and taking care of students, Interviewee E points out that such academics could influence students by their own [prominent] existence and their scholarly work. The professor referred by interviewee E above may be exceptional among Japanese academics; however, it is a valuable account that such academics exist also in Japan. Otherwise, the overall impression of academics in Japan would be that all of them lead education-centred academic life.

countries, there are Japanese academics who devote more time to research than education.

All things considered, the self-perception of Japanese academics tends to be as an educator rather than researcher. This is not necessarily because they prefer to be, but the role of educator is strongly attached to them by the HE policies in Japan. It implies that the many of them are obliged to play the role of educator, while they also seek to remain an academic researcher. Since the timeframe for activities such as teaching hours, frequency of various meetings, and events / ceremonies at universities is quite fixed, time for research tends to be stretched to weekends and holiday periods, in which they are freer from routine work at the university. From comparative perspectives, some of the research participants of this study show their dissatisfaction that the working condition for research in Japan is worse than in other, especially English speaking, countries. That is to say, academics in other countries can spare more time and energy for research, because they are expected to produce concrete outcomes of their research work such as the number of publication in refereed academic journals and the number of their work being cited by others, which are not the expectation / obligation, at least for SSH academics, in the Japanese setting. Similarly, therefore, the notion of 'intellectual' in the Euro-American sense seems less applicable to Japanese academics, due to the strong emphasis of being educator. However, it is doubtful to conclude that academic work in Japan is more education-centred and academic work in other (in this context, it refers more to European and American) countries are more research-centred. As stated by some of the research participants, the limited number of academics working at research universities in Japan may perceive themselves more as researcher than educator, and the same can be said in cases of academics in other countries. Though the extent may vary, there are different roles allocated to respective universities in other countries like in Japan. In other words, not all universities in one country are research universities. There are the limited number of top research universities in each country, while there are many smaller, less research oriented universities. Given that, it is not very persuasive that only academics in Japan practice education-centred academic life against their will to be more research-centred.

Certainly, academic working life is structured and framed, based on types of respective universities, and the framework of academic working life is not necessarily designed to fulfil desire of academic people that they would like to concentrate on what they are academically interested in. What is more, not only policies on science and / or on HE influence what academics should be like, but also demands, requests, and expectations from society towards HE and universities play a certain role to form how universities and academic people should be. Thus, all those aspects above which can be bases of academic work are unlikely to be influenced or changed by individual academic people's efforts. One interviewee says, considering not only working condition for research work but also personal concerns such as family life, "there is no perfectly ideal place" (Interviewee B), since the great majority of SSH academics in Japan belongs to universities which are not classified as research universities. However, in her case, she has a firm motivation to work as researcher, though the working condition is not necessarily ideal for her as a person who would like to pursue research. Interviewee F also states that the majority of universities is not ideal, and that even though one works for a research university, it may not be an ideal place for him / her. Because working for a research university can be only a burden if one does not feel he / she has efficiency that matches to roles and expectation of the research university. What interviewee F means is that it has to be the aptitude that decides one's ideal place. For him, what is important is that one tries his / her best in the given setting with the given environment by making most of such setting and environment. From these accounts, an image of academics emerges. That is, although the place of work "decides who you are" (Interviewee F), that is, whether you are educator or researcher, it seems to be academics themselves who finally decide what they are. If one has a willingness to carry out research, he / she accordingly plans his / her academic activity even with the limited time.

Therefore, it can be concluded that the types of university where one works certainly influence the working conditions and orientation of the work he / she carries out. However, most of academics try to remain as what they wish to be, while they accommodate themselves in the given working situations. For those who know and / or witness the academic working condition of foreign countries, academics in Japan seem to be 'behind' of foreign counterparts. However, academics who could mainly lead such a research oriented life are also the limited number of the whole academic population in these countries. Unless there is a possible condition to be exempted from teaching, academics confront with dilemma between teaching for which they are employed and research for which they were trained. Since there is no other object to compare with the case of Japan, any generalized statements cannot be made. Nonetheless, this can certainly be exploited as a hypothesis for future studies.

7.3 Academic Knowledge: For What?

In the interviews and the questionnaire research, the roles and perception of academic knowledge in society and those for academics are explored, and it is found that academics perceive the role of academic knowledge as something that contributes to society / society members, fosters human resources that could lead their own lives by ability and thoughts which they develop through the HE, and advances and builds up the disciplinary knowledge. Individual aims are phrased in a various way; nonetheless, the main intention seems to be the contribution to the contemporary society, may it be academic or non-academic, with knowledge they generate. If, then, research is a main means for knowledge generation practice, it would be worthwhile to understand how the knowledge generation practice is carried out through research activity, in order to achieve the aim of contribution to society with academic knowledge. Therefore, in this section, starting from the perception of academic knowledge by academics, I will attempt to explore how academic knowledge generation is carried out in practice, what such a knowledge generation practice means for academics, and whether the original aim of academic knowledge to contribute to society is likely to be achieved.

The role and use of academic knowledge is diversely expressed by respective research participants. One may be interested in exploiting the knowledge he / she has generated as a means for improving society and / or solving problems which the society they live in currently experiences, while another may concentrate more on the contribution to the disciplinary field of which he / she is a member. In this sense, academic knowledge seems to be closely attached to the real life world, and it sounds as if these academics sought a connection between academic knowledge and pragmatic aspects of people's life. However, simultaneously, the research participants sense that knowledge generated by them is not really appreciated by society. They feel that academic knowledge is considered useless for non-academic life world. If knowledge in SSH has a value in society, it would be as trivia which relate to people's life. Thus despite academics' will to contribute to society with academic knowledge, they find the ways people in society understand academic knowledge as rather opposite to how they hope it to be. Further, it is also revealed that academics are quite negative about pragmatic exploitation of academic knowledge such as 'collaboration with industries', 'ex-business person researcher', and 'academic research attached too closely to a local administration'. It is quite common that universities collaborate with certain industries in NST research, because the both parties could supplement each other by providing what the other party does not have. That is, universities could provide companies / industries with knowledge based on academic research, and companies could provide facilities for experiments which are specialized for a particular purpose / use. It is not only facilities but also financial support that universities could expect from such university-industry collaborations. However, this collaboration style has not been popular among SSH fields.

> Academics in NST fields take for granted the university-industry collaborations. We are the generation which is strongly against such collaborations and an ideology that research is for development of Japan. (Interviewee E)

> University-industry collaborations used to be considered as wrong in Japanese universities, but now it is considered quite positive. . . . In the university-industry collaborations, knowledge is inevitably used for industry. Knowledge is, in the first place, public good, not a private substance. . . . Exploiting knowledge for profit of a private company is contradictory to the mission of universities. (Interviewee A)

What can be read from the above comments is a strong claim that knowledge should not be considered as a means for development of a particular industry and / or of a nation state. Similar uncomfortableness can be seen in a comment on academics too closely attached to a local administration. While it is noted that there are academics who respect the importance of academic research as well as being committed to a local administration, nonetheless,

> I feel very uncomfortable about notions that working with local administrations / communities as an academic is the only way to face up to social reality. (Interviewee E)

His emphasis seems also to be put on uncomfortableness about a belief that academic knowledge can be contribution to society only when it is useful in pragmatic social aspects such as solving problems which a local community is facing. As a common ground for the above-mentioned aspects, there seems to be a strong opposing view that academic knowledge and academic practice, in a broader sense, should not be utilized only for a particular purpose for a particular group of people. Then, it is a consequent reaction towards ex-business people who teach at universities as professors that "I am different from them, because they discuss things without any theoretical corroboration but only with their own experiences" (Interviewee B). That is to say, though academics work together with ex-business people, they are likely to feel incompatible with those who has no academic background, working in the academic setting. In any of these cases, it seems that utilization of academic knowledge with pragmatic approaches and pragmatic approaches that intrude into the academic space (i.e., universities) are not welcomed by academics. Judging from this point, then, it sounds like a contradiction that they have ideals to contribute to society with academic knowledge while they would like to distance themselves from aspects of the very society they would like to contribute to. Then, a question is raised: What is academic knowledge for? It is understandable that academics have their own missions and ideals about academic knowledge, including knowledge generation practice. Nonetheless, it does not become clear from the empirical research how their ideals are embodied and put into practice. Therefore, this section attempts to clarify how research, which is considered as a core part of knowledge generation activity, is practiced towards knowledge generation and dissemination activities by looking at actual practices as well as the backgrounds of them.

According to the interviews and the questionnaire research of this study, it is noted that there are two types of research: One is research considered as an academic mission of people involved in academic disciplinary practices, and the other is research for one's own career making / prestige. The former refers to a fundamental activity as academics, which is directly related to contribution to building up disciplinary knowledge. It can be stated that it is a natural and genuine intention of academics who entered the world of academe in order to pursue his / her own academic interests in a certain academic discipline. On the other hand, the latter is a type of research which is mainly based on a rather individual motivation for and interests in acquiring better credits / merits for climbing up a career ladder. Though it cannot be asserted that this type of research has no interest in contribution to disciplinary knowledge, it seems that academics, especially those of the younger generations, have a strong tendency to relate knowledge generation and dissemination activities to aspects of job promotion. This dualism is not necessarily that one person can belong to only one of these types, and one can share both types within his / her academic work. However, the emphasis on the latter type in academic work seems quite prominent. What is the background of that knowledge generation, and are dissemination activities connected to the realistic aspect of academic life? As discussed in the other sections, there is a very strong emphasis on ranking, competition, and evaluation within university. In a bigger framework of the entire HE system in Japan, ranking and other aspects which have a competitive nature are seen at the organizational level, which means the comparison is seen between universities. Nonetheless, since the ranking and evaluation among universities are measured and judged by academic productivity of members in respective universities, the individual productivity of the academic members is an important aspect for universities to compete with their counterparts in Japan. Therefore, the pressure is placed on the individual academic members to increase their productivity which is judged by the number of publication.[147] If one can successfully respond to this pressure from a university, one would be provided a reward such as better salary and better job position through the process of annual merit rating for individual academic employee. The reality in such a working situation seems so strong that one cannot simply ignore it, even though he / she does disagree with

---

[147] Evaluating one's work in SSH by the number of citation is not yet so common in Japan.

this evaluation system. It might sound exaggerated, but everything is for credits in today's academic work.[148]

Further, owing to the policy of internationalization of HE, applicants for a university job position are more likely to be successful if they can indicate their potential to make presentations and / or lectures in English and publish internationally. As an example, the following comment is provided:

> Recently, a criterion such as the ability to make a presentation in an international conference and to lecture in English is included when selecting a person for a new job position at my university. As a national university, the pressure from the MEXT is very strong, due to the internationalization policy on HEIs. (GD participant A)

Adoption of the above-mentioned criterion in employment at university is not confined to national universities, which have more direct impacts from the MEXT than private universities. Indeed, for instance, Interviewee C also points out that appreciation of ability in academic English is the standard for employment which is currently introduced to her university,[149] which is a private university. Thus, academic activities in English are gradually considered to be standard, and internationalization in this respect seems to be practiced broadly in universities in Japan.[150] However,

---

[148] The emphasis here is on research / knowledge generation practice in academic work. However, it should not be forgotten that educational work is also evaluated, more or less, in a similar manner, because, as discussed earlier, education has become more important for a number of universities in Japan.

[149] In order to understand and observe the current situation of university recruitment, I looked at some documents for job offers relating to social science subjects at four private universities. All of them required the ability to lecture in English (as well as Japanese), and three out of four required the ability and willingness to have commitment in work related to international cooperation. Thus, we could see what kind of ability is required in Japanese universities to become an academic person through such job vacancy documents. (Doshisha University, 2015: http://www.doshisha.ac.jp/doshisha/recruit.html Ritsumeikan University, 2015: http://www.ritsumei.jp/job/index_j.html Meiji University, 2015: http://www.meiji.ac.jp/koho/recruit/index.html Jochi (Sophia) University, 2015: http://www.sophia.ac.jp/jpn/info/employment all retrieved on 30 March 2015).

[150] Internationalization in this context means as adoption of English language in academic activities. Some might call it 'Englishnization', and the term of 'Englishnization' suits as a description of the phenomena that are seen in Japan as phenomena of 'internationalization'. In the Japanese context, the

in order to carry out such international academic activities, there is a big challenge that the practitioners of them should follow the conventional ways of Western, more precisely English speaking countries', academic work. That is to say, it is not only a matter of language ability but also a matter of ways to generate academic knowledge that SSH academics in Japan have to adjust themselves to the style of knowledge generation activity, especially when they wish to publish their work for foreign publications. Some find it difficult because:

> The work would be accepted in international settings only if one uses a concept which is well-known around the world. Let's take an example of the term 'society'. Concepts of 'society' could be different from one particular country to another, but we have to use one shared concept of 'society' when people from different countries join the discussion. The aspect like this is very difficult to handle. (GD participant D)

Similarly, another person states:

> Just applying a theory which is known in the U.S and Europe to study social phenomena in Japan does not necessarily work, but this is not understood from the Western academic viewpoint. On the other hand, publishing in American or European academic journals is nowadays more and more appreciated when our work is evaluated. (GD participant A)

This mismatch between application of Western theories and studying social phenomena in Japan is frequently seen (e.g., Okamoto, 2010a; Sato, 2010), and even though one could write his / her articles in English, or could translate them from Japanese into English, the theoretical challenges of rendering them suitable in English publications still remains if they are originally written based on theories and / or concepts known only in Japan.

Methodologically speaking, a similar aspect is pointed out. In international settings, providing empirical data for an article / presentation seems more important. For instance, GD participant D confirms that there is no other way to structure research and to present it but being empirical if one studies in the U.S. Concertedly,

---

notion of 'internationalization' and of 'being international' is often understood in relation to English language and / or English speaking countries.

if one received academic training abroad, he / she knows that statistics and evidence are essential in scientific research. On the other hand, there is a dilemma that statistics and evidence are not the only essential methodological factors in scientific research. . . . Therefore, when I write my articles in English, I put more emphasis on such scientific factors [i.e., statistics and evidence]. (GD participant A)

In other words, articles / presentations based on empirical research, which is mainly quantitative, seem to be more favourable in the Western academic settings than just discussing one's thoughts. Thus, there seem to be some fundamental challenges for academics in Japan in participating in international academic world beyond the foreign language proficiency of academics who are practicing these activities.

While publishing in international journals is valued in SSH in Japan, a question arises about whether publishing internationally means that the quality of work in international journals is really high. A strong critique in this respect is presented as follows:

If the field of Japanese studies is taken as an example, studies which are recognized in Japan as good quality of work are rarely known abroad. On one hand, there are academics who publish their work in English, however; the work published outside Japan is considered as bad quality [by academics in Japan]. On the other hand, the work published in English is accepted in respect of the global standard. . . . Then, I wonder what "being recognized internationally" means. . . . Does it mean that one's work with bad quality becomes the mainstream if one says it louder? (GD participant A)

This comment indicates that high-quality work, which is well recognized in Japan is often not published abroad. It is probably because such work does not satisfy the criteria as discussed above for publication in international journals. Contrarily, those who can command English and know what kind of work would be methodologically and theoretically favoured in settings of English publications are more likely to be motivated to publish in international journals, if such an academic activity is strongly encouraged at the institutional level as well as at the national level, and if it could bring them more merits / credits which would possibly make better career as academics. GD participant C mentions that there are two types of academics in relation to this point. One are academics who publish their work simply for making their way, and the other are those who believe in that their work would be a contribution to society / disciplinary fields. These two types are rarely found purely in an individual, rather these two aspects exist in each person, and the interest in and motivation for making his / her own career better can be stronger than aiming at something that does not seem to directly influence his / her academic life. Indeed, GD participant D refers to this orientation towards academic work, with regard to knowledge generation practice and publication practice in particular:

> It is like a 'knowledge factory'. If you are asked, 'Can you make something like this?', they will produce it. . . . But we cannot accuse them of doing it. There are many competitors, and in order to get a job as an academic, they would have to be able to do things they are expected. Otherwise, they may not get a job anywhere. (GD participant D)

He also mentions that academics have to think about knowledge within a bigger framework than these private motivations and perspectives. However, influences of the working condition and environment are overwhelming to carry out knowledge generation and dissemination practices. Thus, it can be stated that the evaluation criteria which have become popular in Japan, such as the number of publications and whether or not international publications and / or conference presentations were carried out, seem to pull academic work towards the intensification of those internationally related activities. Under such a circumstances, it is not a matter of individual choice but a sense of obligation that one had better fulfil those activities as much as possible to maintain or possibly promote his / her career as an academic.

Although it looks as if the academic work in SSH in Japan moved towards internationalization (or Englishnization), there is still an incorrigible situation in Japan that SSH academics are not so willing to publish their work in English, because, first, writing in English takes much more time, and publishing in an international journal requires a very long process until one's article gets published, Writing a book in Japanese can be done with the same amount of time with less work and energy; also, due to enough publication demand in Japanese language and the sufficient number of audience / readers within the country,[151] it is a difficult

---

[151] A report on internationalization of SSH in Japan which is released by JSPS (2011) also points out that there are still a number of academics in SSH who believes in academic values in publication in Japanese among respective disciplines. Behind this belief, the report states that the Japanese society

condition to cultivate motivation among SSH academics in Japan to publish outside the country. That is, there is little incentive to work internationally from the Japanese academics' perspective.[152] If the number of publications in any language counts for annual merit rating, publishing in Japanese is certainly much easier for Japanese academics. Given the working conditions in which SSH academics in Japan have to struggle to keep some time for research activity including writing academic articles and books, writing in Japanese would be, in that respect, a better compromise between the limited time for research work and acquiring merits / credits for their own job evaluation.

To summarize, although individual academics have noble and lofty ideals of academic knowledge, that is, what it is for, how it is to be used, and what it is, the practical situation is different from them. In practice, academic knowledge, or rather the productivity of academic knowledge, is used for a means of evaluation for academic work in universities in Japan. This tendency can be a consequence of the adoption of university evaluation / accreditation system and faculty evaluation in Japan, due to the university reform around the late 1990s and the beginning of 2000s. Moreover, internationalization in academic work brought the evaluation framework which is based on citation databases, and other academic publication conventions in mainly English-speaking countries. As a result, academic work, especially from the perspective of knowledge generation activity, is benchmarked by the number of publications, which urges today's academics to publish more. As for the contents / styles of knowledge generation practice, the mainstream seems the problem-solving type of research with empirical data, which is easy to understand with quantitative data, and this type of research seems particularly favoured when the audience of the research is international. It is probably because quantitative data does not necessarily require logical explanation and understanding by a language but 'evidence' by numerical data, which seems to a number of academics to be indisputable when such evidence is shown by graphs and tables

---

obtains proper quality of academic work and moderate number of audience for such publications (ibid.: 202).

[152] As a comparison, GD participant D states that Korean academics whose work is published in well-known international journals or by a prestigious publisher would be given a great amount of money as a reward.

with numbers. Thus, standardization of academic knowledge generation practice is advanced, and the phenomenon can be explained as globalization of academic work, and of academe in the world. On the other hand, some research participants suggest that style of academic work in Japan would not be totally changed towards this standardized type of work, because there seems to be a big enough demand and a market for academic work in the Japanese language within a country and also academics believe that the Japanese peculiar style of research and research dissemination activity would be obtained as ever before, due to the academic relevance towards Japanese academics. Indeed, a certain group of SSH academics, particularly those who studied abroad and obtain academic degrees, may join the standardized type of academic work, because they may have been studied and trained in this very standardized style of academic work as a norm. Simultaneously, universities which are classified as research university (top global university) would also have stronger orientation towards the standardization of knowledge generation practice. However, given that the rest of the universities in Japan do not have a role to play in the international academic scene, it would also be understandable that they keep the conventional Japanese way of academic work in terms of knowledge generation practice, unless members of those universities are individually motivated and / or interested in the standardized type of academic work. In other words, while standardization of knowledge generation and dissemination practice, owing to the internationalization of academic work, would be advanced, there would be academic people and organizations which remain as the conventional style of those above-mentioned practice in a country, since there seems to be little incentive to shift their work towards internationalization. In both styles, the number of outcomes of knowledge generation practice, which are publications, are valued as a means of evaluation of academic work. As the emphasis of the number of publication (and of being cited in the international sphere of academic work) is so strong, academics have busied themselves in publishing as much as possible and have filled their curriculum vitae with them. One research participant calls it as "knowledge factory" whose image is that knowledge is spit out continuously by academic people for their own sake, not for the advancement of academic knowledge, in most cases. (Further, even if they are asked to research something that they are not originally interested in, they would try to respond to the request of their 'client'.) Although, originally, academics would like to make contribution to society and / or the academic circle that they belong to by knowledge they generate, it seems that today's knowledge generation practice is strongly influenced by competition. If not the competition, it seems to be used for making one's evaluation at university look better. This use of academic knowledge generation practice as a means of academic evaluation is far away from what academics would like to do with academic knowledge. However, once they come to a point of career in which they are established, senior academics, they seem to be able to leave this competition and pursue the original aims by knowledge generation practice. That is, today's academic work is strongly connected to and constructed as the results oriented system, and it is when academics become mature, established, and senior that they are able to pursue their ideals to make contribution to society and / or the discipline with knowledge generation practice. This could imply that most of the life as an academic would be spent in competition, which is only quantitatively judged. Although such a type of evaluation for academic work is questioned by some academics who doubt that the number of publication guarantees the 'quality' of work, this competition would continue unless other evaluation framework is introduced.

7.4 Towards International Collaborations

Similar to the structure of the analysis of academic work, which is classified as academic environment and academic practice, discussing perspectives of different parties requires the arrangement of level of perspectives. Therefore, in this section, perspectives of international collaboration are respectively discussed from the national and political perspective and the academics' perspective. After each of those perspectives is discussed, how those diverse perspectives could take effect in international collaborative work with regard to knowledge generation practices will be understood.

7.4.1 National Perspectives of International Collaborations

In the case of Japan, multi-national / international collaborations are urged to strengthen and develop knowledge generation practices by multiplier effect of collaborations between excellent academic researchers from different global regions. It has been scarce in Japan to find a national initiative towards international collaborations in SSH. JSPS recently launched a new funding programme specialized in the social sciences to encourage academics in Japan to carry out joint research with European countries, which are France, Germany, the Netherlands, and the United Kingdom, by joining the existing funding programme of "Open Research Area for the social sciences (ORA)."[153] Since it is still in the selection process of applications, which universities are selected, what kind of research projects they are, and the amount of the rewarded fund are yet unknown. Nonetheless, judging from the above-mentioned political initiative of the Top Global University programme, the intention of this ORA programme seems to be funding research projects whose application were submitted by universities that have a potential for such international projects, i.e., capability in carrying out research in English, existence of institutional administrative support for international academic work, and having global academic connections with foreign universities,[154] among other things. Such potentials are applied to the European counterparts under the notion of that "some of *the best research* can be delivered by working with *the best researchers* internationally" (the emphasis by the author, The French National Research Agency, n.d.). Thus, this project, from both the Japanese and the European sides, is to be the collaborations between not any researchers but the best researchers of respective countries. As already discussed in relation

---

[153] The funding programme is "an agreement between the Agence Nationale de la Recherche (ANR, France), Deutsche Forschungsgemeinschaft (DFG, Germany), the Economic and Social Research Council (ESRC, UK) and the Nederlandse Organisatie voor Wetenschappelijk Onderzoek (NWO, Netherlands)" (The French National Research Agency website, n.d.) to strengthen international research cooperation between those four countries.

[154] In order to submit a project application for this programme, the applications must find at least two foreign partners from the aforementioned four countries.

to the science policy, internationalization and / or international collaborations seems to connote as a means of indicating competitiveness and strength of a nation state. In this sense, therefore, it is quite natural that one or some of the universities which could be a representative of the country would be selected for such a funding programme for international collaboration. Although the word *collaboration* can give us an impression that some people / groups work together, the fundamental aim of working together from a nation state's perspective would be competing through international collaborations by showing their presence and competences in international academic work. Then, international collaborations initiated and planned by national governmental bodies are likely to exploit intellectual interests of academics by funding them, in order to achieve the above-mentioned aim of the nation state in relation to science. Although this interdependent relationship between the nation state and limited groups of academics certainly brings some benefit to academics for international collaborative work, there will be the pitfall that academics would have to respond to demands of the nation state through their work. As a result, academics involved in such a relationship with the nation state are more likely to start sharing the aim of the nation state.[155] That is, the good 'deal' between universities and the nation state is made to achieve their respective aims, and it is inevitable for universities to share the aim

---

[155] Strictly speaking, academics do not *have to* share each other's interests / aims in carrying out academic work. Nonetheless, it would be impossible to get an application for a national funding programme approved if the application does not, at least, express that the applicant share the aim of the funding programme. If we look at the funding programme of the "Top Global University," if the applicants do not put emphasis on their strong motivation to achieve the world ranking top 100 (for the "Top" type) and to enhance international aspects of their educational programmes which would match globalization of HE (for the "Global" type), they would not be selected successfully. This looks as if the applicant universities voluntarily set such aims for them; however, it is also pointed out that whether goals set up by respective successful applicant universities would be really achieved remains questionable (Mainichi Shinbun evening edition on 23 October 2014), and the highly set-up targets seems to indicate universities' desperate intention to be selected for this programme due to the attractiveness of a big amount of fund as well as the possible prestige they would receive as successful universities in Japan. In this context, they may be indirectly forced to share the aim of the nation state as a return for the benefit they receive.

Academic Culture: An Analytical Framework 251

of the nation state as a part of the 'deal' to maintain a good working relationship. A similar logic can be applied to *kakenhi* (the national research funding programme for individual and groups of academics in Japan) application.

> When selecting a research theme for a project, where we get a research fund from could influence the selection of the theme / topics. There are research themes that are likely to be approved for *kakenhi*. . . . In this sense, we are controlled. I have just said that the motivation for research is genuinely based on my own research interest, but we have to change ways of presenting research projects when we apply for the fund. . . . Despite that we claim for autonomy [as academics], we are strongly bound. (GD participant A)

Though the topic in the above comment is about the funding programme for individual research projects, it is easy to imagine that a similar, if not the same, consideration would be taken when universities apply for national funding programmes. Further, if the scope of the discussion is shifted to the type of universities, national universities tend to be influenced by the national policies on science and HE for the same reasons as discussed above.

Thus despite of diverse education systems and roles of HE / HEIs around the world, if a considerable number of countries' governments share the view on internationalization of HE and of academic work that internationalization of science is for showing the presence of the country to the world as is the case of the Japanese government, the strong emphasis of competitive aspects in academic work, represented as world university ranking, around the world is unsurprising. Rather, competitions such as the university ranking could be the ultimate form of achievement that each nation state can accept as an official evaluation of its HE as a whole to measure their competitiveness in science in the world.[156] This is the most fundamental point of what internationalization of academic work / HE means from a nation state's perspective, which should not be forgotten and ignored.

A number of SSH academics has expressed their concerns about internationalization of academic work by using terms such as

---

[156] Despite that organizations which publish such university rankings are not international organizations, rankings published by Shanghai Jiao Tong University and Times Higher Education have been used as reliable sources to evaluate universities' performance. As the case of Japan indicates, appearing in the world university rankings seems to become not only an academic achievement but also a political goal in HE policy.

inequality, hegemony, dependency, periphery, and all the other contrastive terms. However, the advocates do not notice that feeling dependent, hegemonized, etc. is a different way of agreement with the aforementioned view of the nation state on internationalization. [157] As an important evidence of it, the advocates of the skewed knowledge generation practices in the global social sciences always uses a unit of a nation or of a geographical region as a basis of analysis, as if they were representatives of their countries / regions. The starting point of such academic debates may differ from the political goal set by their national governments, nevertheless, what the both parties aim at is of little difference. Earlier, I stated that such debates are rather political than academic. It is because, although they express their views as academic debates in academic writings, the origin of the debates that they would also like to appear in the world academic publication market like 'Western' academics exactly corresponds with the above view of nation states that our country's universities should appear in the top 100 of the world university rankings. As long as debates of international academic work based on such a view continue, so-called international academic collaboration is simply a synonym with international competitions of academic work. Thus the national perspective of international collaboration is mainly based on the view that it is the global competition *through* various academic activities including international collaboration. Within this perception of international collaboration and internationalization of academic work in general, interactions between academics while working together, academic stimuli through collaborative work with foreign counterparts, and fruitfulness of such work for academics are not of its interest. Instead, outcomes and consequences of such work are everything that is required to be known. Then it is understandable that the contents and academic significance of academic collaborations which cross the national borders have rarely been discussed in the context of the national perspective. After all, only the rankings / positions of a country matter.

---

[157] Some may notice and purposefully express it if they share the view with policy makers in their countries. I do not eliminate this possibility, but I am not certain if the most of them are really conscious of this point.

Academic Culture: An Analytical Framework 253

7.4.2 Different Perspectives among Academics in Japan

If we consider the aforementioned national perspective of international academic work / collaboration as fundamental surroundings of academic work in relation to international academic activities, there would be individual and practical perspectives of such work from academics, who are the practitioners of it. However, this does not intend to separate these national / political and academic perspectives and discuss them as if they had nothing to do with each other. The major intention here is rather reverse, and is to discuss perspectives from academics on the aforementioned issue under the circumstance in which international academic work is strongly defined by the national policy, since academics cannot escape from this working condition as long as they are based in universities in Japan.

Then, a question is: What kind(s) of prospects as well as perspectives on international academic work do they have under this working circumstance? Due to the limited amount of academic literature on similar issues, the discussion inevitably tends to rely on the comments of the research participants in this study, nonetheless, as a starting point, it has to be pointed out that the majority of academics who publish their work on internationalization of HE and / or of Japanese universities seems to share the national perspective on such issues. That is to say, the political aim towards internationalization of HE and HEIs underlies their work, may they be conscious or unconscious of this point. It is frequently seen that such work written by academics in Japan contains implemented HE policies in Japan in relation to internationalization, and many of them end their academic articles by making suggestions how Japanese universities can be better 'internationalized' like the United States and the European countries.

> This paper explores the current situation of internationalization and its effect through a comparison of Japanese universities with universities of other countries. . . . this paper will also discuss how Japanese universities will be able to grow and strengthen their status in comparison to their competitors. (Okugawa, 2014: 119)

The above is taken as an example of typical style of article on internationalization of HE in Japan. What is typical about this article is, firstly, that the article looks at what kind of policies on internationalization of HE in Japan have been implemented, which is expressed as "the current situation of internationalization" (ibid.). Secondly, the article attempts to make a comparison "with universities of other countries," and these "other countries" are normally the so-called the Western countries such as the United States and the countries of the European Union. They rarely make such a comparison with other Asian countries, and why other Asian countries are not compared to the situation in Japan implies that authors of such articles consider that Japan does not have to catch up with situations of Asian counterparts. In other words, the motivation to compare the situation in Japan with those in the United States and the European countries seems that the authors think that there would be clues in situations of the aforementioned countries for the Japanese HE to successfully internationalize. Thirdly and finally, the last sentence of the above quotation is quite revealing: The author understands that it is a competition for which the Japanese universities should "grow and strengthen their status" to beat "their competitors" (ibid.). A statement like this is not particular of this author, but can be found in numerous academic articles written by Japanese academics on this issue (Yonezawa, 2007; Yonezawa, 2009; Yonezawa, 2010).

Thus, it is indicated that such academic articles share the political interests in the issue of internationalization of HE / HEIs in Japan. For those who write this type of article, there seems to be little discrepancy between the national perspectives and the perspectives of their own on international academic work. Rather their academic interests accord with the political interests in this issue. Then, regarding the interconnection between the national perspective and the academic one, academics who share the national perspective are less likely to experience a dilemma between the national and their own perspectives to approach and deal with international academic work, given that the contents of their work discussing internationalization of HE / HEIs indicate little difference from the national perspective. In order to distinguish this perspective from the followings, this perspective is labelled as 'type 1: Sharing the national perspective'.

If the above type is at the one extreme end of various perspectives of academics, the other extreme end may be formed by academics who would like to emancipate themselves from the national framework that forms their academic activities and work with strong, sometimes even irresistible, influence on them. As seen, the factors which influence academic work in the academic environment, such as roles of HE / universities and the science policies, cannot be changed by any individual efforts whether or not individual academics like the contents of those influential factors. Nonetheless, it is also not impossible to obtain diverse working styles, work philosophies, and perspectives on academic work, which do not necessarily agree with the national perspectives on and aims for international academic work.

Judging from the empirical evidence of this study, this type of academic seems to be active not only in the national academe but also academic activities which take place outside of the country. This does not mean that they are only appearing at big international conferences, or just publishing anything for the sake of acquiring merits for evaluation at work. Rather, academics who are able to command English to communicate with their foreign counterparts seem to be committed to academic activities which are often classified as international / cross-national academic activities, because they are firstly curious about what their colleagues in other geographical settings think and do in the same disciplinary field, and secondly they are aware of significance of international / cross-national academic activities in which they could exchange diverse views and opinions, which may not be noticeable within the domestic academic discourses, about the similar / same research topics and themes. Although such activities might result in academic articles, co-authoring with foreign colleagues, or a presentation at an international conference, their main interest does not necessarily seem to be such outcomes, but the processes which stimulate their intellectual curiosity. Moreover, they tend to be inclined to such activities in order to develop academic knowledge, and they appear to be less concerned with personal prestige and status as an academic, nor about the status and competitiveness of the nation state, which can be measured by outcomes of academic activities. Although this study does not focus on aspects of international / cross-national academic activities as a part of academic work, some of the participants of the study refer to them.

256 Discussion of the Case Study

> As an academic, I have continuously established academic networks by exchanging students and academics with those in foreign countries as well as by exchange programmes between universities. . . . It is not for earning merits / credits for my career but for practising what I claim in my own work. If I wanted to do something for career making / job promotion, it would be much better to write academic articles or publish a book with a collection of my articles than going abroad, getting exhausted, making a presentation, and wasting time by doing all these things. (Interviewee E)

> If one is interested in his / her own career making and / or in only advertising him / herself in academic world, he / she would not organize, say, international events / conferences, because it is just so time-consuming and demanding [to organize such events]. (GD participant D)

To avoid any misunderstanding, it should be additionally mentioned that GD participant D notes that the majority of academics nowadays attempt to appear in international conferences for improving their own work profile. However, the emphasis of international activities which the above two participants express is not just appearing in international academic scenes but more organizing and establishing ties between academics of different countries in order to simply exchange academic discourses. That is, international academic work is not always, and not necessarily about enhancing the competitiveness of a nation state through outcomes of the work, that is, how frequently one's work is cited, and how many articles written by academics of one country appear in prestigious international academic journals. Instead, from a perspective of those who pursue academic work and try to develop academic knowledge for development of academic disciplinary field, international / cross-national academic activities is part of the core of their work, due to the globalised academic activities, internationalization of HE around the world, and globalization of academic knowledge flow that enables academics to reach the massive amount of academic writings, information, and communications between academics via websites and other means such as blogs and social networking services. All these aspects and phenomena of internationalization / globalization related to academic work also influence development and generation of academic knowledge, and some academics see the necessity for discourses with their foreign counterparts in order to develop academic knowledge which is relevant for not only the academic circle of a particular country but also the globalized sphere of academe, whichever places on the globe it may be.

Therefore, academics who are more interested in discourses / interactions between foreign colleagues for the aforementioned purpose place greater emphasis on this part of academic work than on career making. In other words, they have freedom not to participate in competitions for career making. Indeed, it can be seen in some comments and responses in the empirical study that the more senior and established they are, the more they are interested in overall academic knowledge generation / development activities rather than academic work which could directly influences their position at work. Although this does not mean to be a generalized statement, there seems a tendency that senior and established academics take this position in relation to international academic activities, compared with the younger generation. Certainly, it is not simply a matter of age and position as academics that lead them to this orientation towards international activities, and many other aspects and belief in their academic life would also influence their view on international academic work. However, the most significant emphasis here is that there are some academics who carry out and sometimes attempt to organize international academic activities, and that they practice them neither for their career making nor for growth and position of the nation state in the world.

As observed in the various parts of this study, influences of the academic environment of academic work, such as the role of HE / HEIs and the science policy are unignorable. Nonetheless, it is significant to note that the environmental aspects of academic work do not necessarily force all academics to follow what the academic environment aspects, which is closely bound to the view and standpoint of a nation state towards academic work. The number of academics who share this view that international / cross-national academic activities are for development of knowledge may not be large, and other academics may find such a view too utopian. However, it is certain that some academics carry out academic work outside of their own country for development of knowledge with little concern about the national perspective or their own career perspective. This perspective can be labelled as 'type 2: International collaboration for academic knowledge development / generation'.

Among the aforementioned two different types of perspectives on international academic activities for academics, another type of perspective can be described. This type is located in the middle of other two types, and probably the greatest number of academics would belong to it. That is to say, whether or not they share the national perspective, they tend to work within the framework which is broadly used for the evaluation of work carried out by academics and / or universities. This framework could make many academics, especially who are in the middle and at the beginning of their academic career, mistake the aim of academic work for the aim of evaluation of academic work. Or, to put it differently, although they are aware of the fundamental roles of academic work, which includes contribution to the development of disciplinary / academic knowledge, the reality that their work is the basis for the decision, which is made by their employer and other stakeholders of their work, about how 'good'[158] they are is "overwhelming" (GD participant D). As discussed, such decisions are made based on the number of publications, of conference presentations, and research projects which he / she participated in, and as a result of the pressure that such activities would influence their position, promotion at work, salary, and other future perspectives as academics, they more intend to concentrate on those activities which indicate their academic 'productivity'.[159] Even though it is understood that it cannot help academics working in such a way because of this quite strongly fixed evaluation framework in today's universities, such an attitude towards academic work including international academic activities seems only introverted and individualistic, which concerns with the evaluation. In other words, any academic activities which can give credits / merits would be carried out, but the main motivation for those activities could also be only acquiring credits for the annual merit rating. Therefore, for those who see academic work with this orientation, international / cross-national academic activities can only be one of the most

---

[158] This judgement whether they are good or not would be made by, according to the employer's and the stakeholders' own interests and standards, and it does not necessarily coincide the quality and / or relevance of work in terms of the contribution to the disciplinary fields.

[159] This style of working is known as "knowledge factory" by GD participant D, meaning that today's academics produce anything that they were asked to produce. He simultaneously states that this type of work would not necessarily contribute to development of academic knowledge, but it is just consumed.

interesting work *items* which would provide them more credits. Although they do not express it so openly, for instance, when they are asked about the importance of publication practices as a part of academic work, some of the research participants respond that publication is very important because it is counted as an academic achievement that is connected to and useful for job promotion and job hunting (Questionnaire respondent B, C and E). This is not to accuse them of connecting academic work with credits, job promotions, and other benefits which may bring them prestige and status, but to clarify that it is the evaluation system that makes them concentrate on the productivity in their work. In this context, international academic activity is a mere means to achieve this particular aim for the academic productivity, and thus, it tends to foster competition between individual academics, unlike the national perspective towards international academic activity, which is the competition between the nation states. The difference between this individual academic perspective and the national perspective in relation to international / cross-national academic activity is not clearly distinguished, and it is often mixed up with each other. However, as described above, it is clear that each of them has different motivations and consequences for international academic activity, even though both of them have a common nature, which is competitiveness. Finally, this perspective is labelled as 'type 3: Bound to evaluation'.

Thus the diverse perspectives towards international academic activity have been discussed. Although they are discussed separately to avoid any confusion, it has to be remembered that they all coexist in today's academic work. While some perspectives such as the national perspective and the 'type 1' of academics' perspective are similar, there are contrastive ones among the academics' perspectives, as seen between the type 1 and 2. Needless to say, I make no judgement about which perspective is correct and which not; nonetheless, it is possible that the most visible perspective is considered as the perspective which has validity and therefore is the norm for those who are concerned with international academic activity. In the case of Japan, it seems that a great number of academics share the view with the national perspective towards international academic work, as the publication on this issue written by Japanese academics indicates. In other words, international academic activity in different contexts is rarely seen as academic publication,[160] and this implies that any other academic debates are less likely to emerge under this circumstance. Some might conclude that it is the evidence that the national perspective and the academics' perspective towards international academic activity perfectly match. However, as shown earlier, there are some academics who have a totally different perspective (type 2) from the national one (and the type 1 of the academic perspective), and this perspective that international academic activity is to engage in discourses with foreign counterparts in order to further develop academic knowledge is the only perspective that exhibits the sole interest in knowledge or knowledge generation, compared with other perspectives.

Today's academic work is generally connected with aspects of competing with others, may it be individual academics or nation states, due to the introduction of and strong emphasis of ranking and evaluation. Particularly, when thinking about the reasons why

---

[160] The reason why discussions of international academic activity in different contexts are rare may have something to do with the peer review / referee system. One of the drawbacks of the peer review system is that discussions which are not common and unfamiliar to peer reviewers of publications are more likely to be declined, as they are not considered by the peer reviewers / referees as a contribution to 'a body of knowledge'. According to Murakami (1994: 69), whether or not one's work is accepted to be published is decided by referees, based on their judgement that this work would put additional value as "something new" on the body of knowledge. However, being "something new" does not mean that anything which suggests new aspects with new approaches. Murakami continues, "Academic articles which deviate from the existing body of knowledge in various aspects would be rejected. . . . Even if a non-expert in one academic field found something new that would add academic value to the field of knowledge, it is most unlikely that such an article is accepted and published. The reason for this is a problem of style of writing. Experts would know what has to be written, what can be written, what better not to write, and what must not to be written. . . . The sense of [the submitted article] 'being not suitable' [in the field of knowledge] can be a legitimate reason to reject the piece of work to publish in the field.. . . It also frequently happens to experts, who acquired a number of academic achievements, when they try to publish their articles in other fields than they belong to." (translation of my own,1994: 69–70) Thus, while "something new" is appreciated in the development of knowledge, "something totally alien" to peers of a field would not be favoured, even though it might open up new field of knowledge in a discipline. As a result of it, entirely new perspectives / views are less likely to appear as academic publications, unless they simultaneously repeat what has been said before.

it is the case, it is inevitable to consider the influence of the national perspective and policy towards international academic activity on individual academic work. However, this strong influence coming from the national policy and / or the views of nation state on academic work does not justify academics following the national perspectives and policy on HE / universities and international academic activity. Although it is certain that some academics in Japan are committed to playing roles in policymaking by being members of committees, councils, and boards as a part of government-initiated work, generation and development of knowledge is fundamentally not an exclusive activity for the development of a nation state and / or a particular society. In other words, such policy relevant academic work can be a part, but cannot be the whole of work of academics.

In the context of international academic activity, this orientation of academic work which shares the political and national view on academic work would be very problematic, because such a type of academic work tends to consider and be interested in how country A would be able to be bigger and stronger than country B, or hopefully, than the rest of the world. Nishihara refers to this very aspect:

> Isn't the line between the mindset that wishes only the development of own country (by academic work) and the nationalism as thin as a knife's edge? In the academism of modern Japan, the national budget is preponderantly provided in the name of progress of international competitiveness. . . . I wonder if those who are concerned are too unaware of that there is a kind of ethnocentrism [in such a mindset]. (translation of my own, Nishihara, 2010: 57–58)

Nishihara also admits that academic work, knowledge / academic theory generation in particular, for the development of a nation state can be a legitimate goal; nonetheless, in the era of globalization of academic work, he suggests that it is more important to think about how academics from different global regions can cooperate and collaborate beyond the national borders (ibid.). In thinking about the development of knowledge, his claim is to the point, because, otherwise, international academic activity would be only the confrontation of national frameworks, perspectives, and views on academic work and knowledge among different nationals. As a consequence of the above confrontation of nationals, it is not hard to imagine that a collection of country-specific studies of any topics would be generated as outcomes of 'international collaboration'. It might be considered as a new type of knowledge generation because of the fact that academics of one country would not be able to gather case study materials from different countries. However, such a consideration lacks another consideration that the collection of different countries' case study would not generate new knowledge. Such 'international collaborations' are only patchworks of country's report from different countries, and what academics who are committed to such 'collaborations' can do at the most is just comparing *my* country with *your* country. From the national perspective, such work may be interesting and useful enough, but it seems to be neither collaborative nor international academic work from the academics' perspective which pursue collaborative knowledge generation with foreign colleagues, as the above type 2 academics advocate.

As is seen in the case of Japan, the international research collaboration in the social science is also urged at the national level, and this emphasis is not particular to the Japanese social science but exists in the social science fields in other countries. On one hand, this national initiative looks as if it would promote international research collaborations with academics of other countries; however, on the other hand, the aim of such national initiatives can be simply to feature Japanese academics / universities with other, possibly academically renowned academics / universities from countries outside of Japan, in order to exhibit that the Japanese academe is as good quality as their counterparts.[161] As long as international academic collaborations mean activities strongly underlain by the aforementioned political

---

[161] International research collaborations can also be collaborations between Japan and any African, Latin American, ASEAN countries. However, as an example of the ORA programme that promotes collaborative research projects in social sciences between Japan and European countries (France, Germany, U.K, and the Netherlands), the national initiative in Japan for promoting international collaborations mainly suggests collaborations with so-called advanced countries such as the United States and the G8 countries. This implies that international collaboration has a quite ambitious meaning not academically but politically to position one country's academe in the same position that the country politically locates in the world. Thus, international academic collaboration in this context concentrates on showing Japan's presence via joint research activity.

aim, mutual academic knowledge generation, which is not the patchwork of individual country case studies but generating a piece of knowledge through academic discussions and interactions among academics from different parts of the world, would not be achieved. It would consequently impact the development of knowledge, since repeating / reproducing country-specific studies would be limited in contributing to mutual knowledge generation, due to the nature of such studies, which they are completed when they finish describing how situations are in one country.

Although the emphasis of significance of international academic collaborations is seen in various places, if such academic work remains within the national framework of each country, the contents of it would also remain national, contrary to what international academic collaborations look like. It seems that a relatively large number of academics do not realize that what they understand as international academic activities can be bound to the nation, though they outwardly looks international, in terms of locations of activities, nationalities of project partners, and use of foreign language(s). It is very similar to the idea that one goes to a foreign country on holiday and is convinced of being international, despite that he / she only looked at some tourist attractions. Probably, the above assumption that most of the international academic activities are intrinsically national is not confined to Japan, but is applied to many other countries. Then, what is important and is required for academics to carry out international academic collaborations in the context of knowledge generation would be the realization of this delusion: What they consider as international academic activities is often very national. Without overcoming the delusion, academic knowledge generation practices in international collaborations will also remain as a collection of nationally confined knowledge.

Since the academic work in Japan is strongly influenced by the national political framework, due to the centralization of education system, it is also realistic to consider that there are a number of aspects in their academic work which cannot be easily changed by academics themselves. For instance, the evaluation system, the pressure for teaching / supervising students, the limited time for research, and the different roles of and expectations to respective universities, as seen in the empirical part of this study, are obviously the working conditions / environments in which they carry out their work. Needless to say, the political agenda on HE and academic research activity is beyond academics' influence. Nonetheless, it would be still possible for academics to ask themselves why they carry out academic work, what the aim of academic work is, what they would like to do with academic knowledge, and what their *raison d'etre* is in the given work setting / circumstance. Therefore, what lies beyond all these competitions and evaluations in academic work is simply such above questions no matter which country one works in, and academics would be able to start academically (not politically) fruitful international collaborations by responding to these questions.

Certainly, as long as the world university rankings and alike exist, it is not deniable that universities around the world and people working in them are involved in academic competitions. However, whether or not academics seriously think about the above questions would make differences in generation of knowledge, especially when they collaborate with their foreign counterparts. Because, if they do not ask themselves these questions, they would take for granted that their work exist for the competitions between universities within their own country as well as universities around the world. Moreover, showing individual productivity is also used for academics' own promotion and evaluation at their workplaces. From this viewpoint, only the productivity, that is, the number of publications and of citations, counts in order to quantitatively compete among colleagues and universities. The accumulation of all of these result in the competition between nation states by considering individual academics and universities as representatives of the countries. In this context, there is no discussion other than the productivity which can be visible and countable. Thus academics consequently tend to consider that the more they produce, the better, as if they were machines that spit out academic work. Imagine academics of this type collaborating together. It would be again a competition between them and can no longer be called 'collaboration'. This is the fundamental difficulty in discussing not only international academic collaboration but also international academic work in general. In the existing debates on international academic work, the actual situations / working conditions are that being more productive than others is the almost only way to survive, and to succeed as an academic person is likely to be considered as the ultimate aim of academic work. For some, it may be the case, but it may not be for the others. This is the reason why I suggest a careful consideration of what academic work is for those who are engaged in it.

Judging from the empirical part of this study, at least, the research participants do not seem to connect their work with the national / political perspective and aim. On the other hand, the confusion between what they *have to* do as a job and what they *hope to* do by academic work / knowledge generation can be seen, and uncomfortableness of being among two different aspects of academic work is also often observed. Therefore, in order to avoid the confusion for future academic debates on this topic, it would be important to think separately about what they are expected to do as academics in the given situation / working environment and what they would like to do through academic work. Further, in order to develop this field of knowledge, exploring more perspectives from academics, in other words, not being confined to the national perspective, would be beneficial. As seen in this study, academics' voices and views could only emerge from qualitative research, not from the statistical data that depicts a mere overall picture of HE in one country. The quantitative research which is the mainstream, if not the only, approach has the limitations when discussing the issue related to international academic activity. Although it can be admitted that the quantitative research in this field of knowledge has significance for the development of knowledge, it has largely been lacking for those seeking alternative and / or diverse discussions beyond the nationally confined analyses. It might sound heretical with such a background of this field of knowledge to attempt to introduce much less nation state-related analysis of international academic activity; however, given that individual academics do not necessarily share the views on international academic activity with their country's government, the current conventional research approach would not be sufficient to explore broader aspects that academic work embraces. The observation that there are mainly three types of perspectives from the academics' side towards international academic activity certainly implies and suggests that there would be more spheres of knowledge to investigate in the context of and in relation to international academic activity.

8. Discussion of the Concept of Academic Culture in the Light of the Case Study

Up to the last section, I have focused on the analyses of aspects that have emerged out of the empirical study about the Japanese SSH. Such analyses are necessary to understand how academic work is actually undertaken, what kind(s) of factors other than academic practice itself influence academic work, especially, in this context of studying knowledge generation practice, why they are influential, and so forth. This study has queried some academics in Japan working for fields of SSH in order to closely observe the above-mentioned aspects of academic work, and consequently these aspects are clarified in detail as discussed and explained in the findings and the discussion section.

Although such analyses certainly have significance because they inform us how academic work operates in the given setting of this country study, the motivation for this study originally arose from the realization that there has almost never been any other alternative ways / approaches to discuss international academic activities in SSH than classifying national and / or regional science communities by world rankings of HEIs and bibliometrics based on citation indices. While the current approach tends to marginalize scholars in less-privileged academic environments compared to, for instance, their colleagues in Anglo American countries, this study seeks another approach which will not involve the orientation of the current approach. That is to say, an emancipation from the contrastive descriptions of environment / condition that each national and / or regional science community has experienced is the fundamental aim of this study. Therefore, it is necessary to verify in the light of this case study about academic culture in Japanese SSH if the concept of academic culture has the potential to offer the aforementioned alternative framework for studying international academic activities in SSH.

In order to achieve this aim, this section will focus on four aspects to verify the validity of the concept and the methodology of academic culture as an analytical framework for studying international academic activities / collaborations in SSH. First, the methodological aspects will be reviewed to see whether or not the way in which the empirical research in this study was implemented was relevant to respond to the aim of the study. If any aspects did not seem to work well with regard to the methodology of the empirical research, how it can be improved will also be discussed in this part. Second, the overall construct of academic culture will be scrutinized. Academic culture is composed by two aspects shaping academic work, academic environment and academic practice, and some factors make up these respective aspects. Since there has never been a similar study to this study of academic culture, I suggest to revisit the classification of the two aspects and the selection of the studied factors. Therefore, the main focus here is whether the classification and the selection of their subcomponents are valid, and whether there would be any possible other classifications and other selections of the components to study academic work in a more precise way. Third, the relationship between academic culture and international academic activities / collaborations will be clarified in the light of the case study about Japan. If one pays attention to the contents and analysis of the empirical research, this study would simply appear as a study that investigates how SSH academics in Japan work with regard to knowledge generation practices. Of course, the outcomes of the empirical research are stimulating and interesting, therefore, it is worth discussing them in depth. Nonetheless, the main reason why I proposed to establish the framework called academic culture is to establish another platform to discuss international academic activities / collaborations. Thus, this part will explain more about the relationship between academic culture and international academic activities by exploiting the framework of academic culture in the light of the case study. Fourth, and finally, after all the above three points are considered, I will suggest how academic culture could be exploited in future studies in the context of international academic activities / knowledge generation, and an overall conclusion about whether academic culture can be a new analytical framework to contribute to debates of international activities / collaborations in SSH will follow.

8.1 Relevance of the Implemented Research Methods

Research methods in any research projects are selected according to the aims of the study, and should hold clear rationales about why they are necessary and appropriate to the study. In other words, inappropriate methods to the aims of research will not be able to achieve what the research project aimed at (Payne & Payne, 2008). In this sense, the selection of research methods which matches the aim(s) of research plays a very important role. In the methodology section, on the one hand, the reasons why the research methods in this study were selected are intensively discussed from various methodological perspectives. On the other hand, these research methods are reviewed and scrutinized to determine whether they are relevant for the purpose of this study, which is the establishment of academic culture as a new analytical framework. There are three research methods exploited in this study: Interview, questionnaire, and focus group discussion, all of which are qualitative. The relevance of each of those methods will be reviewed to evaluate whether they fulfill the role of constructing the study of academic work appropriately. If any other method as an option for the research method in this study is seen, it will also be suggested and discussed.

8.1.1 Interview

Because I have chosen qualitative research, in-depth, individual, semi-structured interviews were implemented in this study. The interview research in this study is the main part of the entire empirical research, and it can be said that these interviews provided very rich descriptions and statements of interviewees' working life as academics. Although some interviewees had a very limited timeframe for the interview, others could sometimes afford to spend more than twice as much time as originally planned. Consequently, such opportunities fed this study with other aspects than the ones in the original interview questions. This was totally unexpected at the beginning of the research, but brought favourable outcomes that were hidden in the interview questions and / or were totally overlooked when the interview questions had been formed.

For instance, most of the interviewees could provide insightful descriptions and analyses of the national funding programmes and their mechanism, which directly and strongly influence their work as academic researchers. Similarly, notions of university-industry relationship that emerged out of the interviewees' comments were also helpful in understanding how research in today's universities operate as well as how some practitioners of research feel about it. Such aspects of academic work are in many cases likely to be unwritten anywhere, because they are taken for granted as conventions and norms in academic work of a country. Internally, there would certainly be little necessity to document ordinary academic working life, as everyone who belongs to the same geographical setting as an academic person knows how his / her working life is through his / her own academic experiences. However, what is considered as norms and conventions in one national academic circle may not be known to academics who work in other national academic circles. This does not necessarily refer only to differences between different national academic communities but commonalities hidden by an assumption that people would work differently if work locations vary. Of course, some scholars have been interested in the academic profession in a restricted sense, and higher education studies in a broader sense, as discussed earlier in this thesis; nonetheless, a large number of such studies rely more on data derived from quantitative research methods, statistics published by national organizations such as ministries, and any other numerical data. Despite their relevance in other contexts, these numerical data and statistics would not be able to provide us with detailed descriptions of academic work and perceptions of it by academics themselves. In this sense, qualitative interviews to study academic work have a significance by (1) providing profound insights about academic work, (2) deriving general descriptions of ordinary aspects in academic work that are not normally documented in academic writing, and therefore (3) opening up a possibility to evolve a new type of study of academic work. Thus, qualitative interview is certainly the core method in the study of academic culture.

8.1.2 Questionnaire

Questionnaire research in this study was implemented as a supplementary means to the interview research, since it had been expected that there would not be sufficient time for both the interviewer and the interviewees to explore all aspects of academic work that are listed as the construct of academic culture, due to the work schedule of the study participants. Therefore, some aspects that focus on activities of their daily working life were removed from the interview questions and shifted to the questionnaire research. Had there been sufficient time to ask about all the aspects, only the interview research would have been necessary to arrive at the information I sought. Considering the financial and time constraint of this study, this supplementary questionnaire was useful and meaningful; however, carrying out further qualitative interviews would have been a better choice to obtain more elaborate accounts from the research participants.

8.1.3 Focus Group

The focus group discussions in this study has twofold aspects: One is, as with the other research methods, to collect empirical data by a different method. The other is to allow the focus group participants to preliminarily analyse / interpret some parts of data collected by the interview research. It is uncommon for focus group to be given two different roles, and the data analysis activity by focus group may be particularly unusual, since the focus group is normally a method of data collection. As expected before the implementation of the focus group discussion, giving these two roles to the focus group was most valuable, because the focus group in this case are academics who are most familiar with the topics of this study as with the ways analyzing data. The focus group as a means of data collection activity could provide data that further detailed and supported what had been given by the interviewees. More importantly, even though there were some conflicting comments between the interviewees and the focus group participants, the latter could reinterpret and / or complement the comments of the former. Thus, this activity could not only provide new comments but also evolve more refined comments and descriptions out of the existing data and thus substantially helped to interpret the data gained from the questionnaire and the interviews. Regarding qualitative research, obtaining quality data has confirmed to be crucial and influential to validate the entire research project. Especially in the context of this study, that academics provided their own views of academic work in the interviews and other academics responded and interpreted them worked well, since all of them are practitioners of the academic work, which, needless to say, involves analysis of data. This refinement and analysis of data by the focus group should be one of the major research methods that the study of academic culture exploits, inviting academics to reflect jointly about the data they provide through other data collection modes, such as individual interviews

8.1.4 For Future Studies

As seen above, the core research methods for the study of academic culture would be qualitative interviews and focus group. It can be assumed that these two methods would work well on studies of academic work using this methodological framework of academic culture in any country. It is supposed that focus group could provide more refined accounts and interpretations of what other participants meant, and this would surely feed the study with richer data and a part of data analysis. Nevertheless, what is obtained from focus group can still be subjective views of research participants, and in this respect, data obtained from focus group discussion can be classified as raw data. As the contents of those data are all about their academic work, it would be also desirable to observe some aspects of their work by participant observation, in order to verify what was informed by interviews and focus group is actually carried out as the participants' accounts revealed or not. For instance, observing some conferences held by academic associations / societies would offer data about how disciplinary communities operate, how members and participants of such disciplinary communities communicate, and whether any different / common activities and interactions are seen between national and international disciplinary meetings if there are opportunities to observe both meetings. Of course, observing all aspects of academic work raised in this study will not be possible, as many aspects of work in SSH are very individual and work at university may not be open to outsiders. However, I believe that it is worth to consider carrying out participant observation to cross-check some aspects of empirical data from the interviews.

Methodologically, the greatest emphasis in the study of academic culture is that the study is based on qualitative research, which will enable it to better reflect academics' own voices. Therefore, any qualitative oriented research methods would be favourable, but interview and focus group with the help of participant observation can offer a fruitful set of research methods to the methodological framework for the study of academic culture.

8.2 Scrutinizing the Construct of Academic Culture

After the review of research methods which this study employed, the construct of academic culture will be also scrutinized in this section. Academic culture consists of two aspects of academic work: Academic environment and academic practice. The respective aspects contain various factors that are assumed to influence academic work in international settings as well as in the local setting in which the research participants carry out their routine work. The purpose of this section is to think about whether there is / are other possible structures, aspects, and factors than this study holds, in search of a possible better construct of academic culture for future studies.

Generally speaking, the construct as a whole seems to work well for achieving the aim of the study.

First, the two broad aspects of academic environment and academic practice are properly defined to understand academic work. Since the study focuses on academic work itself and not other more personal aspects such as political believes,[162] it is sufficient to know the setting in which academic work is situated and the contents of such work, and how it is operated and carried out.

---

[162] Bourdieu's well-known work, *Homo Academicus* (1988) has an interest in investigating academics' personal backgrounds such as educational, social, religious, political, and economic backgrounds. Although his work is also considered as a study of academics, the selected items for the investigation greatly differ from this study.

Second, the factors in these two aspects are appropriate, because they are selected as the factors which particularly relate to knowledge generation. If the focus was not knowledge generation, there must be different factors. Similarly, if the study had a certain firm disciplinary orientation (e.g. sociology, psychology, education, etc.), it would also have to look very much different. However, the aim of the study is to perceive academic work towards knowledge generations in a broad context considering that any forms of joint knowledge productions are the main challenge in international academic activities That is to say, I aimed to describe general and practical aspects of academic work without being bound by a particular academic discipline. Of course, it is certainly possible to take more disciplinary factors into a study of academic culture in future studies. Therefore, I would not deny this possibility, although, in the context of this study, it seems more favourable to obtain the construct as it is.

Third, albeit I believe that the whole construct functioned well in the empirical research of the chosen case, there was a point at which some research participants had difficulties responding to the questions regarding the role of knowledge as the factor "academic knowledge in society". Due to the time constraints of the interview research activity, it was not possible to inquire further about their difficulties in responding to the questions, and consequently, it is still unknown whether the questions were difficult to understand or irrelevant to ask. In any case, it is worth considering the contents of this questions (or phrasing of the questions) for future research and it might also be the case that academics do reflect about knowledge within the academe, but much less about the question how academic knowledge is related to the society and the societal discourses.

Fourth, some other factors than the ones that were originally set emerged from the interview comments. These newly emerged factors suggested by the interview participants were used in the focus group discussion as topics of analysis work. It was obvious in this study that those topics only appeared after the interview; nonetheless, those newly emerged topics could be included in future interviews. These topics are about the origination of knowledge, methodologies and approaches to knowledge, and issues around the application of knowledge. They are quite straightforward factors in understanding how research activity starts, how it is implemented, and how academics handle the outcomes of their research. The original construct of interviews did not include these factors in the aspects of academic practice, and it will be worthwhile to study such factors when investigating how academics approach knowledge generations through actual research activities.

Thus, there are some suggestions, improvements, and considerations with respect to the construct of academic culture. For future research on academic work, the basic construct could be kept, which consists of two broad aspects of academic environment and academic practice and could be further developed by including some additional factors. The main factors, distinguishing between academic practices and academic environment can be fundamentally the same, but the above-mentioned considerations about some additional aspects should be included to improve the essential construct. As pointed out, involving other factors / structuring differently may be possible, however, this is also dependent on different research interests / aims. However, if studies share the fundamental aims and concept of studying academic culture, it will be favourable to apply the same / similar structure of this study.

8.3 Contribution of Academic Culture towards Future Academic Debates on International Collaboration in SSH

Assuming that more diverse cases studying academic culture are accumulated based on the framework of this study, how can academic culture, as it originally understood, contribute to future academic debates on international collaboration in SSH?

For instance, as this pilot case study can exhibit, the aspects of academic environment seem to be quite influential to frame academic work in one country. If the same can be said to other cases, influential factors in the academic environment (e.g. policy, funding system, etc.) will be more clearly identified and defined. Then, how this influence seen in individual cases could further influence international activities / collaborations will generate a new discussion. It is not, however, meant to be a study of science policy on research, but a part of study of academic culture, which emerged from viewpoints of academics. Studies of science / research infrastructure may indicate differences in science policy on research, funding, and other research infrastructure between countries, and some may find discussions of this aspect of academic environment old and repetitive. However, it is actually a new strand of discussions that includes how academics themselves interpret the academic environment and carry out academic work. Of course, some aspects and details of national policy on science should be referred to in such discussions, but the new discussion would be different from the existing discussion strands that are more interested in the relationship between science policy and academic activities which is the consequence of the implemented policy. The new type of discussion values more how academics see the policy, how they digest it, and how they find ways to work as academics, as some parts of this study also showed. That is, the new style of discussion will be able to stay away from politically biased discussions regarding science and academic activities in countries and more focus on how academics deal with them in the everyday's academic practices.

The same can be said about the aspects of academic practice investigated in this study. From the outcomes of this study, it can be for example pointed out that academics of younger generations tend to relate their work more to the evaluation and job promotion at the workplace, while those of more senior and established academics seem to work (i.e., to generate academic knowledge) more towards the development of knowledge in their disciplinary fields. The existing studies, on the one hand, only focus on the aspect of the former by extensively discussing academics' productivity measured and judged by the number of publication and citation. On the other hand, a new path for academic debates can emerge from the latter aspect above striving towards the development of theories, a development which seems to have been quite ignored as an issue to discuss international academic collaboration in respect of knowledge generations.

Thus, by exploiting the framework and concept of academic culture, we can see academic work, knowledge generation, and academic collaborations from much more diverse and more scientific perspectives than the currently available perspective that academic work (especially the publication practice) can be benchmarked only by quantitative data and / or national statistics.

This is not to say that the current perspective is false or inappropriate for discussions of international academic work, but to suggest broader possibilities to construct much wider discussions of this topic, which include the views academics have on the more scientific aspects of academic work. The above-mentioned topics are just examples of how to develop new types and topics of discussions about international academic work / collaboration, and the possibilities are, of course, not limited to those factors mentioned as examples. Nevertheless, the above examples can clearly show that new discussion paths which have rarely been noticed or payed attention to in the context of discussion of international academic work / collaboration can be open to academics to explore and deploy this fresh approach to analysing international academic work from the more scientific perspective of academics and less from the views of national science policies

Though a question whether or not this new analytical framework of academic culture is properly workable in other cases yet remains, it can be assumed that academic culture will be a possible alternative analytical framework for the discussions of international academic collaboration. As already seen, this framework will be able to provide more diverse discussion strands that are based on qualitative research than the current approach does. The original aim of establishing the framework of academic culture is not only to emancipate researchers from the current approach which has limitations and drawbacks to analyse academic work but also to create a way to discuss academic work in global settings without having a political, competitive, and nationally-confined orientation and to give academics again a voice in these debates. Certainly, achieving the final complete form of academic culture will require more time, and this study can only be a first and only one step to shift the discourses towards more scientific concerns and to concerns academics have in the academic life practices. However, I believe that academic culture can shake up the conventional views and the taken-for-granted debates of international academic collaboration. As a consequence of this work, I hope that more cases will be put into practice and the framework will be refined, so that academic culture could be broadly exploited for similar studies to this work.

9. Concluding Remarks

9.1 What Is Achieved in This Study?

This study questions the validity of the existing academic debates on international academic activity, which compare the status of academe in each country, based on quantitative analyses such as citation indices and university rankings. For those who see international academic work as a sort of global academic competition, such debates are surely valid and useful. However, there seems to be a discrepancy between competition / rankings and knowledge generation activity for the development of knowledge which is the core activity in collaborative academic work, may it be national or international. The former is interested in respective parties being higher in the ranking and more visible in the global academic 'market' like prestigious academic journals than others, while the latter means fusion of different knowledge that is developed by individual researchers, and a generation of new knowledge as a result of the fusion of various knowledge seems to have the opposite nature to competitiveness in academic work that has been emphasized in the existing debates.

With my own experiences in working for international research projects under the EU framework programme, this competitive nature of international academic work did not coincide with the motivation of individual academics for participating international research projects. That is, in practice, it seemed that academics were mostly interested in what their foreign counterparts do and think as academic work. It can be assumed that there might be also competitive aspects of such work to join international research activity; however, it did not seem to be *the only and not at all the main* aspect of how academics see international academic work.

Thus this study was structured in order to explore aspects of academic work that could influence academic work when collaborating with foreign counterparts, particularly in the context of the generation of knowledge. Although, Japan was selected as the pilot case to study the above-mentioned aspects, I was not interested in tracing and describing differences and / or particularities of academic working life in Japan by comparing it with the same aspects in other countries' settings. Instead, in this study I have tried to concentrate simply on describing the working condition / environment for academics in Japan and what the research participants have stated through the interviews, questionnaire, and the focus group discussion. The study did not particularly investigate academic experiences in international settings such as international research projects, because it considered that international academic activities do not exist as separate activities from the working condition / environment and conventional academic work that respective academics carry out during their daily working life. Rather, an involvement of international academic activities would be a continuum of such a daily academic life. That is, international academic activities are influenced by various aspects of the daily working life of academics. Indeed, it is true that participating in international academic activities requires particular conditions such as obtaining a foreign language proficiency, connections / networks with foreign colleagues, familiarity with international academic conventions methodologically and theoretically, and others which may not be required when working only domestically. Nonetheless, except for the foreign language ability, any of these activities do not seem to be very peculiar to international academic activities, since they are fundamentally the same that academics do as part of their quotidian work, that is, the generation of knowledge and contribution to the development of knowledge through research. This is the reason why this study attempted to focus on more fundamental aspects of academic work by introducing the concept of academic culture, which is derived from and an extension of the concept of "small cultures" advocated by Holliday (1999).

Yet, there is another major reason to exploit the "small cultures" concept in this study. Whenever people see the word *international*, they often tend to be trapped in believing that anything foreign must be different from something domestic / national / local to him / her. The representative discipline that bases itself on this understanding and tendency towards 'international' is intercultural studies, which heavily uses the essentialist approach. The essentialist approach in cultural studies is mainly interested in seeking differences, particularities, and a uniqueness of one culture that is classified by a unit of one country / ethnic group. Although the essentialist approach may have its own academic values to indicate characteristics of people's behaviours, attitudes, and utterances, it tends to pay so much attention to differences between cultures, which often results in statements / conclusions that we have difficulties in understanding the behaviour of people from other countries / regions due to the fact that our culture is different from theirs in respect of X, Y, and Z. In other words, describing such differences between cultures is simply used to excuse why *we* and *others* cannot collaborate and cooperate well with each other. With the essentialist approach, therefore, reasons why collaborations between people from different cultures do not go well may be found, but not ways in which such people could collaborate. Adding to this aspect, it should be pointed out that national / ethnic cultures is not the one and only influential aspect, nor the only explanation, towards joint activities among different nationalities / ethnicities. Particularly, my previous study, which investigated the influence of national culture in international academic collaborations for Japanese SSH academics in the context of disagreement discourses, indicated that so-called Japanese cultural characteristics were unlikely to influence activities in international research collaborations. This implies that other alternative ways should be sought in order to study international academic activities, rather than exploiting conventional intercultural theories. From this understanding the main grounds for constructing the new approach of academic culture has grown, a view which goes beyond the aforementioned intercultural approach.

The components of academic culture are classified as two aspects: Academic environment and academic practice to explore factors which could influence academic work, in particular, knowledge generation activity. In the academic environment, aspects such as science policy including the national funding system, and the structure of HE / HEIs in Japan, which would greatly influence the working environments / conditions of academics, were closely observed. Also, in the academic practice, more detailed academic practices such as publications, knowledge acquisition, discourse, disciplines, work management practices, and social relations were studied. As a result of the analyses of all, how each aspect is interconnected to construct work of the academics in Japan are clearly depicted and understood. All details have been described and discussed to a great extent, and they are not referred to here, but overall one can state that the national policies on science and HE firmly frame the ways that universities, academic work, academic people function, in order to fulfil the national aims, which are to increase the competitiveness, to show presence of Japanese universities and / or academic work carried out by people working for Japanese universities / research institutes to the world, and to strengthen the status of Japan in the world by science and technology. Under such a regime, universities are hard to be considered as autonomous places where academics could act and work according to their academic / intellectual interests, but rather seem places to foster good employable young people through education and to generate knowledge which would be beneficial for the country. Therefore, possibly a majority of academics in Japan tend to spend more time for teaching and administrative work at the university than research in order to react to the demands from the nation state, industries, and local societies in Japan, and as a result, some academics even do not feel like calling themselves researchers, but rather consider themselves as teachers (*sensei*). Thus there is the tension between what they are expected to do and what they would like to do, and it seems that they are likely to be pulled towards playing a role of a mere educator, especially when they are in their prime as academics. This tendency seems to be lessened as they approach the retirement age, which is sixty-five years old in national universities. Obvious reasons for this were not traced in the empirical study. However, one can assume that they would be more relaxed about aspects of job promotion and evaluation at work, because the more senior they are, the more established they are in terms of career / status. Then, they could also much more think of research activities as the core part of their occupation rather than just being chased around by teaching and by doing administrative work. Despite this shift of work orientation from teaching to research, the fundamental working condition / environment remains the same for all academics working in Japan. If there is anything that drives them to carry out research, it would be the consciousness that they are researchers properly trained to generate academic knowledge and that they would like to contribute to the society with the scientific knowledge they generated.[163]

---

[163] This notion of society is not necessarily confined to society they are physically located and live, but is meant in a broader sense as society of the world.

That is to say, in relation to international academic activities such as international research collaborations, it is the consciousness and the conscience of academic people who are aware of meanings and missions of their work that could go beyond the debates which analyse international academic activities based on the unit of nation states and / or nationalities of academics and their rankings. The major drawback of such debates that divide academic work by a mere classification of nationalities / nation states is that it seems to narrow the debates to national perspectives, despite the declared aim of such debates as being how to make an international / global academic world beyond the national borders. Indeed, as long as any analysis is made from the respective national perspectives, this type of debate would never go beyond the national borders. Instead, quite ironically, these debates would remain national (or regional, at most) while discussing an internationalization of science. This is also obvious from the case of Japan and could probably be applied to many other cases of many other countries.

In this very sense, what is achieved in this study is that the main emphasis of the research is put simply on academic knowledge, that is, what academic knowledge can be for academics and for lay persons in the non-academic society, possible roles of academic knowledge in societies and in the academe, and thus the *raison d'etre* of academic knowledge. In this context, academics are defined as people who generate academic knowledge and are engaged in any activities around it, including teaching. By putting academic knowledge and people in the centre of the discussion instead of the national perspectives (or rather nationalistic views) of academic work, the fundamental aspects in academic work, particularly in knowledge generation activities, are able to be clarified. This point is significant, because when academic people from different global regions collaboratively work to generate knowledge, what really matters to them would be what academic knowledge is, what it is for, how it would be made use of, how it is generated, and why it is to be generated.

Certainly, there would be different working conditions among academics who participate in such activities. One may not have sufficient financial support from his / her institute and / or country, and others may have difficulties in expressing their thoughts in a foreign language. There might be confusions with academic terms /

concepts each of them use, since they were trained in different academic settings. Nonetheless, the aim of and the motivation for international academic collaborative work for individual academics can mainly be the generation of knowledge for further development of knowledge. Then, if we are to see any tension in international collaborative work, it is more likely that participants of such activities have different views on knowledge and knowledge generation practices.

Although the different views on knowledge could originate from different working conditions, environments, situations of the society / country, and other aspects of academic environment which surround academic work in one country, such differences and misunderstandings between the participants can be solved by patiently developing a discussion among them. Discourses between academics from different global regions in the above-mentioned manner would be certainly possible, and the respective national perspectives and any influences of them could be quite easily put aside, if they all are aware of that from a genuine academic point of view international academic collaborations in which they participate are not for growth of any nation states. Indeed, rendering knowledge generation in international academic collaborations mutually fruitful academic activity has little to do with nation states and national perspectives towards academic work, but it depends on academics' own attitudes and minds how they face to such intellectually challenging work.

9.2 For Future Studies

It is certain that this study could suggest a new analytical framework to study academic work in relation to international academic activities such as international research collaboration. Nonetheless, because this study is novel, it should be admitted that it is yet incomplete in some respects. This study is incomplete in two ways: One is some aspects that this study could not investigate in the context of the Japanese academe, due to the time and financial constraint of this particular research project; and the other is the suggestion that future studies verify the applicability of the analytical framework of this study in other academic settings.

Firstly, confined to the Japanese setting, there are some suggestions for future studies. Since this study takes a form of a case study in order to explore aspects of academic work of various types of academic people, some of the research participants did not necessarily have sufficient working condition / environment for research activities in general. This does not mean that they were inappropriate respondents for this study, but rather, it is believed that they are surely typical of academics who make up the Japanese academe. However, exploring various types of academics has its advantages: it could also mean that their respective academic orientations are less likely to focus on research in general, and knowledge generation in particular.

As it has been observed, research work in Japan is concentrated in a certain number of universities, which are classified as research universities. Given this situation in Japan, it can be pointed out that perspectives from academics who work for research universities seem to be lacking in this study.[164] If they are, as it is generally believed, the most active academics in generation of knowledge in Japan, it would be interesting to understand their academic working life in detail with regard to knowledge generation by using the same methodological and analytical frameworks of this study. Simultaneously, focusing on the 'main players' of research activity with bigger samples than this study can be a good future follow-up research, considering that there is a strict segregation of roles of universities and academics working in Japan. It would not only generate a more generalised statement of academic work in Japan, but it would also examine a hypothesis that research carried out by academics working at research / flagship universities is more responsive to the national perspectives on academic research than research carried out by academics working at non-research / flagship universities. Thus, studying academic work in research universities would be able to provide us with a much bigger research sample by focusing on academics who work at the selected number of research-oriented universities, as well as with more qualitative analytical observation of them, which has been little explored in other studies. Similarly,

---

[164] To avoid misunderstandings, it should be noted that some research participants used to study at and work for research universities. Therefore, parts of their experiences and views were assumed to be expressed through such an academic background. However, the study did not intend to exclusively focus on perspectives from those who currently work at research universities.

it would be interesting to understand the academic work of those who are specialised in NST fields as well as SSH fields with new samples. Obviously, the science policy in Japan (as well as in other countries) is focused on science and technology, not only internationalization but also other aspects of science policy. Then, it can be presupposed that academic work in NST fields would receive a more direct and stronger impact / influence of the national, political perspective on academic work. By investigating academic work in NST, a future study would be able to confirm the influence of academic environment factors such as policy on science, funding, and roles of HE / universities, as the finding of this study suggests.

Simultaneously, there may be differences in academic work between in NST and SSH in relation to knowledge generation activity and / or international collaboration. Due to the recent emphasis on interdisciplinary academic collaboration not only among SSH fields but also between NST and SSH fields, including NST fields in the study of academic work would be relevant in the Japanese context as well as the international context.

Another suggestion for future study in the Japanese context is studying the influence of logical constructions when academics in Japan write their work in English and in Japanese. Unlike NST fields, the Japanese language is the major language for academic writing in SSH in Japan. Despite the globalization / internationalization of academic work in Japan, some of the research participants pointed out that academic work, particularly, publication practices in Japan, would remain as they had been, because the market and the demand for such academic writing in Japan is big enough to absorb the knowledge created by Japanese academics. However, if Japanese scholars would have to publish more in English, for whatever reasons it would be, they would have to confront the situation that they should write their work in English. It seems that a number of people in Japan who are concerned with the issue of academic publication in English believe that translation could solve this problem. To a certain extent, it might solve the problem, but what I emphasise here is not what is written but how to convey their academic thoughts in a foreign language. A renowned Japanese linguistic sociologist, Takao Suzuki, refers to academic writing in Japanese, and claims:

> Especially among academic articles of the social sciences [written in Japanese], there are not a few articles in which I wonder why authors of them had to use subtle and roundabout phrases. It can be said that there is a tendency that readers expect to enjoy a kind of mystification by words. (translation of my own, Suzuki, 1975: 32)

That is to say, academic articles in the social sciences written in Japanese appear to be unclear even to Japanese native speakers. The above-mentioned work of Suzuki was published three decades ago, and some may find it outdated; however, the situation does not seem to be dramatically different now. Even though a language can be translated and edited into another language, it would not make sense if foreign readers could not understand the logical construction and the way in which academic thoughts are developed. This is unlikely to be a matter of translation, as long as the "mystification by words" exists in Japanese academic writings. Therefore, as a significant component of academic work in relation to international collaborative knowledge generation activity, it would be important to study the influence of the structure of logical development in Japanese academic writings and those in English. Although this study did not include this aspect as an influential aspect of academic work towards international collaborative academic activities, studying this aspect would certainly have relevance.

Regarding the broader perspective for the development and refinement of the analytical approach, using the framework of academic culture, it would be useful to carry out similar studies in countries other than Japan in order to observe the applicability of this study to the other settings. Since the approach has not been tested and exploited in other geographical settings, its validity is yet unclear. If the approach is applicable to studying academic work in other countries, then, it would bring us a more generalized picture of academic work in relation to the international collaborations. Simultaneously, if different aspects which influence academic work in other settings emerged, it could provide this topic of study with further methodological and theoretical considerations. Although this study originally aimed at generating a new theory / approach to suggest an alternative way to discuss international academic collaborations in SSH, there is a limitation that it is only conducted as a study about academics in Japan, and thus cannot confirm the applicability of the approach to academic work in different academic settings. Therefore, it is hoped that the approach would be exploited to study academic work in any other countries, so that the approach could be verified and refined to achieve a true theoretical saturation, which would finally lead us to theorization of this approach.

Due to the novelty of this study, there can certainly be further studies and refinement of the approach both methodologically and theoretically. Thus this study itself is not yet complete. Nonetheless, if I am allowed to indicate a significance of this study, it would be that it could propose a discussion which does not take for granted that academic work should be discussed by a unit of nation state, and that it could provide narratives of academics to analyse academic work and / or the academic profession. The former is the starting point of this study by questioning why academic people who are keen to discuss international academic work only talk about comparisons between countries and global regions. As I wrote earlier, there would not be American, Japanese, German, Brazilian, or Nigerian academic work, if we think of ways to analyse academic work from an academic people's viewpoint. It is nation states that exploit academic work as a means of development or reinforcement of national power / wealth in the world. To my mind, this view of nation state and views of academic people on academic work are too much mixed up and confused in academic debates on international academic work.

Therefore, this study has attempted to clarify the national perspective and the academic perspective on academic work. The national perspective is not ignorable, since it defines individual academic work to a great extent, and forms academic working life accordingly. However, the national perspective is not identical with the perspective of academics on academic work. Although this study is about academics in Japan, it could have been conducted in any other country, and I believe that I studied academics who happen to work in the Japanese academic setting, rather than the Japanese academics. In this sense, I would not call this study a country-specific study, and hope that any colleagues in the world, wherever they are, would find commonality in this study by considering their working life point of view as this study. I understand that this study has still a long way to go to be more firm and established as the academic analytical approach to studying academic work. However, if any commonalities coinciding with the findings of this study about social sciences in Japan are found by readers in other academic settings, I would say that this study has reached a point of "naturalistic generalization"[165] which is a vicarious experience that readers would find similarities in descriptions and narratives in a study to their own settings. Probably, only then, could I be allowed to claim that this study successfully goes beyond the national borders as a debate dealing with international academic work.

The latter point that the study consists of narratives of academic people on their own work / profession is also rare among existing studies. I have learnt and have been inspired a lot by similar works from Becher and Trowler (2001) or a work of Bourdieu (1988). Nonetheless, it is still scarce to find work on academic work and / or the academic profession that feature academics' own voices. The big scale of quantitative data may be useful when looking only at the overview of general status of academic work, but such data would not be able to explain individual situations or express concerns around academic work confronted by its practitioners. It is probably because the authors of the existing studies on this topic are more interested in combining academic analyses with the national perspective. Or, it might be the case that academics have taken for granted that they know everything about themselves without carrying out research about themselves, but it seems to be overgeneralized by concluding academic work from only his / her own case. Thus, from this viewpoint, there is a call for more qualitative research on what academics do in order to explore academics' own perspectives on their own work. I believe that this study marks the first step of such a new style of research on this topic, and hope that there will be further development of this approach in the near future.

---

[165] Cf. Stake (1995).

10. References

Al-Rodhan, N. R., & Stoudmann, G. (2006). Definitions of globalization: A comprehensive overview and a proposed definition. *Program on the Geopolitical Implications of Globalization and Transnational Security, 6*.

Alatas, S. F. (2003). Academic dependency and the global division of labour in the social sciences. *Current Sociology, 51*(6), 599–613.

Allan, G. (2003). A critique of using grounded theory as a research method. *Electronic Journal of Business Research Methods, 2*(1), 1–10.

Altbach, P. G. (1996). *The international academic profession*. Princeton, NJ: Carnegie Foundation for the Advancement of Teaching.

Altbach, P. G. (2003). Centers and peripheries in the academic profession: The special challenges of developing countries. In *The decline of the Guru* (pp. 1–21). Palgrave Macmillan US.

Altbach, P. G. (2004). Globalisation and the university: Myths and realities in an unequal world. *Tertiary Education & Management, 10*(1), 3–25.

Altbach, P. G., & Teichler, U. (2001). Internationalization and exchanges in a globalized university. *Journal of Studies in International Education, 5*(1), 5–25.

Amano, I. (2006). *Daigaku kaikaku no shakaigaku (Sociology of University Reform)*. Tokyo: Tamagawa University Press.

Ammon, U. (2010). The Hegemony of English. In *The World Social Science Report* (pp. 154–155). Paris: UNESCO.

Andrade, M. S. (2006). International students in English-speaking universities: Adjustment factors. *Journal of Research in International Education, 5*(2), 131–154.

Arimoto, A. (2008). *Henbousuru Nihon no Daigaku Kyoujushoku (in Japanese)*. (A. Arimoto, Ed.) Tokyo: Tamagawa University Press.

Asahi Shinbun. (10-September 2014). 30 percent of academically highly qualified women in Japan do not work: the lowest level among OECD countries. Tokyo. Retrieved 28-February 2015 from http://www.asahi.com/articles/ASG996X2YG99UTIL05T.html

Ayata, S., & Erdemir, A. (2010). Internationalization of Social Sciences and Humanities in Turkey. In M. Kuhn, & D. Weidemann (Eds.), *Internationalization of the Social Sciences* (pp. 265–284). Bielefeld: transcript Verlag.

Bassey, M. (1999). *Case Study Research in Educational Settings* . Buckingham: Open University Press.

Becher, T., & Trowler, P. R. (2001). *Academic Tribes and Territories: Intellectual enquiry and the culture of disciplines* (2nd ed.). Buckingham, U.K: SRHE and Open University Press.

Bedeian, A. G., Van Fleet, D. D., & Hyman, H. H. (2009). Scientific Achievement and Editorial Board Membership. *Organizational Reseach Methods, 12*(2), 211–238.

Benedict, R. (1967). *The chrysanthemum and the sword: Patterns of Japanese culture*. Houghton Mifflin Harcourt.

Billaut, J.-C., Bouyssou, D., & Vincke, P. (2010). Should you believe in the Shanghai ranking? An MCDM view. *Scientometrics, 84*, 237–263.

Blaikie, N. (2007). *Approaches to Social Enquiry* (2nd ed.). Cambridge, U.K: Polity Press.

Boshoff, N. (2009). Neo-colonialism and research collaboration in Central Africa. *Scientometrics, 81*(2), 413–434.

Botschaft von Japan in Deutschland. (n.d.). *Sekaitekina Chishikishakaini okeru Doitu no Yakuwari no kyouka* (Reinforcement of roles of Germany in the world knowledge-based society). Retrieved 1-March 2014 from Botschaft von Japan in Deutschland: http://www.de.emb-japan.go.jp/nihongo/kenkyusha/kokusaikasenryaku.pdf

Bourdieu, P. (1988). *Homo Academicus*. (P. Collier, Trans.) Oxford, U.K: Polity Press.

Boyer, E. L. (1994). *The Academic Profession: An International Perspective. A Special Report*.

Broeckelman-Post, M. (2008). Faculty and student classroom influences on academic dishonesty. *Education, IEEE Transactions on, 51*(2), 206–211.

Brown, A. J., & Dowling, P. C. (1998). *Doing Research/Reading Research: A Mode of Interrogation for Education*. Abingdon, Oxon: Routledge.

Brown, L. (2008). The Incidence of Study-Related Stress in International Students in the Initial Stage of the Internatioanl Sojourn. *Journal of Studies in International Education, 12*(1), 5–28.

Bryman, A. (2008). *Social Research Methods* (3rd ed.). Oxford: Oxford University Press.

Cadman, K. (2000). 'Voices in the Air': evaluation of the learning experiences of international postgraduates and their supervisors. *Teaching in Higher Education, 5*(4), 475–491.

Cano, V. (1996). International Co-operation Patterns in EC Funded Projects. In J. Gaillard (Ed.), *International Science Cooperation* (Vol. 7, pp. 203–218). Paris.

Canto, I., & Hannah, J. (2001). A partnership of equals? Academic collaboration between the United Kingdom and Brazil. *Journal of Studies in International Education, 5*(1), 26–41.

Chalmers, D., & Volet, S. (1997). Common misconceptions about students from South-East Asia studying in Australia. *Higher Education Research & Development, 16*(1), 87–99.

Charmaz, K. (1990). 'Discovering' chronic illness: using grounded theory. *Social sciecen & medicine, 30*(11), 1161–1172.

Charmaz, K. (2005). Grounded Theory in the 21st Century: Applications for Advancing Social Justice Studies. In N. Denzin, & Y. Lincoln, *Handbook of Qualitative Research* (3rd ed., pp. 507–535). London: Sage.

Charmaz, K. (2006). *Constructing Grounded Theory: A Practical Guide through Qualitative Analysis*. London: Sage.

Chiapparino, F. F. (n.d.). *Diversity in organisations: Towards a non-essentialistic, dynamic approach*. Position Paper of Research Task. Retrieved 2014 йил 19-July from http://www.susdiv.org/uploadfiles/RT1.1_PP_Maddy.pdf

Christensen, T. (2011). University governance reforms: potential problems of more autonomy. *Higher Education, 62*(4), 503–517.

Clark, B. R. (1987). *The Academic Life. Small Worlds, Different Worlds. A Carnegie Foundation Special Report*. Princeton University Press.

Cohen, L., Manion, L., & Morrison, K. (2007). *Research Methods in Education* (6th ed.). Abingdon, Oxon, U.K: Routledge.

Cole, S., & Cole, J. R. (1967). Scientific Output and Recognition: A Study in the Operation of the Award System in Science. *American Sociological Review, 32*(3), 377–390.

Connell, R. (2007). *Southern theory: Social science and the global dynamics of knowledge*. Polity.

Corbin, J., & Strauss, A. (1990). Grounded Theory Research: Procedures, Cannons, and Evaluative Criteria. *Zeitschrift für Soziologie, 19*(6), 418–427.

Cronin, B. (2003). Scholarly communication and epistemic cultures. *New review of academic librarianship , 9*(1), 1–24.

Darder, A. (1991). *Culture and power in the classroom: A critical foundation for bicultural education*. Greenwood Publishing Group.

de Boer, H. F., Enders, J., & Schimank, U. (2008). Comparing higher education governance systems in four European countries. In *Governance and performance of education systems* (pp. 35–54). Springer Netherlands.

Doshisha University. (2015). *Kyoshokuin boshuu (Job vacancy for teaching positions)*. Retrieved 30-March 2015 from Doshisha University: http://www.doshisha.ac.jp/doshisha/recruit.html

Dubois, A., & Gadde, L.-E. (2002). Systematic combining: an abductive approach to case research. *Journal of Business Research, 55*, 553–560.

Duggleby, W. (2005). What About Focus Group Interaction Data? *Qualitative Health Research, 15*(6), 832–840.

Duncombe, J., & Jessop, J. (2012). Doing Rapport'and the Ethics of faking Friendship. In T. Miller, M. Birch, M. Mauthner, & J. Jessop (Eds.), *Ethics in Qualitative Research* (2nd ed., pp. 108–121). Sage.

Dunne, C. (2011). The place of the literature review in grounded theory research. *International Journal of Social Research Methodology, 14*(2), 111–124.

Durkin, K. (2008). The Middle Way: East Asian Master's Students' Perceptions of Critical Argumentation in U.K. Universities. *Journal of Studies in International Education, 12*(1), 38–55.

Ebihara, H., & Kuwabara, T. (2009). Nihon no daigakuniokeru kokusaitekina kenkyuukouryuuno joukyouto ronbunseisanno kankeini kansuru kousatsu (Thoughts on relationships between research exchange and production of academic articles in Japanese universities). *Nenji gakujutu taikai kouen youshishuu,* (pp. 840–843). Retrieved April 15, 2014 , from https://dspace.ja ist.ac.jp/dspace/bitstream/10119/8757/1/2H01.pdf

EENEE and NESSE networks of experts. (2008). *European Education and Training Systems in the Second Decennium of the Lisbon Strategy.* Retrieved 22-February 2014 from NESSE (Network of Experts in Social Sciences of Education and training: http://www.nesse.fr/nesse/activiti es/reports/activities/reports/challenges-for-european-education-pdf

Egege, S., & Kutieleh, S. (2004). Critical Thinking: Teaching Foreign Notions to Foreign Students. *International Education Journal, 4*(4), 75–85.

Ehara, T. and Umakoshi, T. (2004). *Daigakuin no kaikaku (in Japanese).* (T. Ehhara , & T. Umakoshi , Eds.) Tokyo: Toshindo.

Embassy of Germany in Japan. (n.d.). *Doitsu no daigaku (German universities).* Retrieved 17-February 2015 from Doitsu renpou kyouwakuku taishikan souryoujikan (Embassy and Consulates of Germany in Japan): http://www.japan.diplo.de/Vertretung/japan/ja/08-kultur-und-bildung/stu dieren-in-deutschland/Hoschschulsystem.html

Epps, E. G. (1989). Academic Culture and the Minority Professor. *Academe, 36*(5), 23–26.

e-Stat. (20-December 2013). *Gakkou kihon chousa heisei 25nendo (Basic research on educational organizations in Japan).* Retrieved 16-May 2014 from e-Stat: http://www.e-stat.go.jp/SG1/estat/List.do?bid=000001051733&cycode=0

e-Stat. (19-December 2014). *Gakkou kihon chousa (Basic research on educational organizations in Japan.* Retrieved 13-February 2015from e-Stat: http://ww w.e-stat.go.jp/SG1/estat/NewList.do?tid=000001011528

European Commission. (10-December 2013). *WP H2020 1. Introduction.* From European Commission Research & Innovation: http://ec.europa.eu/rese arch/participants/portal/doc/call/h2020/common/1597683-part_01_introd uction_v1.1_en.pdf

European Commission. (n.d.). *Funding Opportunities.* Retrieved 15-February 2015from European Commission Research & Innovation: http://ec.europa.e u/research/participants/portal/desktop/en/opportunities/index.html

Fink, G., & Meierewert, S. (2004). Issues of time in international, intercultural management: East and Central Europe from the perspective of Austrian managers. *Journal of East European Management Studies, 9*(1), 61–84. Retrieved 18-July 2014 from http://www.econstor.eu/bitstream/10419/903 04/1/76908351X.pdf

Firestone, W. A. (1993). Alternative Arguments for Generalizing From Data as Applied to Qualitative Research. *Educational Researcher*, 16–22. doi:10.3102/0013189X022004016

Fontana, A., & Frey, J. H. (2003). The interview: from structured questions to negotiated text. In N. K. Denzin, & Y. A. Lincoln, *Collecting and Interpreting Qualitative Materials* (pp. 61–106). London: Sage.

Fox, K. (2004). *Watching the English*. London: Hodder and Stoughton.

Frenken, K., Hoekman, J., & Hardeman, S. (2010). The Globalization of Research Collaboration. In *The World Social Science Report* (pp. 144–148). Paris: UNESCO.

Gaillard, J. F. (1994). North-South Research Partnership: Is Collaboration Possible between Unequal Partners? *Knowledge and Policy: The International Journal of Knowledge Transfer and Utilization, 7*(2), 31–63.

Geertz, C. (1971). *Islam Observed: Religious Development in Morocco and Indonesia*. Chicago: University of Chicago Press.

Geertz, C. (1973). *The Interpretation of Cultures*. New York: Basic Books.

Gibbons, M., & Wittrock, B. (1985). *Science as a Commodity*. Harlow, Essex, U.K: Longman.

Gingras, Y., & Mosbah-Natanson, S. (2010). Where Are Social Sciences Produced? In *The World Social Science Report* (pp. 149–153). Paris: UNESCO.

Glänzel, W., & Schoepflin, U. (1999). A bibliometric study of reference literature in the sciences and social sciences. *Information processing & management, 35*(1), 31–44.

Glänzel, W., & Schubert, A. (2005). Analysing Scientific Networks Through Co-Authorship. In H. F. Moed, W. Glänzel, & U. Schmoch (Eds.), *Handbook of Quantitative Science and Technology Research* (pp. 257–276). Springer.

Glaser, B. G. (1998). *Doing Grounded Theory: Issues and discussions*. Sociology Press.

Glaser, B., & Strauss, A. (1965). *Awareness of Dying*. Chicago: Aldine.

Glaser, B., & Strauss, A. (1967). *The Discovery of Grounded Theory: Strategies for qualitative research*. Mill Valley CA: Sociology Press.

Glaser, B. (1992). *Emergence vs forcing: Basics of Grounded Theory Analysis*. Sociology Press.

Gold, J., Walton, J., Cureton, P., & Anderson, L. (n/a). Theorising and practitioners in HRD-The role of abductive reasoning. Retrieved 27-April 2014 from http://www.ufhrd.co.uk/wordpress/wp-content/uploads/2010/08/9_2.pdf

Goldman, A. (1992). Intercultural training of Japanese for US-Japanese interorganizational communication. *International journal of intercultural relations, 16*(2), 195–215.

Guest, M. (2002). A critical 'checkbook' for culture teaching and learning. *ELT journal, 56*(2), 154–161.

Haigh, M. J. (2002). Internationalisation of the curriculum: Designing inclusive education for a small world. *Journal of Geography in Higher Education, 26*(1), 49–66.

Hall, E. T. (1976). *Beyond Culture*. Anchor Books.

Hammersley, M. (2001). On Michael Bassey's concept of the fuzzy generalization. *Oxford Review of Education, 27*(2), 219–25.

Hasegawa, Y. (2008). Seikatsu jikan (On working time). In A. Arimoto (Ed.), *Henbousuru nihonno daigakukyoujushoku (The Changing Academic Profession in Japan)* (pp. 198–221). Tokyo: Tamagawa University Press.

Hayashi, S. (2004). *Kenkyusha toiu shokugyo (Profession of researcher)*. Tokyo: Tokyo Tosho.

Hayashi, T. (2009). Daigaku no Kenkyuhyouka no Henyou to Kagakukenkyuu no Governance (Changes in Evaluation for Research in Universities and Governance of Scientific Research). *Kenkyu, Gijutu, Keikaku, 24*(3), 231–242.

Hazelkorn, E. (2009). *Impact of Global Rankings on Higher Education Research and the Production of Knowledge*. Paris: UNESCO.

Hicks, D. (2005). The Four Literature of Social Science. In H. F. Moed, W. Glänzel, & U. Schmoch (Eds.), *Handbook of Quantitative Science and Technology Research* (pp. 473–496). Springer.

Hofstede, G. (1984). *Culture's consequences: International differences in work-related values*. Newbury Park: Sage.

Hofstede, G. (1994). The Business of International Business is Culture. *International Business Review, 3*(1), 1–14.

Holliday, A. (1999). Small Cultures. *Applied Linguistics, 20*(2), 237–264.

Holliday, A. (2000). Culture as constraint or resource: essentialist versus non-essentialist view. *Iatefl Language and Cultural Studies SIG Newsletter*(18), pp. 38–40.

Holliday, A. (February 2014). *Innocent and ideological discourses of culture*. Retrieved 6-January 2015 from Adrian Holliday: http://adrianholliday.com/wp-content/uploads/2014/02/discul24b.pdf

Holstein, J., & Gubrium, J. (1995). The Active Interview in Perspective. In J. Holstein, & J. Gubrium, *The Active Interview* (pp. 7–18). London: Sage.

Holstein, J., & Gubrium, J. (1997). Active interviewing. In *Qualitative research: theory, method and practice* (pp. 113–129). Sage.

Horie, M. (2002). The internationalisation of higher education in Japan in the 1990s: A reconsideration. *Higher Education, 43*(1), 65–84.

Horsburgh, D. (2003). Evaluation of qualitative research. *Journal of Clinical Nursing, 12*, 307–312. Retrieved 27-May 2014 from http://www.fctl.ucf.edu/ResearchAndScholarship/SoTL/creatingSoTLProjects/implementingmanaging/content/evaluation%20of%20qualitative%20research.pdf

Huang, F. (2009). The Internationalization of the Academic Profession in Japan: A Quantitative Perspective. *Journal of Studies in International Education, 13*(2), 143–158.

Inoki, T. (2009). *Daigaku no Hansei (Reflections on universities)*. Tokyo: NTT publication.

Ishida, T. (1984). *Nihon no Shakaikagaku (Japanese Social Science)*. Tokyo: University of Tokyo Press.

Ishikawa, M. (2009). University Rankings, Global Models, and Emerging Hegemony: Critical Analysis from Japan. *Journal of Studies in International Education, 13*(2), 159–173.

Jensen, K. (1982). Women's work and academic culture: Adaptations and confrontations. *Higher Education, 11*(1), 67–83.

Jentsch, B., & Pilley, C. (2003). Research relationships between the South and the North: Cinderella and the ugly sisters? *Social Science & Medicine, 57*(10), 1957–1967.

Jöns, H. (2007). Transnational mobility and the spaces of knowledge production: a comparison of global patterns, motivations and collaborations in different academic fields. *Social Geography, 2*, 97–114.

JSPS. (2011). *Jinbungaku shakaikagaku no kokusaikanitsuite (On internationalization of humanities and social sciences)*. Tokyo: JSPS. Retrieved 12-April 2012 from https://www.jsps.go.jp/j-kenkyukai/data/02houkokusho/houkokusho.pdf

JSPS. (n.d.). *Open Research Area for the Social Sciences(ORA)*. Retrieved 1-February 2015 from Japan Society for the Promotion of Science: http://www.jsps.go.jp/english/e-bottom/01_d_outline.html

JSPS. (n.d.). *Grant-in-Aid for Scientific Research*. Retrieved 1-February 2015 from Japan Society for the Promotion of Science: http://www.jsps.go.jp/english/e-grants/index.html

JSPS. (n.d.). *21st CEO Program*. Retrieved 10-February 2015 from Japan Society for the Promotion of Science: http://www.jsps.go.jp/english/e-21coe/index.html

JSPS. (n.d.). *Ibunkayuugouniyoru Houhoutekikakusin wo mezashita Jinbun shakaikagaku kenkyusuishin jigyo (Programme for Promoting Methodological Innovation in Humanities and Social Sciences by Cross-Disciplinary Fusing)*. Retrieved 5-April 2014 from Japan Society for the Promotion of Science (JSPS): http://www.jsps.go.jp/j-ibunya/index.html

Kano, Y. (2008). Koutoukyouikuseisaku to daigakukyoujushoku no henbou (Higher Education policies and changes in academic profession). In A. Arimoto (Ed.), *Henbousuru nihonno daigakukyoujushoku (The Changing Academic Profession in Japan)* (pp. 43–61). Tokyo: Tamagawa University Press.

Katz, J. S. (1999). *Bibliometric Indicator and Social Sciences*. Retrieved 10-July 2014 from http://citeseerx.ist.psu.edu/viewdoc/download?doi=10.1.1.33.1640&rep=rep1&type=pdf

Katz, J. S., & Martin, B. R. (1997). What is research collaboration? *Research Policy, 26*(1), 1–18.

Kim, J., & Meyers, R. A. (August 2012). Cultural Differences in Conflict Management Styles in East and West Organizations: Employing Holism as a Cultural Theoretical Frame to Investigate South Korean and U.S. Employee Conflict Management Styles. Retrieved 19-July 2014 from Journal of Intercultural Communication: http://www.immi.se/intercultural/

Kim, T. (2009). Transnational academic mobility, internationalization and interculturality in higher education. *Intercultural Education, 20*(5), 395–405.

Kitamura, K. (1999). *Gendai no daigaku, koutoukyouiku: kyouiku no seido to kinou (Universities and Higher Education in Modern time: Systems and Functions of Education)*. Tokyo: Tamagawa University Press.

Kitzinger, J. (1994). The methodology of Focus Groups: the importance of interaction between research participants. *Sociology of Health & Illness, 16*(1), 103–121.

Kitzinger, J. (1995). Qualitative research. Introducing focus groups. *British Medical Journal, 311*, 299–302.

Kitzinger, J., & Barbour, R. S. (1999). Introduction: the challenge and promise of focus groups. In R. S. Barbour, & J. Kitzinger (Eds.), *Developing focus group research: politics, theory and practice* (pp. 1–20). London: SAGE Publications.

Klein, D. B., & Chiang, E. (2004). The Social Science Citation Index: A Black Box—with an Ideological Bias. *Econ Journal Watch, 1*(1), 134–165.

Knight, J. (2004). Internationalization remodeled: Definition, approaches, and rationales. *Journal of studies in international education, 8*(1), 5–31.

Knorr Cetina, K. (1999). *Epistemic Cultures: How the Sciences Make Knowledge.* Harvard University Press.

Knorr Cetina, K. (2007). Culture in global knowledge societies: knowledge cultures and epistemic cultures. *Interdisciplinary Science Reviews, 32*(4), 361–375.

Knorr Cetina, K., & Reichmann, W. (2015). Professional Epistemic Cultures. In I. Langemeyer, M. Fischer, & M. Pfadenhauer (Eds.), *Epistemic and Learning Cultures: Wohin sich Universitäten entwickeln* (pp. 18–33). Weinheim & Basel: Beltz Juventa.

Kobayashi, J., & Viswat, L. (March 2014). *3-D Negotiation in a Business Context: Negotiation between Japanese and Americans.* Retrieved 19-July 2014 from Journal of Intercultural Communication: http://immi.se/intercultural/

Kraut, R. E., Fussell, S. R., Brennan, S. E., & Siegel, J. (2002). Understanding Effects of Proximity on Collaboration: Implications for Technologies to Support Remote Collaborative Work. In P. J. Hinds, & S. Kiesler (Eds.), *Distributed Work.* MIT Press.

Kuhn, M. (2013). "Hegemonic Science": Critique Strands, Counterstrategies, and Their Paradigmatic Premises. In M. Kuhn, & S. Yazawa (Eds.), *Theories about and Strategies against Hegemonic Social Sciences* (pp. 31–54). Tokyo: Center for Glocal Studies.

Kuhn, M. and Remoe, S.O. (2005). *Building the European Research Area.* New York: Peter Lang.

Kuhn, M., & Okamoto, K. (2008). *Through international collaborations towards a multipolar SSH 'world order'*. Work package report for the Global SSH project (The Europan Commission Framework Programme 6). Retrieved 2-May 2015 from https://docs.google.com/file/d/0B61cKO6UEgDrUjl5N0NnU2gxWEU/edit?pli=1

Kuhn, M., & Weidemann, D. (2005). Reinterpreting Transnationality—European Transnational Socio-economic Research in Practice. In M. Kuhn, & S. O. Remoe (Eds.), *Building the European Research Area: Socio-Economic Research in Practice.* New York: Peter Lang.

Kuhn, M., & Weidemann, D. (Eds.). (2010). *Internationalization of the Social Sciences.* Bielefeld: transcript.

Kuwayama, T. (2004). *Native Anthropology: The Japanese Challenge to Western Academic Hegemony.* Melbourne: Trans Pacific Press.

Kvale, S. (2006). Dominance through interviews and dialogues. Qualitative inquiry, 12(3), 480–500.

Langemeyer, I., & Martin, A. (2015). "Scientification of Work" as a Challenge to University Education. In I. Langemeyer, M. Fischer, & M. Pfadenhauer (Eds.), *Epistemic and Learning Cultures: Wohin sich Universitäten entwickeln* (pp. 296–307). Weinheim and Basel: Belty Juventa.

Lariviere, V., Gingras, Y., & Archambault, E. (2006). Canadian collaboration networks: A comparative analysis of the natural sciences, social sciences and the humanities. *Scientometrics, 68*(3), 519–533.

LaRossa, R. (2005). Grounded Theory Methods and Qualitative Family Research. *Journal of Marriage and Family, 67,* 837–857.

Larsson, S. (2009). A pluralist view of generalization in qualitative studies. *International Journal of Research & Method in Education, 32*(1), 25–38. Retrieved 27-May2014 from http://liu.diva-portal.org/smash/get/diva2:209423/FULLTEXT01.pdf

Lassegard, J. P. (2006). International Student Quality and Japanese Higher Education Reform. *Journal of Studies in International Education, 10*(2), 119–140.

Leask, B. (2001). Bridging the gap: Internationalizing university curricula. *Journal of studies in international education, 5*(2), 100–115.

Lechuga, V. M., & Altbach, P. G. (2006). *The changing landscape of the academic profession: The culture of faculty at for-profit colleges and universities.*

Leisyte, L., Enders, J., & de Boer, H. (2009). The balance between teaching and research in Dutch and English universities in the context of university governance reforms. *Higher Education, 58*(5), 619–635.

Littlewood, W. (1999). Defining and developing autonomy in East Asian contexts. *Applied linguistics, 20*(1), 71–94.

Liu, N. C., & Cheng, Y. (2005). The Academic Ranking of World Universities. *Higher Education in Europe, 30*(2), 127–136.

Luff, D. (1999). Dialogue Across the Divides:Moments of Rapport'and Power in Feminist Research with Anti-Feminist Women. *Sociology, 33*(4), 687–703.

Lunt, P., & Livingstone, S. (1996). Rethinking the focus group in media and communications research. London: LSE Research Online. Retrieved 8-June 2014 from http://eprints.lse.ac.uk/archive/00000409

Luukkonen, T., Persson, O., & Sivertsen, G. (1992). Understanding Patterns of International Scientific Collaboration. *Science Technology Human Value, 17*(1), 101–126.

Machimura, T. (2010). Doing Sociology in Native Languages in a Globalizing World: Thinking about its Significance and Difficulty in Japan. In M. Burawoy, M. Chang, & M. F. Hsieh (Eds.), *Facing an Unequal World: Challenges for a Global Sociology* (Vol. 2: Asia). Taiwan.

Mainichi Shinbun Newspaper. (23-October 2014). Super Global daigaku: "kuni ga kakuzuke" no hamon (Super Global University: A sensation that the nation state rank universities). (Evening). Tokyo, Japan: Mainichi Shinbun Newspaper. Retrieved 31-March 2015 from http://mainichi.jp/shimen/news/p20141023dde012000020ooc.html

Major, E. M. (2005). Co-national support, cultural therapy, and the adjustment of Asian students to an English-speaking university culture. *International Education Journal, 6*(1), 84–95.

Malinowski, B. (1922). *Argonauts of the Western Pacific: An account of native enterprise and adventure in the archipelagoes of Milanesian New Guinea.* London: Routledge and Kegan Paul.

Marginson, S. (2000). Rethinking academic work in the global era. *Journal of higher education policy and management, 22*(1), 23–35.

McCabe, D. L., Trevino, L. K., & Butterfield, K. D. (2001). Cheating in academic institutions: A decade of research. *Ethics &Behavior, 11*(3), 219–232.

McLafferty, I. (2004). Focus group interviews as a data collecting strategy. *Journal of Advanced Nursing, 48*(2), 187–194.

Meiji University. (10-March 2015). *Kyouin koubo (Job vacancy for teaching positions)*. Retrieved 30-March 2015 from Meiji University: http://www.meiji.ac.jp/koho/recruit/index.html

Melin, G. (2000). Pragmatism and self-organization: Research collaboration on the individual level. *Research Policy, 29*(1), 31–40.

Merton, R. K. (1942). The Sociology of Science. In N. W. Storer (Ed.), *The Normative Structure of Science*. Chicago: University of Chicago Press.

Merton, R. K. (1968). The Matthew Effect in Science. *Science, 159*(3810), 56–63.

Merton, R. K. (1988). The Matthew Effect in Science II: Cumulative Advantage and the Symbolism of Intellectual Property. *ISIS, 79*(4), 606–623.

METRIS. (n.d.). Retrieved 1-March 2014 from Monitoring Emerging Trends on Social Sciences and Humanities in Europe: http://www.metrisnet.eu

MEXT. (2008). *Heisei 20nenndo Monbukagaku hakusho dai1bu dai2shou1 (FY 2008 The White Paper of Education, Culture, Sports, Science and Technology)*. Retrieved 5-May 2015 from MEXT (Ministry of Education, Culture, Sports, Science and Technology, Japan: http://www.mext.go.jp/b_menu/hakusho/html/hpaa200901/1283098_004_01.pdf

MEXT. (19-August 2011). *Kagakugijutu kihonkeikaku (Basic plan for science and technology policy)*. Retrieved 14-February 2015 from MEXT: http://www.mext.go.jp/component/a_menu/science/detail/__icsFiles/afieldfile/2011/08/19/1293746_02.pdf

MEXT. (2013). *Heisei 25nendo gakkoukihonchousa (sokuhouchi) no kouhyounitsuite (On release of basic educational research of the year 2013)*. Tokyo: MEXT. Retrieved 21-March 2015 from http://www.mext.go.jp/component/b_menu/houdou/__icsFiles/afieldfile/2013/08/07/1338338_01.pdf

MEXT. (2014). *Heisei 26 nendo kakenhi (hojokinbun, kikinbun) no haibun ni tsuite (On distribution of kakenhi for the fiscal year 2014)*. Retrieved 11-February 2015 from MEXT: http://www.mext.go.jp/a_menu/shinkou/hojyo/__icsFiles/afieldfile/2014/10/20/1352401_2.pdf

MEXT. (January 2014). *Heisei 26nendo "chi no kyoten" seibijigyou kouboyouryou (Call for application for "Base of knowledge" programme for the year 2014)*. Retrieved 3-February 2014 from Ministry of Education, Culture, Sports, Science and Technology, Japan: http://www.mext.go.jp/component/a_menu/education/detail/__icsFiles/afieldfile/2014/01/28/1343326_01_1.pdf

MEXT. (2014). *Kenkyu daigaku kyouka sokushin jigyo (Project for research universities to strangthen and develop research environment)*. Retrieved 6-January 2014 from MEXT.

MEXT. (September 2014). *Selection for the FY 2014 Top Global University Project*. Retrieved March 23 2015 from Ministry of Education, Culture, Sports, Science and Technology, Japan: http://www.mext.go.jp/b_menu/houdou/26/09/__icsFiles/afieldfile/2014/10/07/1352218_02.pdf

MEXT. (n.d.). *Kokuritsudaigakuhoujinhou no gaiyou (Outlines of national university corporation law)*. Retrieved 22-March 2015 from Ministry of Education, Culture, Sports, Science and Technology Japan: http://www.mext.go.jp/a_menu/koutou/houjin/03052704.htm

MEXT. (n.d.). *On overhead costs in Grants-in-Aid for Scientific Research*. Retrieved 6-February 2015 from Ministry of Education, Culture, Sports Science and Technology, Japan,: http://www.mext.go.jp/a_menu/shinkou/hojyo/07071108/007.pdf

MEXT. (n.d.). *Shiritsu daigaku no yakuwari (Roles of private universities)*. Retrieved 22-March 2015 from Ministry of Education, Culture, Sports, Science and Technology, Japan: http://www.mext.go.jp/b_menu/shingi/chukyo/chukyo9/shiryo/attach/1319879.htm

MEXT. (n.d.). *Shiritsudaigaku senryakuteki kennkyukiban keiseisien jigyo (Strategic research base development project for private universities)*. Retrieved 13-February 2015 from MEXT: http://www.mext.go.jp/a_menu/koutou/shinkou/07021403/002/002/1218299.htm

Mimura, M., Monk, B., & Ozawa, K. (2003). Attitudes to language learning: A case study. *NUCB journal of language culture and communication, 5*(2), 101–116.

Möller, K., & Svahn, S. (2004). Crossing East-West boundaries: Knowledge sharing in intercultural business networks. *Industrial Marketing Management, 33*(3), 219–228.

Morgan, D. L. (1996). Focus Groups. *Annual Review of Sociology, 22,* 129–152.

Morgan, D. L. (1997). PLANNING AND RESEARCH DESIGN FOR FOCUS GROUPS. In D. L. Morgan, *Focus Groups as Qualitative Research* (pp. 32–46). Thousand Oaks, CA: Sage Publications. doi:10.4135/9781412984287

Morita, L. (2010). The Sociolinguistic context of English language education in Japan and Singapore. *electronic journal of contemporary japanese studies.*

Murakami, Y. (1994). *kagakusha towa nanika (What is a scientist?).* Tokyo: Shinchosha.

Murakami, Y. (2010). *ningen nitotte kagakutowa nanika (What is science for human beings?).* Tokyo: Shinchosha.

Murphy-Shigematsu, S. (2002). Psychological barriers for international students in Japan. *International Journal for Advancement of Counselling, 24*(1), 19–30.

Nakayama, S. (1989). Independence and choice: Western impacts on Japanese higher education. In P. G. Altbach, & V. Selvaratnam (Eds.), *From Dependence to Autonomy: The Development of Asian Universities* (pp. 97–114). Springer Netherlands.

Nikkei online. (5-March 2015). Daigakude 'shokugyoujin' ikuseiwo kyouiku saisei jikkoukaigi ga teian (Foster 'professionals' at university: Suggestions from Education Rebuilding Executive Council). Tokyo. Retrieved 5-March 2015 from http://www.nikkei.com/article/DGXLZO83966380U5A300C1CR800 o/

Nisbett, R. E. (2005). *The Geography of Thought: How Asians and Westerners Think Differently-Any Why.* London&Boston: Nicholas Brealey.

Nishihara, K. (2010). *Kanshukansei no shakaigakuriron (Sociological Theory of Inter-subjectivity).* Tokyo: Shinsensha.

Nonaka, I. (1994). A dynamic theory of organizational knowledge creation. *Organization science, 5*(1), 14–37.

Oba, J. (2011). Daigaku no Governance Kaikaku: Soshikibunka to Leadership wo megutte (University Governance Reform: Organizational Culture and Leadership). *Nagoya koutou kyouiku kenkyuu, 11,* pp. 253–272.

OECD. (1996). *The Knowledge Based Economy.* Retrieved 22-February 2014 from The Organisation for Economic Co-operation and Development: http://www.oecd.org/science/sci-tech/1913021.pdf

Okamoto, K. (2010a). Challenges for Japanese Social and Human Scientists in International Collaborations (Unpublished Masters Degree Thesis submitted to the University of London).

Okamoto, K. (2010b). Internationalization of Japanese Social Sciences: Importing and Exporting Social Science Knowledge. In M. Kuhn, & D. Weidemann (Eds.), *Interntaionalization of the Social Sciences* (pp. 45–65). Bielefeld: transcript.

Okamoto, K. (2013). What is Hegemonic Science?: Power in Scientific Activities in Social Sciences in International Contexts. In M. Kuhn & S. Yazawa (Eds.), *Theories about and Strategies against Hegemonic Social Sciences* (pp. 55–73). Tokyo: Center for Glocal Studies.

Okugawa, I. (2014). Internationalization of Higher Education in Japan: The Aim and Challenge at the University of Tsukuba. *Inter Faculty, 5*. Oxford University Press. (1999). Concise Oxford English Dictionary.

Payne, G., & Payne, J. (2008). *Key Concept in Social Research*. (K. Kousaka, A. Ishida, Y. Nakano, K. Hasegawa, H. Hamada, & K. Miura, Trans.) Tokyo: Shinyohsha.

Peltokorpi, V. (2007). Intercultural communication patterns and tactics: Nordic expatriates in Japan. *International Business Review, 16*(1), 68–82.

Reichertz, J. (2004). Abduction, Deduction and Induction in Qualitative Research. In U. Flick, E. Kardorff, & I. Steinke, *A Companion to Qualitative Research* (pp. 159–164). London: Sage.

Reichertz, J. (2010). Abduction: The Logic of Discovery of Grounded Theory. *Forum: Qualitative Social Research, 11*(1). Retrieved 4-May 2014 from http://www.qualitative-research.net/index.php/fqs/article/view/1412/2902

Research Excellence Framework (REF). (2014). Retrieved November 29, 2015, from REF 2014: http://www.ref.ac.uk/

Ribeiro, G. L. (2006). World Anthropologies: Cosmopolitics for a New Global Scenario in Anthropology. Critique of Anthropology, 26(4), 363–386.

Ritsumeikan University. (2015). *Saiyou jouhou (Information for job vacancy)*. Retrieved 30-March 2015 from Ritsumeikan University: http://www.ritsumei.jp/job/index_j.html

Rizvi, F., & Walsh, L. (1998). Difference, globalisation and the internationalisation of curriculum. *Australian Universities' Review*, 7–11.

Ryan, J., & Viete, R. (2009). Respectful interactions: learning with international students in the English-speaking academy. *Teaching in Higher Education, 14*(3), 303–314.

Said, E. W. (2003 [1978]). *Orientalism*. London: Penguin Books.

Sato, Y. (2010). Are Asian Sociologies Possible? Universalism versus Particularism. In M. Burawoy, M. Chang, & M. F. Hsieh (Eds.), *Facing an Unequal World: Challenges for a Global Sociology* (Vol. 2, pp. 192–200). Taiwan.

Schimank, U. (2005). New public management'and the academic profession: Reflections on the German situation. *Minerva, 43*(4), 361–376.

Science Council of Japan. (28-March 2013). *Correspondence to Great East Japan Earthquake*. From Science Council of Japan: http://www.scj.go.jp/ja/info/kohyo/pdf/kohyo-22-t170-1.pdf

Scollon, R., Scollon, S. W., & Jones, R. H. (2011). *Intercultural communication: A discourse approach.*

Seglen, P. O. (1997). Why the impact factor of journals should not be used for evaluating research. *BMJ, 314*, 498–502.

Shao, C. F. (2008). Japanese policies and international students in Japan. referred *Proceedings of Asian Studies Association of Australia Conference.*

Shattock, M. (2001). The academic profession in Britain: A study in the failure to adapt to change. *Higher Education, 41*(1–2), 27–47.

Shin, K.-Y. (Forthcoming). Post-colonialism and Social Theory Revisited. In M. Kuhn, & H. Vessuri (Eds.), *The global social science world-under the 'European' universalism* (pp. 23–40). Stuttgart: Ibidem.

Siepmann, D. (2006). Academic Writing and Culture: An Overview of Differences between English, French and German. *Meta: Translators' Journal, 51*(1), 131–150.

Sophia University. (2015). *Kyouin shokuin tou saiyouannai (Employment information for teaching positions and administrators).* Retrieved 30-March 2015 from Sophia University: http://www.sophia.ac.jp/jpn/info/employment

Stake, R. E. (1995). *The Art of Case Study Research.* Thousand Oaks, CA: Sage Publications.

Stapleton, P. (2002). Critical thinking in Japanese L2 writing: rethinking tired constructs. *ELT Journal, 56*(3), 250–257.

Stewart, D. W., Shamdasani, P. N., & Rook, D. W. (2007). Conducting the Focus Group. In D. W. Stewart, P. N. Shamdasani, & D. W. Rook, *Focus groups: Theory and practice* (2nd ed., pp. 89–109). Thousand Oaks, CA, U.S: Sage Publications.

Strauss, A. L. (1987). *Qualitative Analysis for Social Scientists.* Cambridge University Press.

Strauss, A., & Corbin, J. M. (1990). *Basics of Qualitative Research: Grounded Theory Procedures and Techniques.* Sage Publications.

Suzuki, T. (1975). *Tozasareta gengo Nihongo no sekai (The closed langugage: the world of Japanese).* Tokyo: Shinchosha.

Tanaka, T., Takai, J., Kohyama, T., & Fujihara, T. (1994). Adjustment patterns of international students in Japan. *International Journal of Intercultural Relations, 18*(1), 55–75.

Teichler, U. (2004). The changing debate on internationalisation of higher education. *Higher education, 48*(1), 5–26.

Teichler, U. (2009). Internationalisation of higher education: European experiences. *Asia Pacific Education Review, 10*(1), 93–106.

Teichler, U., & Höhle, E. A. (Eds.). (2013). *The work situation of the academic profession in Europe: Findings of a survey in twelve countries.*

The French National Research Agency. (n.d.). *Open Research Area Plus for the social sciences - 3rd call for proposals*. Retrieved 2-April 2015 from The French National Research Agency: http://www.agence-nationale-recherche.fr/ORA-2015-en

Thorstensson, L. (2001). This business of internationalization: The academic experiences of 6 Asian MBA international students at the University of Minnesota's Carlson School of Management. *Journal of studies in International Education, 5*(4), 317–340.

Tierney, W. G. (1988). Organizational culture in higher education: Defining the essentials. *The Journal of Higher Education, 59*(1), 2–21.

Umakoshi, T. (1997). Internationalisation of Japanese higher education in the 1980's and early 1990's. *Higher Education, 34*(2), 259–273.

UNESCO, & International Social Science Council. (2010). *World Social Science Report*. Paris. Retrieved 10-April 2014 from http://unesdoc.unesco.org/images/0018/001883/188333e.pdf

Usami, K., Hara, H., & Takasugi, H. (2010). Kokusaikenkyuukouryuu ni kansuru daikibo ankeetochousano kokusaikenkyuukouryuushienjigyouunei no tekiyou (Application of big-scale questionnaire survey on international research collaborations to management of international research support programme). *Nenji gakujutu taikai kouen youshishuu*, (pp. 717–720). Retrieved April 15, 2014, from https://dspace.jaist.ac.jp/dspace/bitstream/10119/9395/1/2E25.pdf

van Leeuwen, T. N., Moed, H. F., Tussen, R. J., Visser, M. S., & van Raan, A. F. (2001). Language biases in the coverage of the Science Citation Index and its consequences for international comparisons of national research performance. *Scientometrics, 51*, 335–346.

Walsh, J. P., & Maloney, N. G. (2007). Collaboration Structure, Communication Media, and Problems in Scientific Work Teams. *Journal of Computer-Mediated Communication, 12*(2), 712–732.

Weber, M. (1980). *Shokugyou toshiteno gakumon (Wissenshaft als Beruf)*. (K. Odaka, Trans.) Tokyo: Iwanami shoten.

Weidemann, D. (2010). Challenges of International Collaboration in the Social Sciences. In M. Kuhn, & D. Weidemann, *Interntaionalization of the Social Sciences* (pp. 353–378). Bielefeld: transcript.

Weidemann, D., & Kuhn, M. (2005). Speaking the Same Language? Lingua Franca Communication in European Research Collaboration. In M. Kuhn, & S. O. Remoe (Eds.), *Building the European Research Area: Socio-Economic Research in Practice*. New York: Peter Lang.

Weingart, P. (2005). Impact of bibliometrics upon the science system: Inadvertent consequences? *Scientometrics, 62*(1), 117–131.

Williams, M. (2000). Interpretivism and Generalisation. *Sociology, 34*(2), 209–224.

Wong, J. K.-K. (2004). Are the Learning Styles of Asian International Students Culturally or Contextually Based? *International Education Journal, 4*(4), 154–166.

Yamanoi, A. (2007). *Nihon no Daigakukyouju Shijou (in Japanese)*. (A. Yamanoi, Ed.) Tokyo: Tamagawa University Press.

Yomiuri shinbun newspaper. (8-October 2011). Making students tougher by introducing 'autumn entrance' to university. Japan: Yomiuri Shibun Newspaper.

Yonezawa, A. (2007). Japanese flagship universities at a crossroad. *Higher Education, 54*(4), 483–499.

Yonezawa, A. (2009). The Internationalization of Japanese Higher Education: Policy Debates and Realities. *Nagoya koutoukyouiku kenkyuu (Nagayo Higher Education Studies)*, pp. 199–219.

Yonezawa, A. (2010). Much ado about ranking: why can't Japanese universities internationalize? *Japan Forum, 22*(1-2), 121–137.

ibidem-Verlag

Melchiorstr. 15

D-70439 Stuttgart

info@ibidem-verlag.de

www.ibidem-verlag.de
www.ibidem.eu
www.edition-noema.de
www.autorenbetreuung.de